Oxford **Word Skills**

Idioms and Phrasal Verbs

Advanced

Ruth Gairns and Stuart Redman

OXFORD
UNIVERSITY PRESS

OXFORD
UNIVERSITY PRESS

Great Clarendon Street, Oxford OX2 6DP

Oxford University Press is a department of the University of Oxford.
It furthers the University's objective of excellence in research, scholarship,
and education by publishing worldwide in

Oxford New York

Auckland Cape Town Dar es Salaam Hong Kong Karachi
Kuala Lumpur Madrid Melbourne Mexico City Nairobi
New Delhi Shanghai Taipei Toronto

With offices in

Argentina Austria Brazil Chile Czech Republic France Greece
Guatemala Hungary Italy Japan Poland Portugal Singapore
South Korea Switzerland Thailand Turkey Ukraine Vietnam

OXFORD and OXFORD ENGLISH are registered trade marks of
Oxford University Press in the UK and in certain other countries

First published 2011
2022
14

ISBN: 978 0 19 462013 0

Printed in China

This book is printed on paper from certified and well-managed sources.

ACKNOWLEDGEMENTS

*The authors and publisher are grateful to those who have given permission to
reproduce the following extracts and adaptations of copyright material*: p.54
Unit 16 Exercise 1, p.88 Unit 27 Exercise 1, p.143 Unit 53 Exercise 1,
and p.160 Unit 59 Exercise 1 based on an exercise from *Oxford Idioms
Dictionary for Learners of English* 2nd edition, ISBN 9780194317238
© Oxford University Press. Reproduced by permission.

Source: pp.10-11 *Oxford Idioms Dictionary for Learners of English* 2nd edition,
ISBN 9780194317238

Cover illustration by: Carol Verbyst.

Illustrations by: Chris Davidson pp.43, 153; Colin Elgie pp.9, 162; Clive
Goddard pp.40, 114, 132, 148; Andy Hammond p.112; Sarah Kelly
pp.12, 28, 33, 144; Harry Venning pp.10, 107.

*We would also like to thank the following for permission to reproduce
photographs*: Alamy Stock Photo (Alex Segre, Ben Birchall/
PA Images, Clarissa Leahy/Cultura RM, David Vargas, David Wall,
Dundee Photographics, Edd Westmacott, Gary Roebuck, Ilene
MacDonald, Iuliia Iun, Kablonk/Purestock, Norbert Michalke/
imageBROKER, Norman Pogson, Piero Cruciatti, Radius Images/
Design Pics, RichardBaker, Roman Stetsyk, Sandy Young, Sigrid
Olsson/PhotoAlto, tbkmedia.de, Ted Horowitz); Getty Images (alashi/
DigitalVision Vectors, Dave & Les Jacobs/DigitalVision, David Laurens/
PhotoAlto, Digital Vision/Photodisc, DigitalVision/Colin Anderson
Productions pty ltd, Fuse/Corbis, Image Source/Stockbyte, lisegagne/
E+, mediaphotos/iStock, Photodisc, Scott Barbour, Stockbyte, Thomas
Northcut/Photodisc, Zero creatives/Cultura); Photodisc (David Chasey);
Photolibrary (Corbis, Pixtal Images); Shutterstock (Bangkok Click
Studio, Ben Harding, Casper1774 Studio, Elena Sherengovskaya, ESB
Basic, fizkes, godrick, Iakov Filimonov, iurii, Juice Dash, Kinga, Kiselev
Andrey Valerevich, Kyryk Ivan, LightField Studios, Ljupco Smokovski,
mimagephotography, Monkey Business Images, naluwan, Novikov
Aleksey, photoyh, Pressmaster, robuart, Shutterstock, sirtravelalot,
VALUA STUDIO, Vectors Bang, Vixit, Willy Barton, Ysbrand Cosijn).

Artwork sourced by: Suzanne Williams/Pictureresearch.co.uk

*The authors and publishers would like to thank the teachers and students from
Argentina, Brazil, Czech Republic, France, Greece, Indonesia, Italy, Norway,
Serbia, and Poland who helped with the development of this book.*

They would also like to thank: Rachel Godfrey, Carol Tabor, and Michael
Terry for their valuable comments on early drafts of the text; and
Suzanne Williams for the picture research.

Contents

Communication

Human behaviour

Styles of language

Types of idiom

Introduction

Idioms and Phrasal Verbs

Idioms and Phrasal Verbs forms part of the *Oxford Word Skills* vocabulary series. It is a series of two books for students to learn, practise, and revise everyday English idioms and phrasal verbs.

Intermediate:	intermediate and upper-intermediate (CEF levels B1 and B2)
Advanced:	advanced (CEF levels C1 and C2)

There are over 1,000 new idioms and phrasal verbs in each level, and all of the material can be used in the classroom or for self-study.

How are the books organized?

Each book contains 60 units of vocabulary presentation and practice. Units are one to three pages long, depending on the topic. New vocabulary is presented in manageable quantities for learners, with practice exercises following immediately, usually on the same page. The units are grouped together thematically in modules of four to nine units. At the end of each module there are further practice exercises in the review units, so that learners can revise and test themselves on the vocabulary learned.

At the back of each book you will find:

- an answer key for all the exercises
- an answer key for the review units
- a list of the spotlight boxes
- a list of all the idioms and phrasal verbs taught, with a unit reference to where each item appears
- a separate list of key words with unit references
- a page featuring the histories behind some of the idioms in the book (👁 look on the website **www.oup.com/elt/wordskills** for more).

What are idioms and phrasal verbs? Why teach them together?

Idioms are usually defined as groups of words whose meaning is different from the individual words. So, *under the weather* has nothing to do with the literal meaning of 'the weather'; it means 'feeling ill'. If you *sweep something under the carpet*, you try to keep something secret; and if you *put someone in the picture*, you give them the information they need to understand a situation. As these examples illustrate, in some idioms the meaning can be almost impossible to guess out of context, while others are more transparent.

Phrasal verbs consist of two and occasionally three words: a base verb and at least one particle (preposition or adverb). Many phrasal verbs are idiomatic: in other words, the meaning of the verb and particle is different from the base verb on its own. For example, the meanings of *give up* and *give in* are quite different from the meaning of *give*. As with idioms, some phrasal verbs are more transparent then others, e.g. *stand up* and the most common meaning of *stand* are very similar in meaning, as are *sit down* and *sit*. In other words, phrasal verbs can be seen as a type of idiom, although they are often singled out for specific attention in language-teaching materials.

Putting idioms and phrasal verbs together has a linguistic rationale, but perhaps an even greater pedagogic one. A relatively short passage of text – a practical necessity in most language-teaching materials – does not normally produce nine or ten naturally occurring phrasal verbs, but it can easily yield that number if the target language includes both phrasal verbs <u>and</u> idioms. This makes it easier to present the target language in continuous text rather than disconnected sentences, and gives learners more opportunity to see the expressions being used naturally, and to use them themselves in a realistic way.

Which idioms and phrasal verbs are included?

When people think of idioms, they tend to think of the more imaginative and colourful examples: *kick the bucket, have a bone to pick with someone, full of beans, be barking up the wrong tree,* etc. These vivid expressions can be extremely difficult to understand, so they are often the ones that teachers are called upon to explain in the classroom. It is also undeniably true that idioms – especially the more vivid ones – hold a particular fascination for some learners. However, there are thousands of idioms, less exotic and often more transparent than the ones above, which are of a higher frequency and probably greater value to the vast majority of learners. Here are some typical examples:

bear sth in mind, get your own way, by far, come in handy, fair enough, a happy medium, have your doubts about sth, hours on end, I thought as much, if all else fails, in all probability, last but not least, leave it at that, life's too short, little by little, no wonder, not necessarily, odds and ends, on the surface, play a part in sth, rightly or wrongly, so what?, take it personally, that's life, the sooner the better, to put it mildly, two years running, use your head, you'll be lucky.

Some of these will appear so mundane that they often pass unnoticed as idioms. In some cases the meaning may be quite easy to guess, especially in context, but the same concept may be expressed in a different way in the learner's mother tongue, so these expressions need to be learnt, and are equally deserving of our attention.

In both books, we have concentrated on high-frequency idioms and phrasal verbs which are likely to be of greatest value to learners in everyday English. To this end, you will find some vivid and colourful examples, but the majority are closer to the list above.

One final note on selection. Dictionaries do not always agree on what constitutes an idiom: *hold the line* is listed as an idiom in one dictionary, but a collocation in another. The same is true for *under the influence, be on sb's side, at risk from sth, come to no harm,* etc. Equally, a phrase listed as an idiom in one dictionary may have a separate headword entry in another, e.g. *lost cause, lame duck.* Our criterion for inclusion in this series is that an item has to be listed as an idiom in at least one of the following ELT dictionaries (and they are almost always in more than one):

Oxford Advanced Learner's Dictionary

Oxford Wordpower Dictionary

Oxford Idioms Dictionary for learners of English

Longman Dictionary of Contemporary English

Macmillan English Dictionary for Advanced Learners

Cambridge Advanced Learner's Dictionary

Collins COBUILD Advanced Learner's English Dictionary

How can teachers use the material in the classroom?

New idioms and phrasal verbs are presented through different types of text, including dialogues, tables, and visuals. The meaning of the new vocabulary is explained in an accompanying glossary unless it is illustrated in visuals or diagrams. Important or additional information is included in the 'spotlight' boxes.

Here is a procedure you could follow:

- Students study the presentation for five to ten minutes (longer if necessary).

- You answer any queries the students may have about the items, and provide a pronunciation model of the items for your students to repeat.

- Students do the first exercise, which they can check for themselves using the answer key, or you can go over the answers with the whole class.

- When you are satisfied, you can ask students to go on to further exercises, while you monitor them as they work individually or in pairs, and assist where necessary.

- When they have completed the written exercises, students can often test themselves on the new vocabulary. The material has been designed so that students can cover the new vocabulary and look at the meaning, or vice-versa. This is a simple, quick, and easy way for learners to test themselves over and over again, so there is no pressure on you to keep searching for different exercises.

- After a period of time has elapsed, perhaps a couple of days or a week, you can use the review exercises for further consolidation and testing.

- You will often notice the heading ABOUT YOU or ABOUT YOUR COUNTRY. This indicates a personalized exercise which gives learners an opportunity to use the new vocabulary within the context of their own lives. Students can write answers to these in their notebooks, but they make ideal pair-work activities for learners to practise their spoken English while using the new vocabulary. If you use these as speaking activities, students could then write their answers (or their partner's answers) as follow-up.

- To extend page 162, which gives the histories behind a number of idioms in this book, go to the website **www.oup.com/elt/wordskills** to find a regular feature. You and your students should find this interesting.

How can students study alone?

- Choose the topics that interest you. You don't need to do the units in any particular order.

- Each page will probably take you about 20–25 minutes. Firstly, spend at least ten minutes studying the presentation, which may be a text, a dialogue, a table, etc. Use the glossaries to help you understand the meaning of new items. Practise saying the idioms and phrasal verbs a few times to help you remember them.

- Keep a notebook where you can write down the new idioms and phrasal verbs with the meaning and an example sentence to help you remember them. If you are using a bilingual dictionary, you could also add a translation.

- Do the exercises in pencil: then you can rub them out, and do them again in a few days' time. Check your answers in the answer key on pages 163–79. At the end of many units you will find a section called ABOUT YOU or ABOUT YOUR COUNTRY. This gives you an opportunity to use the vocabulary more freely to write in your notebook about yourself, your country, etc.

- You can usually **test yourself** on the new vocabulary. Look at the idioms and phrasal verbs in the glossaries and tables, and cover the meanings. See if you can remember the meanings. You can do this when you have finished the exercises, or several days later as a way of revising the idioms and phrasal verbs.

- You can use the further practice exercises in the review sections which follow each module. Either do them immediately after a unit, or do them a few days later as a form of revision.

- We think it is probably better for you to do one unit at a time on a regular basis, e.g. two or three times a week, rather than study irregularly but try to do a lot of units at the same time.

- If you haven't got a good dictionary in English, we recommend *The Oxford Advanced Learner's Dictionary*. You may also be interested in two specialist dictionaries: *Oxford Idioms Dictionary for learners of English* and *Oxford Phrasal Verbs Dictionary for learners of English*.

- Go to the website **www.oup.com/elt/wordskills** to find a regular feature on the origins of a number of idioms in the book.

Abbreviations

The following abbreviations are used:

N	noun	sth	something
V	verb	sb	somebody
ADJ	adjective	etc.	You use 'etc.' at the end of a list to show there are other things, but you aren't going to say them all.
ADV	adverb		
PL	plural		
OPP	opposite		
SYN	synonym	i.e.	that is
INF	informal	e.g.	for example
FML	formal		

1 I can understand idioms

Idioms are fixed or semi-fixed phrases, and many of them are difficult to understand.

*The situation is improving, but we're **not out of the woods** yet.*	**not out of the woods** INF not yet free from difficulties or problems.
*I'll probably **take a back seat** and let Marco do most of the work.*	**take a back seat** deliberately become less actively involved in sth, and stop trying to control things.
***My heart sank** when I saw the hotel room they'd given us.*	**my heart sank** used to tell sb that you suddenly felt sad or worried about sth.

Idioms are particularly common in spoken English. Some are easier to understand, but you will need to learn many of them as fixed phrases.

'It's an expensive restaurant. **Having said that**, the food is very good.'

'… and then **the next thing I knew**, the cat had jumped out of the window …'

'Pete and Sue have split up. ~ Mmm. **I thought as much**.'

Glossary

having said that	used to say that sth is true despite what you have just said.
the next thing I knew	used to say that sth happened very quickly and unexpectedly.
I thought as much	used to say you are not surprised that sth is true.

The glossaries and tables in this book will also show you that some idioms have a choice of words or a particular style. (See Units 49–54 for more on style.)

Idiom	Meaning	Special feature
*Will they lose? ~ **More than likely**.*	very likely.	a choice of words with different meanings: **more than likely/happy/ready**, etc.
*She can't do the gardening. ~ I'd be **more than happy** to help her.*	very happy.	
*I'd be **hard pressed to** name all the countries in Europe.*	find it very difficult to do sth.	a choice of synonyms: **be hard pressed/pushed/put to do sth**.
*I think Ann **got out of bed on the wrong side** this morning.*	used to say that sb is in a bad mood.	the style is HUMOROUS.

Most of all, you need to be aware that idioms come in all shapes and sizes (= are of many different types), and they are not always obvious. When you read a text, look for possible idioms and check in a good dictionary to see if you are right.

I asked Sue about her essay and she just ignored me.

~ Yes, I think it's a bit of **a sore point** because she got a very low mark for it.

Oh dear. I **put my foot in it**, then.

~ No, **it serves** her **right**. She **didn't do a stroke of work**, so don't **take it personally**. She'll just have to work harder next time.

Glossary

a sore point	sth that makes you upset, angry, or embarrassed when sb mentions it.
put your foot in it	INF accidentally say sth that embarrasses, upsets, or annoys sb.
it serves sb right (**for doing sth**)	used to say that you think sb deserves sth unpleasant that happens to them.
not do a stroke of work	INF not do any work at all.
take it/sth personally	feel that a failure is your fault, or feel offended by sth/sb.

1 Which idioms are suggested by these pictures?

2

1 ....

2 ....

3 ....

4 ....

Complete the sentences with words from the box. Then underline the full idioms.

> having   pushed   serves   stroke   foot   more   sore   thing   much   personally   woods ✓

▶ There's been a slight improvement in his health, but he's <u>not out of the woods</u> yet.
1 Is Karen still upset about you taking her dress? ~ Yes, I'm afraid it's a .... point.
2 My brother hasn't done a .... of work all day; he's so lazy.
3 The seat collapsed under me, and the next .... I knew, I was on the floor.
4 You didn't say that I was upset with her, did you? ~ Yes, I'm afraid I put my .... in it.
5 New York is incredibly exciting. .... said that, it's very expensive these days.
6 I was .... than happy to help, but she wanted to do it on her own.
7 We'll be hard .... to finish this work by the end of the day.
8 Sam lost the race. ~ I thought as .... He looked very dejected.
9 They made Mandy repeat the test. ~ Good. It .... her right for trying to cheat.
10 Donna wasn't very nice to me. ~ Don't take it .... She's just in a bad mood.

3 Look at the idioms in bold in these sentences, then use a good dictionary to find out what special features they have (choice of words, grammar, or style). Write at the end, or in your notebook.

▶ He **landed on his feet** with that job at the bank. *Could also be 'fall on your feet'.*
1 It won't be easy; you've just got to **hang on in there**. ....
2 **If my memory serves me correctly**, the first moon landing was in 1969. ....
3 My sister's just bought a new car. Basically, it's just **keeping up with the Joneses**. ....
4 He's unreliable at the best of times, but forgetting my birthday was **the last straw**. ....
5 You may **rest assured that** we will do everything we can to help. ....

4 Read the text then answer the questions.

On the first morning we met our instructor, Kevin, and he made it clear we were going to hit the ground running. We had to build a raft and then sail it down a river; he said it would sort out the sheep from the goats. That made me feel very uneasy, but I put a brave face on it. The next day was even worse – abseiling down a cliff – but I was determined not to throw in the towel. By the third day I was beginning to realize we were all in the same boat, and probably all feeling equally vulnerable. That made me feel much better, and by the end of the week I'd also realized that Kevin's bark was worse than his bite. I survived.

1 The text contains six idiomatic phrases that are being used figuratively. Underline them.
2 Match the phrases with these explanations:
  a admit you've been defeated and stop trying. ....
  b distinguish the able people from the less able people. ....
  c he is not as aggressive as he sounds. ....
  d start doing something and proceed quickly and successfully. ....
  e be in the same difficult situation. ....
  f pretend you feel confident and happy when you do not. ....

2 Idiom and metaphor

Many idioms begin as phrases with a literal meaning, which then develop a figurative/metaphorical meaning. For example, somebody can **be in the driving seat** (of a vehicle), which means they are literally in control of the vehicle. When we use the phrase metaphorically, we mean the person is in control of a situation. Other examples are:

They've decided to **wait for the dust to settle**.	Literal meaning: 'wait to be able to see more clearly'. Metaphorical meaning: 'wait for an unsettled situation to become calm'.
I'm sure we're **on the right track**.	Literal meaning: 'on the right road, path, or track'. Metaphorical meaning: 'acting in a way that will bring a desired result'. OPP **on the wrong track**.

Metaphors from particular areas of activity can sometimes describe particular thoughts, ideas, etc. For example, boxing expressions often describe people in difficult situations:

The minister is *on the ropes* now.
INF = having serious problems and likely to fail.

The boss found himself *in a tight corner*.
INF = in a difficult situation. SYN *in a tight spot* INF.

Idioms derived from card games are sometimes connected to keeping plans and ideas hidden.

She *plays her cards close to her chest*.
= keeps her plans or ideas secret.

I think he's *got something up his sleeve*.
= has a plan or idea he will keep secret until needed.

With some idioms, the literal meaning has become lost over time, and we only use the metaphorical meaning. For example, in the past a blacksmith was a person who made things out of iron. He had to strike (= hit) the iron while it was still hot in order to bend it into the shape he wanted. From this we get the idiom strike while the iron is hot = make use of an opportunity immediately because now is the best time to do it.

The idiom have a chip on your shoulder (= be sensitive about or feel offended by sth, as a result of sth that happened in your past) comes from a 19th-century American custom. If a boy wanted to fight, he would put a piece of wood on his shoulder; he fought against the first person who knocked the piece of wood off.

 You can find the histories behind some of the idioms in this book on page 162 (look on the website www.oup.com/elt/wordskills for more).

1 Complete the sentences.

1 It'll take a while to finalize the plans, but I think we're on the right _____ now.
2 Katrina hasn't told us everything. I think she's still got something up her _____ .
3 That boy has a _____ on his shoulder about his height. I don't know why it bothers him.
4 I think we should wait for the _____ to settle before we decide what to do.
5 After the recent criticism, I think she's in quite a tight _____ .
6 I don't understand why he always plays his cards so close to his _____ .

2 Rephrase these situations using a suitable idiom.

▶ She's got a secret plan. *She's got something up her sleeve.*
1 She's in control of the situation. _____
2 I'm sure we're doing the right things. _____
3 Now is the time to do it; don't wait. _____
4 Wait until the situation is much clearer. _____
5 The company is doing badly and is likely to fail. _____
6 She's in a difficult situation right now. _____
7 He always seems to think the world has treated him unfairly. _____
8 She always keeps her ideas secret. _____

3 What is the common idea linking the idioms with 'head' and the common idea linking the idioms with 'heart'? And what is the meaning of the final idiom?

have your head screwed on ⎫
lose your head ⎬ _____
use your head ⎭

break sb's heart ⎫
take sth to heart ⎬ _____
not have the heart to do sth ⎭

I let my heart rule my head. = _____

4 Where do you think these idioms come from? Put them in the correct column below.

be on the same wavelength   be in the saddle
bite the bullet   get your wires crossed
beat a hasty retreat   learn the ropes
take the wind out of sb's sails   keep a tight rein on sth/sb

Ships and sailing	Radio and telecommunications	Horse riding	Weapons and war

5 Thinking about the literal meaning of the idioms in Exercise 4, can you now match the idioms with their metaphorical meanings?

▶ *bite the bullet* _____ force yourself to do sth unpleasant or difficult that you have been avoiding.
1 _____ be in a position of control or responsibility.
2 _____ learn how to do a particular job.
3 _____ think in a similar way.
4 _____ go away quickly from an unpleasant place or situation.
5 _____ make sb less confident by saying or doing sth unexpected.
6 _____ control sth/sb carefully or strictly.
7 _____ become confused by what sb is saying because you think they are talking about sth else.

3 Introduction to phrasal verbs

A phrasal verb consists of a base verb and one or two particles (adverbs or prepositions).

MEANING

Some particles extend the meaning of the base verb:

Eat up your supper.[1] 'Up' here adds the idea of eating all of something.

Some particles create a new meaning, but still with a connection to the base verb:

Let's eat in this evening.[2] = eat at home this evening.

Some particles change the meaning of the base verb from literal to figurative:

These big bills are eating into my savings.[3] = using up my money.

GRAMMAR

Some phrasal verbs are <u>intransitive</u>, i.e. they don't take an object:

We got up early to watch the sun come up. = rise.

Many phrasal verbs are <u>transitive</u>, i.e. they take an object. Transitive phrasal verbs are of two types: separable and inseparable. With separable phrasal verbs, the object can usually go before or after the particle; with inseparable phrasal verbs, the object must go after the particle. Dictionaries often show the difference like this:

| tear sth up |

Here, 'sth' comes between the verb and particle. This shows you that the object can go before or after 'up':

Don't tear up the letter. / *Don't tear the letter up.* = destroy it by tearing it to pieces.

But note that, if the object is a pronoun, it must go between the verb and particle:

Don't tear it up. (NOT *Don't ~~tear up it~~.*)

There are also a small number of phrasal verbs where the object always goes before the particle:

I showed the students around the school. (NOT *I ~~showed around the students~~.*)

| take against sb/sth |

Here, 'sb/sth' comes after the verb and particle. This shows you that the object cannot go between 'take' and 'against'; it must go after the particle:

He took against Sam after that. = started to dislike Sam. (NOT *He ~~took Sam against~~.*)

DIFFERENT FORMS, DIFFERENT MEANINGS

With some phrasal verbs, a difference in grammatical structure indicates a difference in meaning.

The plane **put down** in a field.	**put down** (intransitive) land.
1 I'll **put** your number **down** here. 2 The cat had to **be put down**.	**put sth down** 1 write sth, especially a name or number, on a piece of paper or a list. 2 (usually passive) kill an old or sick animal with a drug.
Don't **put yourself down** so much!	**put yourself/sb down** criticize yourself or sb else in front of other people.
I **put** my name **down for** the day trip to the seaside.	**put sb / sb's name down for sth** write sb's name on a list so that they can take part in sth.
I **put** her anger **down to** stress.	**put sth down to sth** believe sth is caused by sth.

OTHER POINTS

As some of the examples on page 12 illustrate, some phrasal verbs have two particles (an adverb and a preposition), and some phrasal verbs can be used with another phrase or clause.

put sb up to sth INF	*She's usually very good; Danny must have **put** her **up to** it.*	encourage or persuade sb to do sth wrong or stupid.
talk sb into / out of (doing) sth	*I tried to **talk** her **out of** resigning, but she went ahead.*	persuade sb to do / not to do sth.
count on sb to do sth	*I'm **counting on** you **to** help us.*	trust sb to do sth.
work out + *wh* clause	*I can't **work out what** this means.*	find the answer to sth.

1 Circle the correct word.

1 If you've got time, I could show you *in | around* the old part of the city.
2 The service was slow and the bill was incorrect. I put it down *for | to* poor management.
3 You'd better tear that cheque *up | out* into small pieces so that no one can cash it.
4 Do you fancy going to the pizza place, or shall we just eat *into | in* as usual?
5 I don't feel I can really count *on | in* Alec to do the work in the way we agreed.
6 We were planning a big barbecue and Aiden put me down *for | on* making the salads.
7 I haven't got much work, so payments on the house are eating *in | into* my savings.
8 You'll never succeed in business if you keep putting yourself *down | up* all the time.

2 Complete the definitions.

1 *She took against me* means 'she began to _____ me for no particular reason'.
2 *He put me up to it* means 'he encouraged me to do something _____!'
3 *The helicopter put down near the river* means 'the helicopter _____ near the river'.
4 *She talked me out of leaving* means 'she _____ me not to leave'.
5 *The dog was put down* means 'the dog was _____ by an injection'.
6 *She put my address down* means 'she _____ down my address'.

3 Complete the sentences with the correct particle.

1 I worked _____ what he meant.
2 The sun came _____ at 5.00.
3 Show us _____ the exhibition.
4 Don't count _____ him for help.
5 Put his name _____ on the list.
6 I tore the note _____ deliberately.
7 What do you put it _____ to?
8 He talked me _____ buying the car.

4 Here are some phrasal verbs which do not appear on page 12. Underline the phrasal verb and its object. Check your answers on page 164 before you do Exercise 5.

▶ The man in the bureau de change <u>did me out of about €10</u>.
1 In the mountains you have to watch out for snakes.
2 It's crucial to stand out against discrimination, especially in the workplace.
3 They weren't supposed to be there, but the police let both of them off.
4 We were having a meeting when the cleaner burst in on us.
5 He married the girl I was in love with; I try very hard not to hold it against him.

5 Using the context to guess the meanings, write the verbs in Exercise 4 next to the definitions.

▶ stop sb from having sth that they should have, especially in a dishonest way. *do sb out of sth.*
1 be careful of sth or sb. _____
2 suddenly enter a room and interrupt something that is happening. _____
3 say or show publicly that you oppose sth. _____
4 feel angry with sb for sth that they have done in the past. _____
5 give sb little or no punishment for sth they did wrong. _____

4 I can use phrasal nouns and adjectives

A Phrasal nouns

Phrasal nouns are sometimes formed from phrasal verbs, e.g. **take off** (of a plane) and the related noun **take-off**, **look on** and **onlooker**. Nouns formed from phrasal verbs may be hyphenated, e.g. **passer-by**, or may be written as one word, e.g. **breakout**.

Police are interviewing **passers-by** who witnessed the **breakout** at Hyde Prison last night.

Onlookers watched in shock as the thief stole a police car and made a quick **getaway** from the scene of the crime …

The government has been forced into a **climbdown** after the revelations of a **cover-up** …

There was a sharp **intake** of breath from the public gallery during the judge's **summing-up** …

Following the **outbreak** of violence, the police have requested **backup** from the army.

Glossary

breakout	an escape from prison by a group. **break out (of sth)** v.
getaway	1 an escape or quick departure, especially from the scene of a crime. 2 a short holiday. **get away** v.
climbdown	an act of admitting that you were wrong. **climb down** v.
cover-up	a course of action taken to hide a mistake or illegal activity from the public. **cover sth up** v.
intake	an act of taking sth in, especially breath, food, etc. **take sth in** v.
summing-up	a legal statement made by a judge, magistrate, or lawyer which gives a summary of the evidence in a court. **sum up** v.
outbreak	a sudden start of violence, war, disease, etc. **break out** v.
backup	extra help or support you can get if necessary. **back sb/sth up** v.

spotlight *passer-by, bystander, onlooker*

A **passer-by** (PL **passers-by**) is someone who is walking past something by chance, especially when something unexpected happens. **pass by sb/sth** v. A **bystander** is someone who watches what is happening, e.g. an accident, without taking part. **stand by** v. SYNS **onlooker**, **look on** v.

1 Rewrite the sentences, forming phrasal nouns from the phrasal verbs.

1 Will the union climb down? Will there .... ?
2 Did the police cover up the facts? Was .... ?
3 We asked someone who was passing by. We ....
4 Someone broke out of prison last night. There ....
5 The judge summed up briefly. The ....
6 Will the team back us up? Will .... ?

2 Complete the sentences with a suitable phrasal noun.

1 When the men had been fighting for a few minutes, we realized there were about a dozen .... watching them.
2 Most people would benefit from a reduction in the .... of salt in their diet.
3 This move represents a .... over plans to change the school meals policy.
4 Security cameras showed that during the prison ...., the guards did nothing.
5 The party was really boring; we made a quick .... and went to a club instead.
6 If Marianne can't look after the dog this weekend, I've got my uncle as ....
7 The authorities are extremely worried about the threatened .... of flu this winter.
8 I stopped a .... and asked him to call the police.

B Adjectives formed from phrasal verbs

Throwaway society contributes to global warming

Breakaway republic holds first elections

FRENCH TEAM WINS **KNOCKOUT** COMPETITION

DOCTOR'S MANNER DESCRIBED AS 'OFF-PUTTING'

MONTHS LATER, FLOOD RECOVERY STILL **ONGOING**

Outspoken critic of government loses job

WATERED-DOWN PLANS FOR BROADBAND SPEEDS

SUPERVISORS DECIDE ON FATE OF **LEFTOVER** LIBRARY FUNDS

Worn-out mums dream of more support from dads

Glossary

throwaway	(of goods) produced cheaply and intended to be thrown away after use (also **throwaway society**). **throw sth away** v.
breakaway	(of a group, organization, or part of a country) having separated from a larger group or part. **break away from sb/sth** v.
knockout	A **knockout** competition is one in which players or teams continue competing until there is only one winner left. **knock sb out** (**of sth**) v.
off-putting	INF If sb or sth is **off-putting**, they are strange or unpleasant, in a way that prevents you from liking them. **put sb off** v.
ongoing	continuing to exist or develop. **go on** v.
outspoken	saying what you think, even when it upsets people. **speak out** (**against sth**) v.
watered down	A **watered-down** plan, statement, etc. is weaker and less powerful than it was originally. **water sth down** v.
worn out	1 (of a person) very tired because they have been working hard. 2 (of a thing) too old or damaged to be used. **wear sb/sth out** v.
leftover	remaining after you have finished or used what you want or need, e.g. *leftover* food. **leftovers** PL N. **be left over** (**from sth**). v

3 True or false? Write T or F.

1 *Ongoing* talks are finished. ....
2 An *outspoken* critic says very little. ....
3 *Worn-out* shoes are useless. ....
4 *Leftover* food can be eaten later. ....

5 An *off-putting* manner is a good thing. ....
6 If you lose a *knockout* round, you're out. ....
7 A *watered-down* comment is less powerful. ....
8 A *throwaway* product is valuable. ....

4 Complete the dialogues using a phrasal verb, noun, or adjective.

1 Did your team get through the first stage? ~ No, they ....
2 Is Bess having a rest? ~ Yeah, that was a long walk. She's completely ....
3 The article isn't as strongly worded as it was. ~ No, it's been ....
4 What's for dinner? ~ I think there are some .... from lunchtime.
5 She coughed throughout your performance. ~ I know, I found it really ....
6 Why did they form a .... group? ~ They were unhappy with the way things were.
7 He's strongly against fox-hunting. ~ That's right; he has often ....
8 Have the discussions come to an end yet? ~ No, they're still ....

Review: Introduction to idioms and phrasal verbs

Unit 1

1 Complete the crossword. The letters in the grey squares spell out an expression. What is it?

1 If you put your _____ in it, you say something embarrassing by accident.
2 If you say, 'it serves you _____', you mean that the person deserves the unpleasant thing that has happened to them.
3 If you say, 'the _____ thing I knew', you're going to describe something very surprising that happened after that moment.
4 If something is a _____ point for you, it makes you feel upset, annoyed, or embarrassed if someone mentions it.
5 If you got out of bed on the wrong _____ today, you're in a bad mood.
6 If you're trying to _____ up with the Joneses, you're trying to have all the possessions and achievements that your friends or neighbours have.
7 If you _____ the ground running, you start doing something and proceed quickly and successfully.
8 If you haven't done a _____ of work, you've done no work at all.
9 If your _____ is worse than your bite, you aren't really as unkind or angry as you seem.
10 If your heart _____, you suddenly feel sad or worried about something.
11 If you throw in the _____, you give up on a problem and admit you are defeated by it.
12 If you take a back _____, you become less active and stop trying to control things.
The expression in the grey squares is _____ .

Unit 2

1 Match 1–10 with a–j.

1 That man's got a real chip on his _____
2 I can't understand him; we aren't on the same _____
3 I had to beat a hasty _____
4 The announcement took the wind out of my _____
5 It's nothing personal: you really mustn't take it to _____
6 I think he must have some trick up his _____
7 This idea isn't working. I think we're on the wrong _____
8 She's the boss and she likes to be in the driving _____

a seat.
b heart.
c sleeve.
d retreat.
e shoulder.
f track.
g sails.
h wavelength.

2 Complete the idioms.

ABOUT YOU

1 I tend to play my _____ close to my _____ .
2 I like to _____ while the iron's hot.
3 If I'm in a tight _____, I generally ask for help rather than trying to deal with things on my own.
4 I've got my head _____ on when it comes to finance.
5 I occasionally let my _____ rule my _____ .
6 If someone criticizes me, I tend to take it to _____ .

3 Are the sentences in the questionnaire in Exercise 2 true about you, sometimes true, or not true? Write your answers, or talk to another student.

Unit 3

1 Complete the sentences in a logical way.

▶ The school organized the visit, and I put my name down _for it_ .
1 That was a stupid thing to do. Who put you up _____ ?
2 If you go to the market, watch out _____ .
3 I'm very willing to give you a hand; you know you can count _____ .
4 It wasn't her fault but he still took it _____ .
5 The boys were just being stupid, so the policeman let them off with _____ .
6 This is a very complicated sentence. I can't work out what _____ .

2 Rewrite the part of the sentence in italics, using a phrasal verb that keeps a similar meaning. Make any other additions that are necessary.

▶ They are *trusting* us to help them. _counting on_
1 The helicopter had to *land* in a field. _____
2 The sun *rose* just after six o'clock. _____
3 The children *finished* their dinner. _____
4 He *criticizes himself* a lot. _____
5 We had to have our dog *killed*. _____
6 She just *started to dislike* me; I don't know why. _____
7 We decided to *have dinner at home* last night. _____
8 He *persuaded me to go*. _____

Unit 4

1 What related phrasal nouns and adjectives are formed from these phrasal verbs? Write them in the correct column below.

pass by ✓   speak out   look on   water sth down   break out (of war)   wear sth out
sum up   go on (= continue)   stand by (of a person)   put sb off (= distract)

Phrasal verb	Phrasal noun	Phrasal verb	Phrasal adjective
pass by	passer-by		

2 Agree with the first speaker in each dialogue, using a suitable phrasal verb, noun, or adjective.

▶ The government tried to hide their mistakes, didn't they? ~ Yes, there was a _cover-up_ .
1 Weren't your team eliminated? ~ Yes, I'm afraid they were _____ .
2 We didn't eat everything, did we? ~ No, we've still got some _____ salad.
3 The minister was lying, wasn't he? ~ Yes, it was obviously a _____ . He's finished.
4 The police will be there to support you. ~ Yes, they'll provide plenty of _____ .
5 You always have a holiday, don't you? ~ Yes, I like to _____ every year.
6 You must've been exhausted after that work. ~ Yes, I was _____ .

5 I can describe character

A What are they like?

Star Theatre

For the Love of Alice – Cast List

Gideon Beck: Ex-army major, **loves the sound of his own voice**; **doesn't suffer fools gladly**. Thought to be **tough as old boots**. Very protective of daughter, Alice.

Alice Beck: Attractive and charming **on the surface**, Alice likes to **play it cool** with men, but **deep down**, she's quite shy. Loves her father, but very much **under** his **thumb**.

Jocelyn Beck: Gideon's wife. **Has a quick temper**; friends think she's **mad as a hatter**.

Andrew Elder: Neighbour, in love with Alice. Sadly, **thick as two short planks**.

Glossary

like/love the sound of your own voice	DISAPPROVING talk too much, usually without listening to other people.
not suffer fools gladly	not be polite or patient with people you think are less intelligent than you.
(as) tough as old boots	INF very strong and able to bear pain, criticism, etc. without complaining.
on the surface	when you consider obvious things. OPP **deep down**.
play it cool	INF hide your feelings so that you appear calm and controlled.
under sb's thumb	controlled or influenced by sb.
have a quick temper	become angry easily and often.
(as) thick as two short planks	INF (of a person) very stupid.

> **spotlight** *mad*
>
> *She's (as) mad as a hatter.* INF = strange or crazy. SYN **barking (mad)** INF.
> *He's mad keen on Alice.* INF = likes her very much.
> *I was hopping mad.* INF = very angry.

1 Circle the correct word.

1 Keep out of the new boss's way; apparently he's got a very *quick | fast* temper.
2 *Low | Deep* down, Joe's a true romantic. It just doesn't look that way on the *surface | top*.
3 That was a really crazy thing to do. ~ Yeah, I thought she was *barking | hopping* mad.
4 You'll find that Mr Waters doesn't suffer fools *gladly | happily*, so watch what you say.
5 She's a very dominant woman; she certainly has her husband under her *finger | thumb*.
6 My aunt's *rough | tough* as old boots, so I'm sure she'll get through the operation.

2 Complete the second sentence so that it paraphrases the first.

1 My brother's furious about the money. In other words, he's _____ mad.
2 John's really stupid. In other words, he's thick as _____ _____ .
3 Ella didn't show Luis her true feelings. In other words, she played _____ .
4 Ana adores horse-riding. In other words, she's _____ it.
5 Don just talks and never listens. In other words, he loves the sound of his _____ _____ .
6 I love Caz, but she's crazy. In other words, she's mad _____ .
7 Mona does everything Pete tells her to. In other words, she's under _____ .
8 Grandad can put up with anything. In other words, he's tough _____ .

B Noun phrases describing character

Idiom	Meaning
My sister goes to bed at exactly 10.30 every night; she's **a creature of habit**.	**a creature of habit** a person who likes to do the same thing at the same time on a regular basis.
Most of the group are very quiet – we need **a live wire** like Jez to get us talking.	**a live wire** a person who is lively and full of energy and enthusiasm.
We could do with **a bright spark** here to bring in new ideas. Some **bright spark** left the door unlocked! How stupid.	**a bright spark** INF 1 a lively and intelligent person. 2 IRONIC = a person who has done sth stupid.
She always asks Dad for help with cash because she knows he's **a soft touch**.	**a soft touch** INF a person from whom you can easily get money because they are kind or easy to deceive.
I don't know if Ash would be right for the job; he's a bit of **an unknown quantity**.	**an unknown quantity** a person or thing whose qualities are abilities are not yet known.
Mrs Andrews runs the business and people think she's **the salt of the earth**. Drug dealers are **the scum of the earth**.	**the salt of the earth** a good, reliable, honest person. OPP **the scum of the earth** INF, INSULTING a person or group considered to be extremely unpleasant or evil.
He's tough, ambitious, and he's **nobody's fool** – he's our best hope as a manager.	**nobody's fool** a person who is too clever to be tricked by other people. SYN **no fool**.
I hate dealing with Rupert; he's **a nasty piece of work**.	**a nasty piece of work** a person who is unpleasant, unkind, or dishonest.
He's a bit of **a cold fish**. He hardly every speaks to us or even smiles.	**a cold fish** DISAPPROVING a person who shows little emotion or seems unfriendly.
If he said he would help you, I'm sure he will; he's **a man of his word**.	**a man**/**woman of his**/**her word** a person who always does what he/she has promised to do.

3 Are these descriptions positive or negative? Write P or N.

1 He's a live wire. ....
2 She's a nasty piece of work. ....
3 He's the salt of the earth. ....
4 She's a woman of her word. ....
5 She's nobody's fool. ....
6 Which bright spark left the light on? ....
7 She's a cold fish. ....
8 He's the scum of the earth. ....

4 Complete the descriptions of Angela's colleagues. Then circle the full idioms.

Andy Crocker is a great boss: hardworking, honest, and a man of his (1) .... He's a real family man too and he adores his kids. They only have to ask for something and they get it; he's a (2) .... touch.

Mrs Bolton's been here for years and she's now approaching retirement. She's the salt of the (3) .... , and will do anything for Andy. But things have to be done in a particular way – 'Mrs Bolton's Way'; she's a (4) .... of habit.

Mandy O'Neill is new in this department, so at the moment she's a bit of an (5) .... quantity. She used to be in sales, and my friend Sally says she's a bright (6) .... and (7) .... fool. I'll reserve judgement on her till I get to know her better.

Tim Richards – What can I say? I just can't stand him. I don't trust him at all; I think he's a nasty (8) .... , actually.

5 ABOUT YOU Can you think of five people that you know who could be described by any of the idioms in the table? Write in your notebook, or talk to another student.

A Selfless behaviour

Best mum competition

[Please write your application in not more than 120 words.]

All mums **have** the family's **best interests at heart**, and **will go out of their way to** help their kids, but what makes a great mum? Well, ours has all the qualities. When things went wrong and Dad left us, Mum **went to great lengths to hold** the family **together**. She **was always there for** us, but trusted us to make our own decisions. When we needed **a shoulder to cry on**, it was Mum we **turned to**, not our friends. But what **sets** her **apart from** the other mums is her concern for others. She**'s** always **giving** someone or other **a helping hand**. We **thank our lucky stars** that she's our mum!   (Patti, 16)

Glossary	
have sb's (**best**) **interests at heart**	care about sb and want to improve their situation.
go out of your way (**to do sth**)	do sth that you do not have to do and that involves making a special effort to help or please sb.
go to great lengths to do sth	try in a determined way to achieve sth.
hold sth together	keep a group of people, a marriage, etc. united in difficult circumstances.
be there for sb	be available and supportive if sb wants to talk to you or needs your help.
a shoulder to cry on	a person who gives you sympathy.
turn to sb/sth	go to sb/sth for help or advice.
set sb apart (**from sb**)	make sb different from or better than others.
give/lend (**sb**) **a helping hand**	help sb.
thank your lucky stars	feel very grateful and lucky about sth.

1 Put the words in order and add one more word.

▶ them | way | out | help | she | went | of | to   *She went out of her way to help them.*

1 help | lengths | dad | to | them | went | to   ....

2 writing | our | given | helping | we | were | a | with   ....

3 hold | managed | their | they | to | marriage   ....

4 best | have | heart | she | doesn't | your | at   ....

5 healthy | I'm | stars | I | thank | my | that   ....

6 on | a | she | to | needs | shoulder   ....

2 Write a phrase with the same meaning as the words in italics.

▶ They *helped me* with the housework.   *gave me a helping hand*

1 Who would you *seek advice from* if you had a problem?   ....

2 Her positive attitude *makes her different* from her colleagues.   ....

3 She needs a *sympathetic person to talk to about her problems*.   ....

4 She is always *available to talk to if I need help*.   ....

5 Dad always *makes a special effort* to keep them amused.   ....

6 My sister *tried very hard* to get the medicine I needed.   ....

7 I *am so grateful* that I have such a great family.   ....

8 Somehow Mum managed to *keep the family united*.   ....

3 ABOUT YOU What would you write in a best mum, best dad, best sister, or best brother competition? Write in your notebook, or talk to another student.

B Selfish behaviour

Do you suffer from selfish or bossy siblings?

 KIM ▶ Yeah, my sister always wants to **have things her own way**, so I have to **put my foot down** with her. She thinks she can **twist** me **round her little finger**, but she can't!

 AYRON ▶ My brother's very **sure of himself** and he**'ll stop at nothing** to get what he wants. He**'d walk all over** my parents if he had the chance.

 CARMEN ▶ When we were kids, my older sisters used to **push** me **around** and **pick on** me because I was small. It took me years to learn to **stick up for myself**.

 PRINCESS ▶ My sister **never lifts a finger** to help around the house; she just **takes it for granted that** we'll clear up after her. If it weren't for me, her room would be disgusting!

Glossary

have things/it (all) your own way	get or do what you want, even when other people want sth different (also **have/get your own way**).
put your foot down	INF use your authority to stop sb doing sth.
sure of yourself	OFTEN DISAPPROVING very confident.
stop at nothing	do anything to get what you want, without caring about its effect on others.
walk all over sb	INF treat sb badly by always doing what you want to do.
push sb around	give sb orders in a rude or unpleasant way.
pick on sb	treat sb unfairly by blaming or criticizing them.
stick up for sb/yourself	support or defend sb/yourself.
not lift a finger (to do sth)	INF do nothing to help sb.
take it for granted (that …)	expect sth to happen because it usually does. (Also **take sb for granted** be so accustomed to sb that you don't appreciate them.)

spotlight Persuading people

If you can **twist sb round your little finger** INF, you can persuade them to do anything you want. If you **get round sb**, you persuade them to do what you want, often by being nice to them. If you **win sb over**, you get their support by persuading them you are right.

4 True or false? Write T or F.

1 If someone can *stick up for* themselves, they can defend themselves. ....
2 If someone *won't lift a finger*, they probably have an injury. ....
3 If someone *takes you for granted*, they can persuade you to do anything they want. ....
4 If someone *wins you over*, they have persuaded you that they are right. ....
5 If you *have things all your own way*, you do what everyone else wants. ....
6 If you will *stop at nothing*, you won't do anything to help. ....

5 Complete the dialogues.

1 Jun has no self doubts and is very confident. ~ Yes, she's very ....
2 Dad refused very firmly to let us stay out late. ~ Yes, he put ....
3 She criticizes me, but not the others. It's not fair! ~ Yes, I think she's .... you.
4 He tells me what to do and he's horrible about it. ~ Yes, he .... around.
5 Li's only nice to me because she wants my help. ~ She's just trying to .... you.
6 I can make her do anything. ~ Yes, you can twist ....
7 She's really bossy and I hate it. ~ Well, don't let her .... you!
8 Ed only wants to do what he wants. ~ Yes, he just wants to .... way.

7 I can talk about relationships

A Being married

> # How to make your marriage work
> You think you're **made for each other**, you **tie the knot**,
> then the hard work begins!
>
> ---
>
> ▶ You have to **meet** your partner **halfway** – compromise is everything. Don't let things like finance or household chores **drive a wedge between** you.
>
> ▶ If you're upset with each other, should you try to **clear the air** or **walk away**? Remember that things said **in the heat of the moment** can be hard to forgive later. On the other hand, if you walk away, you may **be storing up** problems for the future. My advice is: go for a short walk to calm down, then you can discuss the matter sensibly.
>
> ▶ Don't **live in each other's pockets**. You'll need to give each other space in the marriage.
>
> ▶ All marriages **go through a bad patch**; use laughter to keep things in perspective.

Glossary

be made for each other	INF be perfect partners.
tie the knot	INF get married. SYN **get hitched** INF.
meet sb halfway	reach agreement with sb by giving them part of what they want.
drive a wedge between people	make the relationship between two people or groups suffer. (👁 See page 162.)
clear the air	improve a difficult or tense situation by talking about it.
walk away	leave a bad situation.
in the heat of the moment	at a time when you are too angry or excited to think carefully.
store sth up	do sth that will make a problem worse in the future.
live in each other's pockets	be too emotionally close or spend too much time together.
go through a bad/sticky patch	INF experience a difficult period in your life.

1 Good news or bad news? Write G or B.

1 Talking cleared the air between us. ......
2 I said it in the heat of the moment. ......
3 We're going through a sticky patch. ......
4 They're made for each other. ......
5 They tied the knot last Saturday. ......
6 We agreed to meet each other halfway. ......
7 It drove a wedge between us. ......
8 They're living in each other's pockets. ......

2 Put the words in order and add one word.

▶ of | it | I | the | moment | said | in | the   *I said it in the heat of the moment.*
1 for | Dom | are | Janet | other | and | each   ....
2 they | think | hitched | do | you | will   .... ?
3 be | trouble | could | later | storing | for | you   ....
4 argument | walk | an | easy | it | isn't | to | from   ....
5 marriage | a | through | went | bad | their   ....
6 each | they're | other's | in | living   ....

3 ABOUT YOU Look at the advice in the text at the top. Do you agree with all the points? Why/why not? Write in your notebook, or talk to another student.

B Being single

Is it fun being single?

DOZYJOE Yes! You're free – nothing**'s holding you back** and no one's nagging you because the dishes **are piling up** in the sink. You can **do as you please** any time, day or night.

RUDY Not for me. I'm bored and lonely. Yes, you **answer to** no one, but **I'd far sooner** be in a loving relationship. **I'd give anything to** meet the right person.

BELLA My previous boyfriend **messed** me **around**; I felt he **let** me **down** badly, and I was really hurt. Now that I**'ve finished with** him, the thought of going through the same thing again **doesn't bear thinking about**. I don't want another distressing **break-up**.

Glossary

hold sb back	stop sb being as successful as they should be.
pile up	increase in quantity or amount.
do as you please	be able to do whatever you like. SYN **please yourself**.
answer to sb (**for sth**)	have to explain your actions or decisions to sb.
mess sb around/about	treat sb badly, especially by changing your mind a lot or breaking promises.
let sb down	not help or support sb as they had hoped or expected.
finish with sb	end a romantic relationship with sb.
not bear thinking about	be too shocking or unpleasant to think about.
break-up	the ending of a relationship or marriage. **break up** (**with sb**) v.

spotlight Expressing wishes

I'd (far) sooner be married. = I would (much) prefer to be married.
I'd give anything to meet her. = I would very much like to meet her.
I'd give my right arm to have Anya back. = I would very much like to have Anya back.

---

4 Write the opposite using an idiom or phrasal verb.

▶ I can do whatever I want. OPP *I can't do as I please / please myself.*
1 Her boyfriend treated her really well. OPP Her boyfriend ....
2 I don't have to explain my actions to my boss. OPP I have to ....
3 There's less and less work. OPP The work ....
4 I've just started going out with Pilar. OPP I've just ....
5 He didn't stand in the way of my success. OPP He ....
6 She gave me the help I was hoping for. OPP She ....

5 Complete the texts with one word in each case. Then underline the full idioms, phrasal verbs, or phrasal nouns.

Danny was quite possessive, so when I (1) .... with him, I was relieved that at last I could do (2) .... I pleased. But not long after the (3) .... of the relationship I was terribly lonely, and I regretted what I'd done. Now I'd give (4) .... to have him back.

I feel guilty about Donna. I know I (5) .... her down badly, and I'm sure she was sick of me (6) .... her about. But the truth is, I'd far (7) .... be single and be able to please (8) .... in what I do. And getting married just doesn't (9) .... thinking about; I'm far too selfish.

I'm sure there's a little sign above my head that says, 'I want to get married'! I'd give my right (10) .... to meet Mr Right!

6 ABOUT YOU Which speaker at the top of the page do you agree with most, and why? Or do you have a different point of view? Write in your notebook, or talk to another student.

8 I can talk about families

A Why do families argue?

What is it about **your own flesh and blood**? I've got two sisters. They used to **fight like cat and dog** when they were kids, and **there's little love lost between them** now. But as soon as an outsider criticizes either of them, they immediately **close ranks** and **turn on** them. It's a bit the same with me and my wife. When we're together we argue, but when we're apart, we're **miserable as sin**. How do you **account for** that? I guess living **on top of** each other doesn't help, and I'm sure we **take** each other **for granted** a lot of the time. But families are strange!

Glossary

your own flesh and blood	a person or people that you are related to.
fight like cat and dog	(of two people) often have angry fights.
there's little/no love lost between them	= they don't like each other.
close ranks	If people **close ranks**, they join together to protect themselves, especially when they are being criticized.
turn on sb	attack sb suddenly and unexpectedly.
(as) miserable as sin	INF used to emphasize that sb is very unhappy.
account for sth	be the explanation or cause of sth.
take sb for granted	be so accustomed to sb that you don't appreciate them.

spotlight *on top of sb/sth*

They live on top of each other. = very close to each other (which often causes problems).
He gets commission on top of his salary. = in addition to his salary.
The books were piled on top of one another. = on, over, or covering one another.

1 Replace the words in italics with an idiom or phrasal verb that keeps a similar meaning.

1 When she left him, he was *so unhappy*. ....
2 *In addition to* all the family problems, he's split up with his girlfriend. ....
3 You can't abandon them: they're *members of your family*. ....
4 She *suddenly attacked* me for no reason. ....
5 His surname's different from his brother's. How do you *explain* that? ....
6 Living *so close to* one another is a problem. ....
7 My brothers *argue bitterly* all the time. ....
8 *They don't like each other.* ....

2 Complete the sentences.

1 Is it true we fight more with our own .... and blood? If so, why?
2 Did you ever fight like cat and .... with any of your brothers or sisters?
3 Do you think members of your family would close .... if criticized?
4 Do you ever feel your family are living on .... of each other?
5 Have any members of your family ever turned .... you? If so, why?
6 Do you ever .... any of your family for granted? If so, who?

3 ABOUT YOU Write your own answers to Exercise 2 in your notebook, or talk to another student.

B Being a middle child

Middle child syndrome

Being the middle child of three can **result in** 'middle-child syndrome'. The firstborn often gets the most attention and **is put on a pedestal**; the last to be born is the baby and tends to **get away with murder**. The middle child, though, can feel neglected, **squeezed out** by their siblings, and **starved of** attention. Some studies **have backed** this **up**, suggesting that middle children who feel **left out** may **distance themselves from** others and become loners. It is important, therefore, that parents **make a point of lavishing** attention **on** the middle child and praising their achievements. And on the positive side, studies show that the middle child is often more creative and artistic than the others.

Glossary

result in sth	cause a particular situation to happen.
put sb on a pedestal	admire sb so much that you do not see their faults.
get away with murder	INF do whatever you want without being stopped or punished.
squeeze sb out	(usually passive) If sb is **squeezed out**, they are no longer included in sth that they were previously involved in.
starve sb/sth of sth	(usually passive) If you are **starved of sth**, you do not have enough of sth that you need.
back sth/sb up	support sth/sb; say that what sb says or writes is true.
leave sb out	not include sb.
distance yourself from sth	become less involved or connected with sth.
make a point of doing sth	make a special effort to do sth.
lavish sth on sb	give a lot, often too much, of sth to sb.

4 One word is missing. Where does it go? Write it at the end.

▶ It can result ⟨ serious problems. *in* ....
1 They lavish far too much money their children. ....
2 There's a danger that they will their son on a pedestal. ....
3 She's very naughty; they let her get with murder. ....
4 Since the divorce, he's distanced from his family. ....
5 No wonder the child was unhappy; she was of attention. ....
6 Try to a point of praising your middle child's creativity. ....

5 Complete this story of one middle child.

It's true that the firstborn is put on a (1) .... and the third child gets away with (2) .... , but in my case it didn't (3) .... in me becoming an underachiever. Quite the opposite. I made a (4) .... of ensuring that I wasn't squeezed (5) .... or (6) .... of attention. In fact, I craved attention and fought really hard to excel in everything. I became an overachiever.

Now, I don't feel left (7) .... by my parents. We have a very good relationship and I feel they (8) .... me up in everything I do. Mind you, they still (9) .... more attention on my younger sister than me. But I don't mind that now.

6 ABOUT YOU Are you the middle child of three, or do you know any middle children? If so, is there any truth in what the text says? Write in your notebook, or talk to another student.

9 I can describe my emotions

A An emotional rollercoaster

A rollercoaster

Since I found out that I was pregnant, I've been on an emotional rollercoaster[1]: my mood seems to change **for no apparent reason**. One minute I'm **on top of the world**, the next I'm **at the end of my tether**, or **crying my eyes out** at some silly romantic movie. I'm so short-tempered – the slightest thing **winds** me **up**. A guy in the office was tapping on the radiator earlier, and I just **went off the deep end** and **screamed my head off** at him. Poor man – I have since apologized. Pregnancy **has stirred up** feelings I didn't know existed! It's such a new experience; I guess I just need time to **take** it all **in**.

Glossary

for no apparent reason	without an obvious cause.
on top of the world	very happy or proud. OPP **down in the dumps** INF.
at the end of your tether	having no patience or energy left to deal with a difficult situation. SYN **at your wits' end**.
cry your eyes/heart out	INF cry in an uncontrolled way and be unable to stop.
wind sb up	INF make sb angry or upset.
go off the deep end	INF suddenly become very angry or emotional.
scream/laugh/shout your head off	scream/laugh/shout very loudly.
stir sth up	make sb feel or think sth, e.g anger, fear, memories.
take sth in	accept sth as real or true (*I can't **take it all in**).*

1 **Rewrite the sentences using the word in capitals. The meaning must stay the same.**

▶ I'm feeling really fed up. DOWN *I'm feeling really down in the dumps.*
1 The news is so bad that I can't believe it. TAKE ....
2 The boy was making a lot of noise. HEAD ....
3 She couldn't stop crying. EYES ....
4 I can't deal with the situation; I'm so upset. TETHER ....
5 He got angry and lost his temper. DEEP ....
6 The news made everyone angry. STIR ....
7 Please don't make her angry. WIND ....
8 I'm feeling extremely happy. WORLD ....

2 **ABOUT YOU** **Complete the questions. Then write your answers in your notebook, or talk to another student.**

1 What kinds of things in life tend to wind you .... ?
2 What makes you feel down in the .... ?
3 Do you ever feel at your wits' .... ? If so, why?
4 When did you last laugh your head .... , and why?
5 When did you last go off the .... end at someone, and why?
6 Do you ever feel incredibly positive for no .... reason?
7 What memories would it .... up to see your old school?
8 Which single thing would make you feel on .... of the world right now?

B Keeping emotions under control

Dealing with office disputes

As head of department, I have to deal with disputes between employees, and I absolutely cannot **take sides**. I try to involve both parties in the dispute, but ensure that I keep any meeting **on an even keel**. **That's easier said than done**, especially if they**'re dying to have a go at** each other. Someone like Zoe, for instance, tends to **rub** her colleagues **up the wrong way**, and **flares up** at the slightest provocation. So, first I spend time alone with her, **cooling** her **down**, then I bring in whoever she has upset. It's a stressful job, and I have to **keep** my emotions **in check**. When I go home, I can **pour my heart out** to my husband: he doesn't mind at all!

Glossary	
on an even keel	happening in a calm way, with no sudden changes or disturbances.
that's easier said than done	= that's a good idea, but difficult to achieve.
be dying to do sth / for sth	INF want to do or have sth very much.
have a go at sb	INF attack or criticize sb.
rub sb up the wrong way	INF do or say sth that annoys or offends sb.
flare up	1 suddenly become angry (as above). 2 (of a fire) suddenly start burning more brightly.
cool (sb) down	become or make sb calmer and less excited. SYN **calm (sb) down**.
keep sth/sb in check	control sth/sb.
pour your heart out (to sb)	tell sb all your problems or feelings. OPP **bottle up your feelings/emotions**.

spotlight *side*

I can't take sides in their argument. = support one person or group and not another.
I'm on your side in this matter. = agree with you and support you.
She always sides with my brother. = agrees with him and supports him.

3 Write sentences using words from each column.

She rubs ✓	side	in check.
He poured	said	on this issue.
Don't take	sides	the wrong way. ✓
He must keep	up	out to me.
Whose	me up ✓	than done.
That's easier	his heart	a coffee.
Don't bottle	for	are you on?
I'm dying	his anger	your feelings.

She rubs me up the wrong way.

4 Complete the dialogues. Then circle the full idioms and phrasal verbs.

1 Has all the chaos subsided at home? ~ Yes, we're back on an .... again.
2 Does your brother support you? ~ No, he always .... with my sister. It's not fair!
3 You seemed angry at the meeting. ~ Yeah, it took me ages to .... down afterwards.
4 Did your boss speak to you about being late? ~ Yes, he had a .... me again.
5 Did you enjoy meeting Louis? ~ Oh yes, I'd been .... to meet him for ages.
6 I thought he was going to explode. ~ Yeah, but somehow he kept his temper in ....
7 Why were they fighting? ~ Well, violence .... up very easily in that area.
8 He needs to calm down. ~ Well, that's easier .... He's incredibly upset.
9 Don't you like Cheryl? ~ She's OK but she just rubs me ....
10 I feel so tense inside. ~ That's because you .... your feelings.

10 I can describe physical actions

She rolled the picture up.

She dealt the cards out.

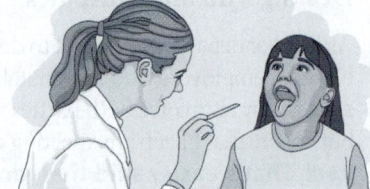
She stuck her tongue out.

He zipped his jacket up.

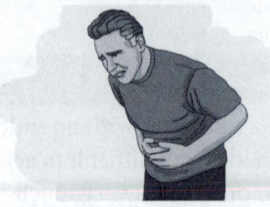
He doubled up in pain (also be doubled up). SYN double over.

She took the skirt up. OPP let sth down.

We propped the tree up.

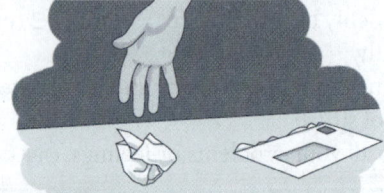
I screwed the letter up.

She curled up on the sofa.

I mopped up the spilt milk.

I chucked the packet away INF. SYN chuck sth out INF.

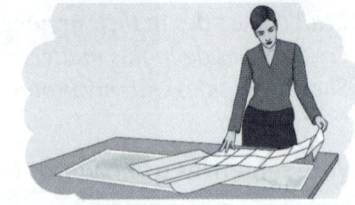
She spread the map out on the desk.

Some of these phrasal verbs also have figurative meanings.

Example	Meaning
The business is in a bad state; we'll have to roll our sleeves up and get on with it.	**roll your sleeves up** start doing a difficult or unpleasant job.
Judge Wallis dealt out tough penalties for people driving without a licence.	**deal sth out** give a punishment to a person or group. SYN **hand sth out**.
She hates her job, but she'll have to stick it out until the end of the year.	**stick it**/**sth out** INF continue to do sth to the end, even though it is boring or difficult.
The new Italian Prime Minister took up his post at the weekend.	**take sth up** start a new job or have a new responsibility.
The government is propping up the ailing car industry. Do you agree with that?	**prop sth up** support sth that is in difficulty. SYN **shore sth up**.
I made a mess of the exam last time, so I don't want to screw it up this time.	**screw sth up** SLANG do sth badly or spoil sth. **screw-up** N.
When she sang, we curled up with embarrassment.	**curl up** INF become very embarrassed.
We just have a few things to mop up before signing the contracts.	**mop sth up** complete or end sth by dealing with a few final details.

1 Tick the logical sentence ending.

1 Jack's trousers need letting down: *he's growing fast* ☐ *I bought a size too big for him* ☐.
2 Could you chuck this out – *that cupboard will do fine* ☐ *we don't need it any more* ☐.
3 She screwed up the notes and *put them in the bin* ☐ *put them in her folder* ☐.
4 I've tried propping the photo up but *it keeps falling off* ☐ *it keeps falling over* ☐.
5 When you've rolled up the rug, *it'll need hoovering* ☐ *it can go in the lorry* ☐.
6 Zip your bag up or *someone might steal it* ☐ *someone might steal your wallet* ☐.
7 The cat curled up on the chair and *fell asleep* ☐ *scratched me* ☐.
8 He was doubled up – I think *he was in pain* ☐ *he was in danger* ☐.

2 True or false? Write T or F.

1 If you prop something up, it's because it isn't stable. ......
2 If you spread something out, you get rid of it. ......
3 If you zip something up, it means it was closed before. ......
4 If you let something down, it's because it was too long. ......
5 If you screw up an exam, it means you make a mess of it. ......
6 If you have to mop some juice up, it's because you spilt it. ......
7 If you're doubled over, you might be laughing or in pain. ......
8 If you curl up, it means you stretch your body. ......
9 If you take up a pair of trousers, you make them shorter. ......
10 If you mop up the details of something, you forget about them. ......

3 The same word is missing in each pair of sentences. Write it in.

1 a I'll have to .... this skirt up.
   b She's hoping to .... up her new job by Christmas.
2 a There are a few details to .... up before we end the meeting.
   b Why didn't anyone .... up this water that's all over the floor?
3 a I just .... up when she said all those embarrassing things about me.
   b I'd had an awful day, so I just went home and .... up in front of the TV.
4 a That little boy .... out his tongue at me. What bad manners!
   b It was an awful job, but I .... it out for six months.
5 a The judge decided to .... out a heavy sentence for the robbery.
   b Can you .... the playing cards out? I've hurt my hand.
6 a Time to .... our sleeves up and get down to work, I think.
   b You'd better .... your trousers up if you're going for a walk on the beach.
7 a I can't see why the government should .... up such a useless industry.
   b I tried to .... the fence up with some large stones, but eventually it fell over.
8 a It's a really important meeting, so make sure you don't .... it up!
   b What made him .... up that note from the boss?

4 Complete the sentences using a phrasal verb from page 28 in a logical way.

▶ I think we can get the carpet in the car if we *roll it up* .
1 I've got another six months with this awful project. I hope I can ....
2 We need to see all the photos at the same time, so you'll need to ....
3 This skirt's too short, but it's easy enough to ....
4 That document's really important – why on earth did you .... ?
5 There's a lot of work to be done, so it's time to ....
6 There's a lot of water on the floor. Could you .... ?
7 He was so weak he kept falling over. I had to ....
8 When my brother did that awful dance at the wedding, I just ....

Review: People

Unit 5

1 Read the text, then answer the questions.

AMAZON ADVENTURE

As group leader, you have to choose four volunteers from the list below to accompany you on a three-week trek down the Amazon. It will be hot, difficult, and you're not sure what to expect. You need people with initiative, who will also work well as a team. Which four would you choose and why? And why wouldn't you choose the other six?

Amy: a bright spark

Syd: tough as old boots

Mandy: a cold fish

Ollie: an unknown quantity

Don: nobody's fool

Clive: likes the sound of his own voice

Bill: thick as two short planks

Brenda: salt of the earth

Isabel: doesn't suffer fools gladly

Alec: a creature of habit

I would choose ....

....

....

I wouldn't choose the others because ....

....

....

....

2 Complete the phrases being defined.

1 hopping .... very angry.
2 have a quick .... become angry quickly and often.
3 a nasty .... of work a very unpleasant person.
4 a live .... someone who is lively and full of energy.
5 a soft .... someone you can easily get money from because they're kind.
6 mad as a .... strange or crazy.
7 under sb's .... completely controlled by somebody else.
8 play it .... hide your feelings so that you appear calm and controlled.

Unit 6

1 Rewrite the sentences using the word in capitals. Keep a similar meaning.

1 He never does anything to help. FINGER ....
2 She'll do anything to get what she wants. STOP ....
3 They tried very hard to help us. LENGTHS ....
4 Her generosity is what makes her different. SET ....
5 Call me if you need a sympathetic friend. SHOULDER ....
6 My sister assumes I'm always there to help her. GRANTED ....

2 Complete the sentences.

1 Does anyone ever pick .... you for no reason?
2 Do you think you can stick .... for yourself in most situations?
3 Can anyone twist you round their little .... ?
4 Who do you .... to when you need a .... to cry on?
5 Who do you usually ask when you need someone to lend you a helping .... ?
6 Does anyone ever put their .... down to stop you getting what you want?
7 Can you remember a time when you went out of your .... to help someone?
8 Is there anyone you sometimes .... for granted?

3 ABOUT YOU Write your answers to Exercise 2 in your notebook, or talk to another student.

Unit 7

1 Complete the conversation.

ANA   I hear that Tina has (1) .... with Graham. I'm amazed – they've been together for a couple of years, haven't they?

DOM   Yeah, but I think the (2) .... was pretty inevitable, actually.

ANA   Why's that?

DOM   Well, they've been going through a sticky (3) .... for a while now, and to be honest I don't think they're really (4) .... for each other.

ANA   Well, Graham's not an easy person. He likes to please (5) .... what he does, and frankly, he's not the kind of guy to (6) .... someone halfway.

DOM   Exactly. I think Tina felt he'd (7) .... her around long enough, and in the end, she decided to walk (8) .... from the whole thing. I don't blame her.

2 Rewrite each sentence, starting with the words given. Keep the meaning the same.

▶ He's going to have to compromise with her.
  He's going to have to _meet her halfway_ .
1 It happened at a time when they were too angry or excited to think carefully.
  It happened in the heat ....
2 It was money which caused them to disagree and argue so much.
  It was money which drove ....
3 It would be much nicer if you came alone.
  I'd far ....
4 They're just spending too much time together.
  They're just living in each ....
5 I hear they've decided to get married.
  I hear they've decided to tie ....
6 I'd love to meet George Clooney.
  I'd give ....

Unit 8

1 Tick the correct sentence ending.

1 There's no love lost between us: a) we're great friends. ☐ b) we just don't get on. ☐
2 He always makes a point of helping; a) why is he so selfish? ☐ b) why is he so kind to us? ☐
3 They started playing and left Michael out: a) that made him sad. ☐ b) that made him feel special. ☐
4 Dan backed me up because a) he knew I was wrong. ☐ b) he knew I needed support. ☐
5 Service was on top of the main charges, a) which made it more expensive. ☐ b) which wasn't so bad. ☐
6 They always close ranks when a) there's an external threat. ☐ b) they're higher up. ☐
7 She turned on me; a) I had expected that. ☐ b) I hadn't expected that. ☐
8 They take Mum for granted, and a) they shouldn't do that. ☐ b) she likes it. ☐

2 Rewrite the sentences using the correct form of the word in capitals. Keep the same meaning.

▶ She didn't include me in the plans. LEAVE *She left me out of the plans.*
1 Shan became less involved in the group. DISTANCE
2 I gave my son a lot of praise. LAVISH
3 Dara doesn't get any affection from her parents. STARVE
4 He's a close relative of mine. FLESH
5 She behaved badly and never got caught. MURDER
6 Those kids argue all day long. CAT

Unit 9

1 Are you happy or unhappy about these situations? Write H or U.

1 I'm at the end of my tether. ....
2 She's on my side. ....
3 He wound me up. ....
4 The news stirred up anxiety. ....
5 I'm on top of the world. ....
6 He had a go at me. ....
7 I'm feeling a bit down in the dumps. ....
8 He went off the deep end. ....

2 Complete the idioms and phrasal verbs being defined.

1 scream your .... off   scream very loudly.
2 that's .... said than done   = that's a good idea, but difficult to achieve.
3 .... your heart out   tell sb all your problems and feelings.
4 take ....   support one person and not another.
5 .... sb up the wrong way INF   do or say sth that annoys sb.
6 for no .... reason   without an obvious cause.
7 cry your .... out   cry in an uncontrolled way.
8 be .... to do sth INF   want to do sth very much.

Unit 10

1 Use a phrasal verb to describe what you can see in each picture.

1 She's ....

2 She's ....

3 She's ....

4 He's ....

5 Somebody has ....

6 She's ....

7 I'm ....

8 I'm ....

2 Circle the correct definition.

1 If you **prop up** a company, you *help a company in difficulty | inherit it*.
2 If you **roll up your sleeves**, you *stop doing sth | start a difficult task*.
3 If you **screw sth up**, you *make a mess of it | forget how to do it*.
4 If you **curl up** with sth, you become very *angry | embarrassed*.
5 If you **stick sth out**, you *continue to do sth difficult or boring | you work hard at sth*.
6 If there are a few things to **mop up**, there are a few things to *remember | complete*.

11 I can talk about money

A Financial worries

Hi Dad

I spoke to Martin yesterday. He'd be too embarrassed to tell you this, but I think he's **pretty much** living **on the breadline**. Last week he had to **fork out** a lot of money **on** his car, which he badly needs, and next month he'**ll be** even **worse off** when his rent goes up. The thing is, I don't think he's got much to **fall back on**. I said I could **lay my hands on** about £200 to help out, but he'll need more than that to **pay off** his debts. I know he desperately wants to **pay his own way**, but would you be willing to **bail** him **out** just this once, or at least have a word with him - without saying I'd spoken to you? Thanks.

Love Tracey

Glossary

pretty much/**well**	INF almost.
on the breadline	very poor; with very little money to live on.
fork sth out (**on sth**)	INF spend a lot of money on sth, usually money you don't want to spend. SYN **pay sth out**.
be worse off	be poorer, unhappier, etc. than before. OPP **be better off**.
fall back on sth	have sth to use when in difficulty (in this case money).
lay/**get your hands on sth**	find or get sth that you want or really need.
pay sth off	finish paying money that is owed for sth.
pay your (**own**) **way**	pay for everything yourself without relying on others.
bail sb out	rescue sb from a difficult situation, usually with money.

1 Correct the mistake in each sentence.

▶ I've always paid my ~~only~~ way. *own*
1 Where am I going to lay my hand on $5,000? ....
2 I had to fork over £30 just to get into the club. ....
3 He still has to pay out most of his debts. ....
4 A lot of families are living on the breadqueue. ....
5 If she spends her salary, she'll have no money to fill back on. ....
6 Now she's got promotion, she'll be better on. ....

2 Complete the text.

When my daughter left university, she said she'd soon be able to pay (1) .... her debts, and then she'd (2) .... much be able to pay her own (3) .... But things didn't work out like that. After she'd (4) .... out almost all her salary on rent, travel, and food, she was (5) .... off than before; and as she hadn't saved anything at university, she had nothing to (6) .... back on – nothing, that is, except her parents. We were naturally the ones who had to (7) .... her out.

3 ABOUT YOU Complete the sentences. Then decide if you agree with them. Write your answers in your notebook, or talk to another student.

1 You should always .... your debts as soon as possible.
2 Once you leave home, you should .... way.
3 If you need to .... hands on some money fast, you should borrow it from a member of your family. That's what families are for: to .... out when things are difficult.
4 Governments should give more to people who are on ....

B Financial investment

TOP TIPS for investing in the stock market

- Don't invest more than you can afford, or you could **land yourself in** trouble.
- Don't invest **off your own bat** – seek proper financial advice first.
- **Err on the side of caution** if you don't **have** a lot of **money to play with**.
- Don't let all the jargon **put** you **off** – you'll pick it up **as time goes by**.
- Once you've bought stocks, **hold on to** them for a while. Fast trading can be expensive.
- Don't forget to **add on** the fees you will have to pay: this could **come to** 3 or 4 per cent.
- Don't expect your investments to **bear fruit** immediately – you need patience.
- Remember shares go down as well as up, so go into it **with your eyes open**.

Glossary

land sb/yourself in sth	INF get sb/yourself into a difficult situation.
off your own bat	INF If you do sth **off your own bat**, it is your idea and you do it without help from others.
err on the side of caution	be careful and not take many risks.
have money/time, etc. **to play with**	have enough money/time, etc. for doing sth.
as time goes by	as time passes.
hold on to / onto sth	keep sth; not give or sell sth to sb else.
add sth on (**to sth**)	include sth extra. **add-on** N.
come to sth	add up to a total amount (*The bill came to £50*).
bear fruit	have a successful result.
with your eyes open	knowing that there could be problems in a situation.

> **spotlight** *put sb off (sth)*
>
> *The accident put her off driving.* = made her dislike it (as above).
> *It's too late to put him off.* = postpone or cancel the arrangement I made with him.
> *Don't put me off when I'm working.* = disturb or distract me.

4 Put the words into correct sentences.

1 the | err | on | should | side | you | caution | of ....
2 it | eyes | went | I | with | open | my | into ....
3 he | an | own | his | account | bat | off | opened ....
4 could | himself | in | trouble | he | land ....
5 she | her | to | shares | held | on | oil ....
6 play | don't | much | with | money | we | to | have ....

5 Complete the texts.

'The shares were going to cost me just under £800, but once you (1) .... on the broker's fee at 2 per cent, and the management fee, it (2) .... to a bit more than £800.'

'My broker told me not to expect shares to bear (3) .... immediately, but he said they would go up as time (4) .... by, and that would give me more money to (5) .... with.'

'I knew the shares were a bit risky and that (6) .... me off. I'm afraid I always (7) .... on the side of caution; that's my nature. My cousin is the complete opposite. He invested £5,000 entirely off his own (8) ...., with no financial advice at all.'

12 I can talk about wealth and poverty

A Wealth

You may think that some people **have more money than sense**, and in my brother's case, you'd be right. He's a city trader **living life in the fast lane**, and he **thinks nothing of** spending £1,000 just on a night out. Michelin-star restaurants **don't come cheap**, and when you **splash out on** expensive wines as well, a meal alone can **cost an arm and a leg** – and that's before he's even **set foot inside** the casino. As far as he's concerned, **money's no object**, and he can lose vast sums in **a matter of seconds**. Would I fancy living **in the lap of luxury** like him? No, not really.

Glossary

have more money than sense	have a lot of money and spend it stupidly.
live life in the fast lane	If sb **lives life in the fast lane**, they live a life full of activity and excitement.
think nothing of (doing) sth	consider an activity to be normal that most people would think was difficult, unusual, etc.
not come cheap	= be expensive.
splash out (on sth)	INF spend an unusually large sum of money on sth.
cost an arm and a leg	INF be very expensive.
set foot in/on/inside sth	enter a place.
money is no object	used to say that sb has a lot of money and can buy what they want.
in the lap of luxury	in the easy and comfortable conditions that result from being wealthy.

> **spotlight** *a matter of …*
>
> **A matter of seconds/minutes/days**, etc. is used to emphasize how short a period of time is.
> *The books you ordered should arrive in **a matter of days**.*
> *It was only **a matter of minutes** before he returned.*

1 True or false? Write T or F.

1 If you *think nothing of doing something*, it means you are not interested in it. ....
2 If *money is no object*, you are able to spend a lot. ....
3 If you say '*in a matter of weeks*', you are saying that something will take quite a long time. ....
4 If you *splash out on something*, you take care of how much you are spending. ....
5 If you live *in the lap of luxury*, you live in very comfortable conditions. ....
6 If you *live life in the fast lane*, you are always moving from one place to another. ....

2 Complete the dialogues.

1 Why did she buy that ugly big house? ~ Because she's got more money than ....
2 I'll bet that boat was expensive. ~ Yes, it was. It cost an arm and a ....
3 Did you have to wait a long time? ~ No, just a .... of minutes.
4 Why are you saving up? ~ I'm going to .... out on a luxury holiday in New York.
5 School books are expensive, aren't they? ~ Yes, they don't .... cheap.
6 You've been to the Ritz before, haven't you? ~ No, I've never .... foot in the place.

3 ABOUT YOU Would you enjoy life in the fast lane? Would you like to live in the lap of luxury? Why/why not? When was the last time you splashed out on something? What was it? Write in your notebook, or talk to another student.

B Poverty

I met Don at a centre for homeless people. He'd been living beyond his means and found himself in arrears with his rent. Then he lost his job and got caught up in a downward spiral that led to him becoming homeless. His only real possession was a guitar, with which he managed to earn a bit of money from busking, but he was living from hand to mouth. He told me he knew of a room going cheap somewhere in Paddington, and if he could just put aside a bit of money, he might be able to put down a deposit. Sadly though, the last I heard, Don had been arrested for stealing. His prospects are not good to say the least, but it's the same old story for many people like him living on the streets.

Busking: playing music in the street for money.

Glossary

live beyond your means	spend more money than you earn.
be/get caught up in sth	become involved in sth which may cause problems.
live from hand to mouth	have just enough money or food to stay alive.
going cheap	If sth is **going cheap**, it is available at a lower price than usual.
put sth aside	save or keep sth for future use.
put down a deposit	pay some money to reserve sth, before paying for it in full.
the last I heard	used to give the most recent news you have about sth.
to say the least	used to say you could have described sth in a much stronger and more extreme way.
it's the same old story	used to say that the present bad situation has often happened before.

spotlight *in arrears (with sth)*

If you are **in arrears with** your rent or other payments, you are late paying the money that you owe. This phrase is slightly formal; a more informal way to say it is *I got behind with the rent / my payments.*

---

4 One word is missing in each sentence. Where does it go? Write it at the end.

▶ You should always put some money ∧ in case of emergencies. *aside*
1 I heard she got with her mortgage payments; she owes over €1000. ....
2 They've been living from hand mouth for months now. ....
3 As soon as he gets any money, he wastes it; it's the same story. ....
4 He's lucky to be alive, say the least. ....
5 I bought these shoes because they were going. ....
6 Where's Joe? ~ The last heard, he was in Scotland. ....
7 He's been living his means. ....
8 You have to put a deposit if you want to keep the flat. ....

5 Rewrite the sentences using the word in capitals. Keep the same meaning.

▶ That's the most recent news I have of him. LAST *That's the last I heard of him.*
1 He got involved in something illegal. CAUGHT ....
2 He's late paying his rent. ARREARS ....
3 I'm saving €100 a month. ASIDE ....
4 She paid a £25 deposit. PUT ....
5 This happens over and over again. STORY ....
6 She's spending more than she earns. MEANS ....

13 I can talk about health

A A nasty bug

LAURA Steph, are you OK? **You're not your usual self** today.

STEPH No, I'm a bit **off-colour**, actually. I **felt like death warmed up** when I woke up this morning. I had a splitting headache, and I thought I was going to **throw up**. I just **keeled over** and nearly **passed out**!

LAURA Oh, no! Poor you. Do you want something for your headache?

STEPH It's OK; I took some tablets and it's just starting to **wear off**. I really hope I'**m** not **coming down with** flu.

LAURA Well, there's a nasty bug **going round** at the moment - you could have **picked** it **up** anywhere. You'd better **take things easy** for a day or two.

Glossary

you're not your usual/normal self	you're not looking or behaving as you usually do.
off-colour	INF looking or feeling ill. SYN **under the weather** INF.
feel/look like death warmed up	INF feel or look very ill or tired.
throw up	vomit; be sick.
keel over	INF fall over, especially when you feel ill.
pass out	faint; lose consciousness for a short time. SYN **black out**. OPP **come round**.
wear off	(of a pain, feeling, or effect) gradually disappear or stop.
come/go down with sth	get one of the common illnesses (flu, a cold, etc.).
go round	spread from person to person. (A rumour can also **go round**.)
pick sth up	INF catch an infectious illness. (Also **pick up a bug** INF. **bug** = bacterium or virus.)
take things/it easy	relax and avoid working hard or doing too much.

1 Circle the correct answer.

1 If you're **under the weather**, you are *depressed* | *off-colour*.
2 If you think you're going to **throw up**, you should go to *bed* | *the bathroom*.
3 If you **pass out**, you *know* | *don't know* what is happening around you at that moment.
4 If you think you're **coming down with** something, you're starting to feel *tired* | *unwell*.
5 If you **pick up** a virus, you *become ill* | *feel better*.
6 If you **keel over**, you will definitely *fall over* | *black out*.

2 One word is missing in each line. Where does it go? Write it at the end.

1 I banged my elbow last week, and the pain is only just starting to off now. ....
2 I had a terrible night, and I feel like death warmed this morning. ....
3 I think I'm coming with a cold. What shall I take for it? ....
4 Her face went white as a sheet and she suddenly blacked; it was terrifying. ....
5 If you're feeling a bit under the weather, you'd better it easy today. ....
6 He's not his self today. What's the matter with him? ....

3 ABOUT YOU Complete the sentences. Then write your answers in your notebook, or discuss with another student.

1 When did you last feel under the ....? What was wrong with you?
2 Have you ever blacked out and then .... round in front of a lot of people?
3 Is there a bug .... round where you live at the moment?
4 If you're feeling ....-colour, do you always take things ....?

B Major and minor illness

> … After the operation Dad seemed to be **on the mend**, but he suddenly **took a turn for the worse** and started to **go downhill**. **It was touch-and-go** for a while, but the doctors reassured us that he **would pull through**. He's doing OK now, **touch wood**, …

> … I woke up **feeling out of sorts** and my eyes were incredibly itchy. When I looked in the mirror, I saw that they **had swollen up**, and I also noticed **I'd come out in** a rash on my neck. After a while, the swelling **went down**, but the rash **hasn't gone away**. I'd better see the doctor and **get** it **checked out**. **Better safe than sorry.** …

Glossary

on the mend	INF getting better after an illness or injury.
take a turn for the worse/better	suddenly become worse/better.
go downhill	get worse in health, quality, etc.
it is touch-and-go (**whether**)	INF = it's very uncertain whether sth will happen or not.
pull through (**sth**)	get better after a life-threatening illness or operation.
feel/be out of sorts	feel/be ill or bad-tempered.
swell up	(of part of the body) become bigger in size. OPP **go down**.
come out in sth	become covered in spots or a rash.
go away	disappear.
check sth out	find out if sth is safe, correct, or acceptable.

spotlight Sayings

I think my back is OK now – touch wood! Said in order to avoid bad luck; the speaker will often touch something made of wood when they say this.

Let's get some malaria tablets – better safe than sorry. = it is wiser to act safely than to act carelessly and later regret it. Also **… to be on the safe side**.

4 Good news or bad news? Write G or B.

1 She's on the mend. ......
2 He didn't pull through the operation. ......
3 I've come out in spots. ......
4 It's touch-and-go at the moment. ......

5 She's feeling out of sorts. ......
6 The symptoms have gone away. ......
7 She's going downhill. ......
8 Mum's taken a turn for the better. ......

5 Complete the dialogues.

1 You'd better ask the doctor about that. ~ Yes, you're right. Better safe than ....
2 Is the dog any better? ~ No, it .... downhill very quickly, and I'm afraid it died.
3 Shall I bring some bandages on holiday? ~ Yes, just to be on the safe ....
4 Have you got over the operation? ~ Mmm, things seem to be fine now – touch ....
5 It was a bee sting, wasn't it? ~ Yes. It started to .... up immediately.
6 I've got a mark on my skin. ~ Probably nothing, but you'd better get it .... out.
7 I've still got this cough. ~ Yes, it can take ages for these things to go ....
8 I see the swelling on your arm has .... down now. ~ Yes, it's much better, thanks.
9 I hear Bryn was in a really bad accident. ~ Yes, it was touch-and- .... for a while.
10 Your mum had a nasty fall, didn't she? ~ Yes, but fortunately she's on the .... now.

14 I can talk about driving and journeys

A Driving irritations

- You come out of a shop to find that another car **has** double-parked and **blocked** you **in**.
- You're in a steady stream of traffic, but there's always someone trying to **cut in** in front of you.
- Someone **flags** you **down**. You **pull over** to help, but all they want is directions!
- You know that **getting from A to B** is two kilometres **as the crow flies**, but after going round various one-way systems, you end up driving ten.
- A friend asks for a lift into town. You know the traffic **is murder** at this time of the day, and they want you to **drop** them **off** in the most difficult place.
- You have an important appointment and you**'re cutting it fine**, but the person in front of you insists on driving **at a snail's pace**.
- You are **miles from anywhere** (and lost), and there are no signposts giving directions.

Glossary

block sb/sth in	stop sb from moving their car out of a place.
cut in (on sth/sb)	(of a vehicle or driver) move suddenly in front of another vehicle, leaving little space between the two vehicles.
flag sb down	signal to a driver to stop by waving at them.
pull over	move to the side of the road to stop or let sth pass.
get from A to B	travel from one place to another.
as the crow flies	in a straight line.
be murder	INF (of a situation) be difficult and unpleasant.
drop sb off	stop driving so that a passenger can get out of your car.
cut it/things fine	INF leave yourself only a very short amount of time to do sth.
at a snail's pace	very slowly.
miles from anywhere	INF in the countryside, a long way from a town.

1 Complete the text.

It's only two miles from home to my office as the (1) .... flies, but the traffic in town is always (2) .... in the mornings, and everything moves at a (3) .... pace. I was (4) .... it fine on that morning as I had to (5) .... a neighbour off at the station before getting to work for an early meeting. In my impatience I (6) .... in on the person in front of me when I was trying to overtake. Unfortunately, a policeman saw what happened and (7) .... me down. I (8) .... over, worrying about what he'd say. Luckily it was just a caution.

2 Replace the words in italics with an idiom or phrasal verb that keeps the same meaning.

1 I want to *travel from one place to another* as quickly as possible. ....
2 The traffic is *extremely unpleasant* during the rush hour. ....
3 *In a straight line*, it's about two miles to the motorway from here. ....
4 Another car *parked too close and prevented me from driving away*. ....
5 If you want to get there by 7.00, you're *not leaving yourself much time*. ....
6 The village is *in the countryside and a long way from town*. ....

3 ABOUT YOU How would you feel, and how would you react, if you were in the situations at the top of the page? Write in your notebook, or talk to another student.

B A metaphorical journey

Some idioms derived from roads and transport describe progress, or the lack of it, and the future.

> Duncan feels that if the company can **step up a gear**, then a couple of years **further down the road**, who knows? They could be one of the biggest firms in the south west.

> Now the council**'s given** us **the green light** for the shopping and leisure centre, let's hope the new development **will** really **put** Barnwood **on the map.**

> It's **the end of the road** for Ken's little corner shop now the supermarket has opened next door. The shop**'s** barely **ticking over**, and at 70, poor Ken**'s running out of steam**.

> Colin**'s gone off the rails** recently and I've already given him one warning. I had enough problems with Rob last month, so I don't want to have to **go down that road again** with Colin.

Glossary

step/**move up a gear**	start working more effectively or faster (also **in top gear** = working very fast and effectively).
(**further**) **down the road**	INF used to talk about the future and what might happen.
give (**sb/sth**) **the green light**	give (sb/sth) permission to start sth. (See spotlight.)
put sth/sb on the map	make sth/sb famous or important.
the end of the road/**line**	the point at which sth can no longer continue in the same way.
tick over	(usually used in the progressive) (of a business) keep working, without producing or achieving much. (See spotlight.)
run out of steam	lose your energy and enthusiasm. (See spotlight.)
go off the rails	INF start behaving in a wild or unacceptable way.
go down that road	take a particular course of action.

spotlight Literal meanings

When a car **is ticking over**, the engine is running but the car is not moving. The **green light** refers to a traffic light (green = go). Early trains were powered by steam engines; this became a source of several idioms, such as **run out of steam**.

4 Good news or bad news? Write G or B.

1 We've been given the green light. ……
2 The company is barely ticking over. ……
3 He's run out of steam. ……
4 It will put us on the map. ……
5 They've moved up a gear. ……
6 She's gone off the rails. ……

5 Answer the questions.

1 What do you have to move up in order to work faster? …………
2 What light do you need to go forwards? …………
3 What is a car doing if the engine is running but it's not moving? …………
4 What have you reached if something can no longer continue? …………
5 What does a person go off when they start behaving wildly? …………
6 What do you run out of when you lose your enthusiasm for something? …………

6 Paraphrase the sentences on the left, starting with the words you are given.

1 They've given us permission to start. They've given us …………. .
2 We won't take that course of action. We won't go …………. .
3 It will make us famous. It will put …………. .
4 We're finished as a company. Our company has reached …………. .
5 We're starting to work faster. We're stepping …………. .
6 We might feel differently in the future. We might feel differently further …………. .

15 I can talk about eating

A What shall we have?

Shall we **grab a bite to eat**? ~ Yeah, I'm starving - **I could eat a horse**!

Would you like some more lasagne? ~ No, thanks. It was delicious but I'**m full up**.

Jo just **picks at** her food. ~ Yeah, she **eats like a bird**. She's on some strange diet.

Gosh, that fish soup smells fabulous. ~ Yeah, it'**s making my mouth water**.

Aren't there any **leftovers**? ~ No, the boys **polished** them **off**.

How did you hear about this restaurant? ~ Just **by word of mouth**.

What a great meal. ~ Yes, it was lovely. Anyway, we'd better be going. I'**ll settle up**.

How was dinner? ~ I left it in the oven and it **was burnt to a crisp**, unfortunately.

Glossary	
a bite (**to eat**)	INF a small meal (**grab**/**have a bite** (**to eat**)).
be full (**up**)	have had enough to eat.
pick at sth	eat only small amounts of food because you are not hungry.
make your mouth water	If food **makes your mouth water** it looks or smells so good you want to eat it immediately. ADJ **mouth-watering**.
leftovers	PL N food remaining from a meal after you have eaten (**be left over** (**from sth**)).
polish sth off	INF finish sth, especially food, very quickly.
by word of mouth	through people telling each other and not through newspapers, advertisements, etc.
settle up (**with sb**)	pay what you owe on a bill or an account.
burn sth to a crisp/**cinder**	cook sth for too long or with too much heat, so that it burns.

spotlight Idioms with *horse*

I could eat a horse! = I'm very hungry.

She eats like a horse. = eats a lot. OPP **eat like a bird**.

1 One word is wrong in each sentence. Cross it out and write the correct word.

▶ The cake was delicious but I'm completely ~~filled~~ up, thanks. *full*

1 There was some chocolate in the fridge but Sam cleaned it all off. ....

2 If you manage to catch the waiter's eye, we can set up with him. ....

3 I'm absolutely starving – I could eat a house! ....

4 We might try and grab a mouth to eat before the cinema. ....

5 I can't eat this toast – it's burnt to a chip! ....

6 Just talking about that dish Mum made is making my taste water. ....

7 He's got an enormous appetite; he eats like a mouse! ....

8 I get all my new clients by word or mouth. ....

2 Complete the dialogues. You may need more than one word.

▶ Are you very hungry? ~ Yes, I could *eat a horse!* ....

1 She hardly eats anything, does she? ~ No, she just .... her food.

2 Would you like some more pie? ~ No, I really couldn't. I'm ....

3 Did you eat everything up? ~ No, look in the fridge. I think there are some ....

4 Do you advertise your restaurant? ~ No, all our customers come ....

5 Jon's very greedy. ~ Yeah, but his sister's the opposite. She eats ....

6 Shall we pay the bill? ~ Yeah, but don't worry. I'll ....

7 It's nearly lunchtime. ~ Yeah, let's go and grab ....

B Metaphors

	*This new phone's **the best thing since sliced bread**!*	**the best/greatest thing since sliced bread** sth you think is excellent.
	*She thinks the world of him; he**'ll have her eating out of his hand**.*	**have sb eating out of your hand** make sb like you so much they agree to everything you say.
	*If this plan fails, I**'ll have egg on my face**.*	**have egg on your face** be embarrassed because sth you tried to do went wrong.
	*My last job was hard enough but this one is awful – it's **out of the frying pan, into the fire**!*	**out of the frying pan, (and) into the fire** used to say that sb who was in a bad situation is now in an even worse situation.
	*That boy's a real **couch potato**!*	**couch potato** INF a person who spends too much time watching TV.
	*He'll never cope in that job. He**'s bitten off more than he can chew**.*	**bite off more than you can chew** try to do too much or do sth that is too difficult.
	*She tells lies and then acts as if **butter wouldn't melt in her mouth**.*	**butter wouldn't melt (in sb's mouth)** used to say that sb looks innocent, kind, etc. but really they are not.
	*He's one of these businessmen who**'s got a finger in every pie**.*	**have a finger in every pie** INF be involved and influential in a lot of different activities.
	*I shouldn't have left her, but it's no use **crying over spilt milk**.*	**cry over spilt milk** waste time worrying about sth that has already happened and that cannot be changed.
	*He's 65 but he's still **full of beans**.*	**full of beans** having a lot of energy.

3 Match the idioms with the topics in the box.

> energy   TV   having influence   regret ✓   looking foolish
> events getting worse   seeming innocent   being overambitious

- ▶ cry over spilt milk *regret*
- 1 have egg on your face ....
- 2 butter wouldn't melt ....
- 3 a couch potato ....
- 4 have a finger in every pie ....
- 5 bite off more than you can chew ....
- 6 full of beans ....
- 7 out of the frying pan, into the fire ....

4 Complete the sentences with an appropriate idiom from the table above.

- ▶ He can lie but look completely sweet and innocent. *Butter wouldn't melt (in his mouth).*
- 1 It's a wonderful invention; in fact, it's ....
- 2 She's taken on too much work; in fact, she's ....
- 3 I know she'll do whatever he wants; he's got her ....
- 4 There's nothing you can do to put it right, so it's no use ....
- 5 If the new scheme doesn't work, the politicians will have ....
- 6 He's in front of the TV all day long; he's just ....
- 7 I thought things were bad, but then this happened! Out ....
- 8 She recovered quickly from the operation and now she's ....

16 I can talk about study

DEZI I wasn't very good at English when I started, but **it wasn't for want of trying**. I worked really hard **night after night**, but I **couldn't make head or tail of** the grammar, and it really **held me back**. Then one day things just seemed to make sense, and I started **showing signs of** improvement. My teacher says it's all part of the learning process. I hope she's right.

MATTEI For a long time I did **next to nothing**, until my teacher told me one day that if I didn't **pull my socks up**, I'd fail my English exams and then I**'d have nothing to show for** three or four years' studying. So, I decided to **turn over a new leaf**. I really began to **apply myself**, and I'm pleased to say I've just passed my university exams **with flying colours**.

ORLA One of my problems is that I make silly mistakes in my writing, and I only just **scraped through** my last exam. My teacher**'s** always **telling me off** for this, and says I should check my work carefully **as a matter of routine**. She's right, because if I don't **cut out** the errors, I**'ll be marked down** in the next exam.

URSULA I went to the States three summers **running**, and that helped me a lot. My English **came on in leaps and bounds** as a result.

Glossary

it is not for want/**lack of trying**	used to say that sb is trying hard even though they are not successful.
night after night	every night for a period of time.
hold sb back	stop sb being as successful as they should be.
show signs of sth	show that sth seems to be happening, e.g. *show signs of* improvement/ *recovery*, etc.
next to nothing	almost nothing.
pull your socks up	INF used to tell sb that they are not doing well and must work harder.
have nothing / **something** / **little** / **a lot to show for sth**	have achieved nothing / something / little / a lot as a result of sth that you have done.
turn over a new leaf	change your life by stopping a bad habit or becoming a better person.
apply yourself	work hard on sth; give your full attention to something.
with flying colours	very well; with a very high mark/grade.
scrape through sth	succeed in doing sth with difficulty, especially passing an exam.
tell sb off	INF talk angrily to sb for doing sth wrong.
as a matter of routine/**course**	as a habit; as the usual way of doing sth.
cut sth out	stop doing sth, especially sth wrong.
mark sb down	reduce the mark/grade given to sb in an exam.
two weeks / **three years** / **four times** etc. **running**	two weeks / three years / four times etc., one after another.
come on	improve.
in/**by leaps and bounds**	very quickly; in large amounts.

spotlight Not understanding

If you **can't make head or tail of sth** INF, you are completely confused by it. You can also say that something **goes over your head** if you don't understand it.

1 **Is the speaker pleased or unhappy with these situations? Write P or U.**

1 The teacher marked me down. _____
2 I'll have to pull my socks up. _____
3 My English is coming on. _____
4 I've cut out the errors. _____
5 My pronunciation is holding me back. _____
6 I passed with flying colours. _____
7 The grammar goes over my head. _____
8 My son has turned over a new leaf. _____

2 **Complete the dialogues. Then circle the whole idiom or phrasal verb.**

▶ Was the dictionary expensive? ~ No, it was second hand, so it cost next *to nothing* _____ .
1 Did she get through the exam? ~ Yes, she passed with flying _____ .
2 Ben's not doing well at school, is he? ~ No, but it's not for want _____ .
3 Was the teacher annoyed with you? ~ Yes, she told _____ .
4 Did you understand the lecture? ~ No, I'm afraid it went over _____ .
5 He's got to work harder, hasn't he? ~ Yes, he needs to _____ himself.
6 Is the writing preventing him from getting better? ~ Yes, it's definitely holding _____ .
7 Are the boys getting better? ~ Yes, they're showing _____ improvement .
8 Is Mariko actually doing some work now? ~Yes, she turned over a _____ .
9 How did you do in the exam? ~ Badly. I think they _____ down for my spelling.
10 Can you understand this article? ~ No, I can't make head _____ .
11 Did you check your spelling? ~ Yes, I use the spelling checker on the computer as a matter _____ .
12 Is Gary working hard enough? ~ No, he'll have to pull his _____ .

3 **Replace the words in italics with an idiom or phrasal verb that keeps a similar meaning.**

▶ I was *given a lower grade* in the exam for lack of clarity. *marked down*
1 His English is *getting better*. _____
2 I can't *understand this at all*. _____
3 She worked *every night for a long period of time*. _____
4 This dictionary cost me *hardly anything*. _____
5 I *only just passed* my exams. _____
6 His lack of qualifications is *stopping him from being more successful*. _____
7 I need to *stop making* these silly mistakes if I want to improve. _____
8 My brother went to Japan three years *ago, and again two years ago, and again last year*. _____
9 I could do well, but I need to *work harder*. _____
10 She's worked hard at her tennis and she's progressing *very quickly*. _____

4 **Complete the sentences.**

1 Has a teacher ever _____ you off in class? If so, what for?
2 Has a teacher ever told you that you need to pull your _____ up? If so, why?
3 Have you passed any exams with _____ colours? If so, which ones?
4 Do you feel your English:
   a) is coming _____ in leaps and _____ ?
   b) is showing _____ of getting worse?
5 When you're studying, are there certain things you always do as a _____ of routine?
6 Do you feel you have a lot to _____ for the years you've been learning English?

5 **ABOUT YOU** Write your own answers to Exercise 4 in your notebook, or ask another student.

A How to do well at work

Tips to help you get on at work

❏ First, you need to **get your foot in the door**.

❏ Learn to **take things in your stride** whatever happens.

❏ Don't **pin your hopes on** others. If necessary, have the courage to **go it alone**.

❏ Don't **put all your eggs in one basket** – try to **keep your options open**.

❏ **Keep in with** your colleagues – you may need their support.

❏ **Keep your ear to the ground** – you hear important things **on the grapevine**.

❏ If you can **make a name for yourself**, things will get easier.

❏ Always **keep your feet on the ground**.

Glossary

get your/a foot in the door	get your first opportunity to work for an organization or business, which could later bring you success.
take sth/things in your stride	accept and deal with sth difficult without letting it worry you.
pin (all) your hopes on sb/sth	hope that sb will help you or that sth will happen because all your plans depend on this.
go it alone	do sth without help from anyone.
put all your eggs in one basket	rely on only one thing for success, having no other possibilities if sth goes wrong. OPP **keep your options open**.
keep in with sb	INF stay friends with sb because you think you will benefit from it.
keep your ear to the ground	make sure you find out about recent developments in a particular situation.
on the grapevine	by talking in an informal way to other people.
make a name for yourself	become well known and respected by many people.
keep your feet on the ground	have a sensible and realistic attitude.

1 Cover the glossary. Then form complete idioms from the key words.

▶ pin | hopes *pin your hopes on sb/sth*

1 take | stride ....
2 get | foot | door ....
3 keep | ear | ground ....
4 put | eggs | basket ....
5 keep | feet | ground ....
6 make | name ....

2 Complete the text.

Sandra got her (1) .... in the door when she was very young, and once she started at Berwick's, she took everything in her (2) .... and quickly made a (3) .... for herself. She was offered jobs in other cities, but wanted to keep her (4) .... open by staying in London where she could keep her ear to the (5) .... and wait for something really exciting to come up. She was (6) .... her hopes on getting a top job with C&M, and when she heard on the (7) .... that they wanted someone to run the Singapore office, she applied for it and got it. In a couple more years, she'll have enough experience to go it (8) .... if she wants to, but I know she has continued to (9) .... in with her old colleagues at Berwick's, so who knows where she'll end up.

3 ABOUT YOU Which is the best single piece of advice in the text at the top? Do you disagree with any of it? Write your answers or talk to another student.

B The production line

'I've been at Benhams **close on** twenty years. People now just think of me as **part of the furniture**. I **got the push** from my first job in a solicitor's office – **my face didn't fit**. Then I came here, and was lucky to meet Cynthia, who **took** me **under her wing** and showed me **the tricks of the trade** – things I now **pass on** to the younger girls. Some would say it's a **dead-end job**, and it's true that it's not a career, but standing at a machine eight hours a day still **takes some doing**. The bosses don't **throw their weight around** with me either; they know I always do a good day's work, and that's enough for me.'

Glossary

close on	(used with time, age, distance, etc.) almost; very nearly (*He's **close on** 60*).
part of the furniture	A person who is **part of the furniture** is so familiar to you that you no longer notice them.
sb's face doesn't fit	used to say that sb won't get or keep a job because they are not the kind of person that the employer wants.
take sb under your wing	look after sb who has less experience than you.
the tricks of the trade	the clever ways of doing things in a particular job.
pass sth on (**to sb**)	give sth to sb else (in this case, knowledge of the job), especially after receiving it yourself.
dead-end job	a boring job with no hope of promotion.
take some doing	INF be difficult to do, or involve a lot of effort or time.
throw your weight around/about	INF tell people what to do in a bossy way.

spotlight Being dismissed

There are several informal idioms that mean to be dismissed from a job.
I got the push/boot/elbow. OR *They gave me the push/boot/elbow.*

4 Correct the mistake in each sentence.

1 You need someone to show you the tricks of the business. ....
2 I've been there all my life, so I'm some of the furniture. ....
3 It's a hard job and it'll make some doing. ....
4 The boss tells me what to do, and I pass it through to the others. ....
5 It was lucky for me that Mary took me under her arm and helped me. ....
6 Simone has worked here close by ten years. ....
7 He was lazy, so he got the pull. ....
8 He's very bossy and likes to throw his size about. ....

5 Complete the dialogues with one or two words.

1 It's a tough job. ~ Yes, it'll take ....
2 They didn't like you, then. ~ No, my face didn't ....
3 He uses his position in an aggressive way. ~ Yes, he likes to throw his ....
4 There are no real prospects for Jun at the office. ~ No, it's a dead ....
5 They haven't sacked you, have they? ~ Yes, I got the ....
6 I'm finding it difficult. ~ Don't worry. You'll soon learn .... of the trade.
7 Does Maurice always help newcomers? ~ Yes, he takes them under ....
8 Roy's been there since the company started. ~ Yeah, he's part of the ....

18 I can talk about business 1

A A company in trouble

Government refuses to **shore up** ailing van company LEV

HOPES RISE OF A **MANAGEMENT BUYOUT** OF LEV

MANAGEMENT BUYOUT **FALLS THROUGH**

Buyer for stricken LEV company emerges **at the eleventh hour**

FUTURE OF LEV SECURED, **THANKS** TO WESTRUN AND £5M GOVERNMENT **BAILOUT**

FUTURE OF LEV **HANGS IN THE BALANCE** ONCE AGAIN

LEV takeover **on the verge of** collapse

Westrun **pulls out of** proposed takeover of LEV

Unions warn government not to **stand aside** and watch 850 jobs **go to the wall**

Glossary

shore sth up	help to support sth that is weak or going to collapse. SYN **prop sth up**.
management buyout	a situation in which the managers of a company gain control by buying most of its shares. **buy sb out** V.
fall through	If a deal or plan **falls through**, it does not happen.
at the eleventh hour	at the last possible moment.
thanks to sb/sth	used to say that sth has happened because of sb/sth.
bailout	an act of giving money to a business, economy, etc. to save it from collapse. **bail sb out** V.
hang in the balance	If the future of sth **hangs in the balance**, it is uncertain.
on the verge of (**doing**) **sth**	very near to the moment when sth happens or sb does sth.
pull out (**of sth**)	withdraw from an arrangement; stop being involved in sth. **pull-out** N.
stand aside	not get involved in sth.
go to the wall	INF (of an organization) fail because of lack of money.

1 Rewrite the sentences using the correct form of the word in capitals. Keep the meaning the same.

1 The deal isn't going to happen now. FALL ....
2 We survived because of the government. THANKS ....
3 Michael White is about to resign. VERGE ....
4 There are fears that the company could fail. WALL ....
5 A management buyout emerged at the last possible moment. HOUR ....
6 Their future looks uncertain. HANGS ....
7 The government will rescue them financially. BAIL ....
8 The company had withdrawn from the deal. PULL ....

2 Complete the text.

The proposed management (1) .... of Wilson Dowling was (2) .... in the balance last night, as it emerged that the government was threatening to (3) .... of the deal altogether. Originally the government had agreed to support the management team with a £20m rescue package, and promised that it would not (4) .... aside and let the 200-year-old company (5) .... to the wall. However, last night that deal was on the (6) .... of falling (7) .... It seems the transport minister is now concerned that the £20m (8) .... will not be sufficient, and the government might have to (9) .... up the company with a much larger rescue package.

B Companies fighting back

Companies profiting from recession

City analysts **were caught on the hop** yesterday when the Big Deal DIY chain announced that profits were up by 5 per cent. It is thought that DIY **is making a comeback** during the recession as people **do up** their own homes rather than **bringing in** the professionals.

Also doing rather well is the bicycle manufacturer Raleigh. Bicycle sales **had fallen off** in recent decades, and after **being in the doldrums** for a number of years, Raleigh had to **slim down** considerably. However, they too **are bucking the trend** as more people give up their cars and opt for bicycles instead. The company is now hoping to **branch out** in an attempt to get new customers, as well as **win back** some old customers.

Glossary

catch sb on the hop	INF surprise sb by doing sth they are not expecting.
make a comeback	If sth **makes a comeback**, it becomes popular and successful again. **come back** v (e.g. *come back* into fashion).
do sth up	repair and decorate a room or building.
bring sb in	ask sb to do a particular job or be involved in sth.
fall off	decrease in quantity or quality.
be in the doldrums	(of a business) not be growing or doing well. (👁 See page 162.)
buck the trend	succeed in doing sth where most others are failing.
branch out (into sth)	start to do a new activity, especially in business.
win sb/sth back	get or have again sb/sth that you had before.

spotlight Food and dieting metaphors

Verbs related to food and dieting are used metaphorically in business.
The firm had to slim down. = cut the number of jobs and become smaller.
Rising oil costs are eating into *our profit.* = using up a part of our profit.

3 **Good news or bad news? Write G or B.**

1 We're winning back customers. ....
2 They've made a comeback. ....
3 It's eating into our profit. ....
4 We're branching out. ....
5 We'll have to slim down. ....
6 They're in the doldrums. ....
7 We've bucked the trend. ....
8 Quality has fallen off. ....

4 **Complete the dialogues using one of these phrases in each response.**

> slim down   comeback   catch somebody on the hop   buck the trend
> bring sb in   do sth up   in the doldrums   branch out ✓   fall off

▶ Will he continue just doing what he's good at? ~ *No, he's decided to branch out.*
1 Did you solve the computer problem yourselves? ~ No, ...
2 Were you expecting the sudden fall in sales? ~ No, ...
3 Has the quality stayed the same? ~ No, ...
4 Is the company doing any better? ~ No, ...
5 Has the company kept all its workers? ~ No, ...
6 Have they had the same poor results as others? ~ No, ...
7 Did you get professional decorators? ~ No, ...
8 Long hair is out of fashion, isn't it? ~ No, ...

19 I can talk about business 2

A A success story

When I started selling my cheese, I thought I was being paid **the going rate**, but I soon realized that supermarkets **were playing** one supplier **off against** another to get the lowest price. So, I decided to **cut out the middleman** and sell direct to the public. As it happens, I **was in the right place at the right time** because local street markets were gaining in popularity, and my decision soon **paid off** – the business was **a roaring success**. **In a short space of time** I trebled my income, but I made sure I didn't **rest on my laurels**. I **ploughed** the profits **back into** the company and expanded, and I'm proud to say that five years on, the company **is** still **going strong**.

Glossary

the going rate (**for sth**)	the usual amount paid for goods and services.
play sb off against sb	make two people or groups compete with each other in order to give yourself an advantage.
cut out the middleman	sell your produce directly to the public instead of selling it to a retailer (the **middleman**), who then sells it to the public.
be in the right place at the right time	be somewhere at a time when you can take advantage of an opportunity.
pay off	INF (of a plan or action) be successful and bring good results.
a roaring success	INF a great success.
in/within a short space of time	before much time has passed.
rest on your laurels	be so satisfied with your achievements that you stop trying to achieve more. (See page 162.)
plough sth back (**in/into sth**)	put money made as a profit back into a business in order to improve it.
be going strong	INF be doing well and being successful.

1 **Tick the correct sentences. Cross out the words which are not necessary in the incorrect sentences.**

  1 We were profitable within a short space of the time. ....

  2 Profits were down so we decided to cut out of the middleman. ....

  3 They tried to play us off against one another. ....

  4 It's important you don't rest up on your laurels. ....

  5 We were fortunate to be in the right place at the right time. ....

  6 The company has been going on strong for years. ....

  7 We made healthy profits last year so we ploughed them all back into the company. ....

  8 She hasn't been getting the going pay rate for her work. ....

2 **Complete the idiom or phrasal verb in each sentence.**

  1 If we sell direct to the public, we can cut out the ....

  2 Sometimes you just need to be in the right place ....

  3 The company started doing well within a short ....

  4 We've been very profitable, but we mustn't rest ....

  5 The business has been a roaring ....

  6 I don't want to be overpaid, but I expect to be paid the going ....

  7 Changing the marketing policy was tough at first, but eventually it paid ....

  8 The company has been very successful, and after 20 years it's still going ....

B Reasons for failure

In retrospect, things started to go wrong even when we were doing quite well.

• You need to **keep one step ahead of** your competitors; we didn't do that.

• We had the opportunity to expand, but we were complacent and **missed the boat**.

• We **deluded ourselves into** thinking we would never go bankrupt.

• Overseas producers started **flooding the market** with cheap goods, and we couldn't compete.

• When things got difficult we tried **cutting corners**; it proved a **false economy**.

• When we realized we **were in deep water**, it took us ages to **cut our losses** and **sell up**.

• Looking back, I think our staff structure was **top-heavy**.

Glossary

in retrospect	when thinking about a past event or situation from the perspective of the present.
keep/**stay one step**/**jump ahead of sb**	keep an advantage over sb, especially your competitors.
miss the boat	miss an opportunity to do sth.
delude yourself (**into doing sth**)	choose to believe sth that is not true.
flood the market	produce sth in such large quantities that competing products suffer.
cut corners	DISAPPROVING do sth in the easiest, cheapest, or quickest way in order to save time or money.
false economy	an action that is intended to save money but which actually costs you more.
be in / **get** (sb) **into deep water**	be in / get (sb) into a serious or difficult situation.
cut your losses	stop doing sth that you can see is going to be unsuccessful before the situation gets worse.
sell up	sell most of what you own, especially your house or business.
top-heavy	having too many people in senior positions and not enough workers.

3 Circle the correct answer(s). Both answers may be correct.

1 It was a great opportunity but I'm afraid we missed the *train* | *boat*.
2 *In* | *By* retrospect, it was not the right decision.
3 We've always tried to keep one *step* | *jump* ahead of our competitors.
4 I'm afraid the company was *top-heavy* | *too heavy*.
5 Selling the other shop was a *false* | *wrong* economy.
6 We could be in deep *waters* | *water* if we don't increase our sales.
7 It's a big mistake to cut *a corner* | *corners*.
8 In the end we decided to cut our losses and *sell up* | *sell out*.

4 Answer the questions.

1 If you have missed the boat, what have you missed exactly? ....
2 Why would someone want to cut their losses? ....
3 If you use the phrase 'in retrospect', what are you talking about? ....
4 How would you probably feel if your main competitor flooded the market? ....
5 If you were in deep water, would you want to get out of it? ....
6 What are two obvious ways to cut corners if you run a café? ....

Review: Everyday life

Unit 11

1 Complete the questions using verbs from the word snake in the correct form.

forkland lay fallbailplayputbeargo

▶ Could you _lay_____ your hands on your cheque book straight away?
1 If you had some money to _____ with, would you invest it in shares?
2 Are you more or less cautious as time _____ by?
3 Would you _____ out $100 on a haircut?
4 Would you _____ out an old friend if they were in trouble financially?
5 If you _____ yourself in financial difficulties, who would you turn to?
6 Is it important to have some savings in the bank to _____ back on?
7 Do you expect financial investments to _____ fruit immediately?
8 If a friend lost a lot of money on the stock market, would it _____ you off investing?

2 ABOUT YOU Write your answers to Exercise 1 in your notebook, or talk to another student.

3 Complete the dialogues.

1 Does his father help him financially? ~ No, he always pays _____ _____ .
2 Do you take risks? ~ No, I generally _____ on the side of _____ .
3 Did someone tell you to do that? ~ No, I just did it off my _____ .
4 How much does it all cost? ~ It _____ to €450.
5 Do you think you'll have more money next year? ~ No, I think I'll be _____ .
6 Have you finished paying for your flat yet? ~ No, but I'll have _____ it _____ by next year.
7 I'm surprised Jack took over the firm. ~ Yes, but he went into it with _____ _____ open.
8 She's living on very little money. ~ I know; it's terrible to see her on _____ .

Unit 12

1 Write the opposite, using the word in capitals at the end of the sentence.

▶ Solar panels aren't very expensive. OPP Solar panels _don't come cheap._ _____ COME
1 He lives in very poor circumstances. OPP He lives _____ . LAP
2 The meal cost him nothing. OPP The meal cost _____ . LEG
3 She's sensible with her money. OPP She has _____ . SENSE
4 The car was very expensive. OPP The car _____ . GOING
5 He never saves any money. OPP He always _____ . ASIDE
6 I often go to that nightclub. OPP I've never _____ . SET

2 Write the last word.

1 My aunt expects the very best quality, and as far as she's concerned, money is no _____ .
2 My life moves at a slow pace, and my needs are very inexpensive to say the _____ .
3 Bernard was living on an island in the Pacific, the last I _____ .
4 Are they getting behind with the payments? ~ Yes, they're three months in _____ .
5 Do you think you would be suited to life in the fast _____ ?
6 They want the power without the responsibility – it's the same old _____ .
7 My neighbour has a terrible life, just living from hand to _____ .
8 I keep warning my sister to be careful: she's living beyond her _____ .

Unit 13

1 Organize the phrases into three groups and give each one a title.

> off-colour   pass out   pull through   under the weather   black out
> on the mend   take a turn for the better   come round   out of sorts

Title:	Title:	Title:

2 Rewrite the sentences using the words in capitals in the correct form. Keep the meaning the same.

▶ George looked absolutely dreadful. DEATH *George looked like death warmed up.*
1 We're not sure if he'll survive. TOUCH
2 He started to vomit. THROW
3 She suddenly got worse. TURN
4 I think he's getting worse. DOWNHILL
5 It won't disappear. GO
6 Check it out – to avoid any risks. SIDE

Unit 14

1 Write the opposite for each sentence, using key words from the box in the correct form.

> crow   drop   snail   steam   cut   miles ✓

▶ The house is in the middle of the city. OPP *The house is miles from anywhere.*
1 She picked me up at 3.00. OPP
2 I had plenty of time. OPP
3 He's full of energy. OPP
4 It's five miles via a very indirect route. OPP
5 She drives really fast. OPP

2 Complete the dialogues.

▶ Look! There's a police car coming! ~ Thank goodness. Go and flag it *down* .
1 Is business going well? ~ Not really; things are quiet and we're just   over.
2 Was it busy in town? ~ Yes, there's a festival on, so the traffic's   !
3 We can't be complacent about the business. ~ No, now's the time to move up a   .
4 We could borrow even more from the bank. ~ No, we mustn't go down that   .
5 Why on earth would someone park here? ~ I don't know, but they've   me in.

Unit 15

1 Complete the idioms in the sentences with words associated with food or eating.

1 My mother's getting on, but she's still full of   .
2 Madeleine will end up with   on her face if she interferes.
3 We can't put the pot back together again, so it's no use crying over spilt   .
4 He does whatever Emily wants. She's just got him   out of her hand.
5 She looks so innocent;   wouldn't melt in her   .
6 I think Eric has   off more then he can   with that job.

2 Replace the words in italics with an idiom or phrasal verb that keeps a similar meaning.

1 Would you like more to eat? ~ No, *I couldn't eat any more*, thanks. ....
2 *I'm really hungry*. ....
3 Can I *pay the bill*, please? ....
4 Where did you hear about the restaurant? ~ *Personal recommendation*. ....
5 There should be some *food remaining after we have finished eating*. ....
6 Shall we *have something* to eat? ....
7 He *spends all his time watching TV*. ....
8 That pudding over there *looks fantastic and I really want to eat it*. ....

Unit 16

1 Put the dominoes in the correct order to make a joined sequence of idioms, starting with 'Mark' in the second domino. Write the correct order of dominoes below.

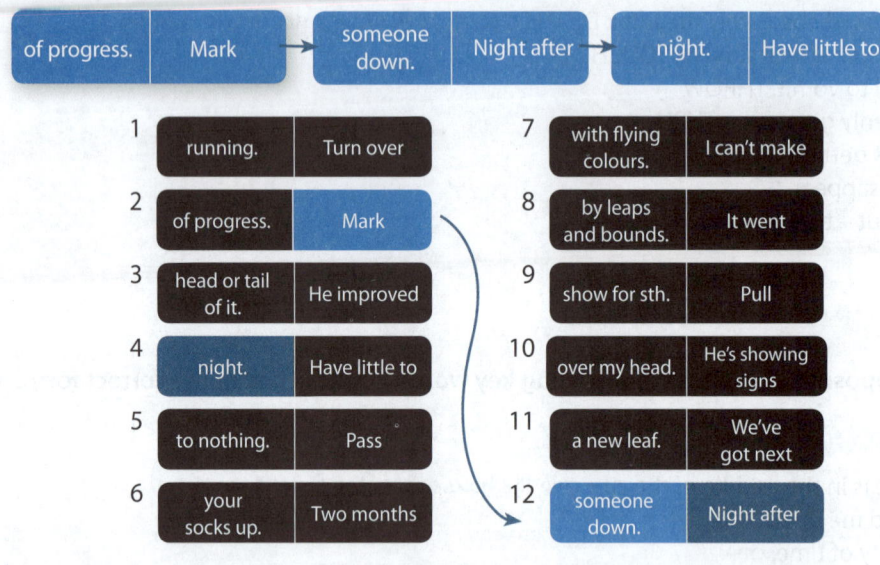

| of progress. | Mark | → | someone down. | Night after | → | night. | Have little to |

1	running.	Turn over		7	with flying colours.	I can't make
2	of progress.	Mark		8	by leaps and bounds.	It went
3	head or tail of it.	He improved		9	show for sth.	Pull
4	night.	Have little to		10	over my head.	He's showing signs
5	to nothing.	Pass		11	a new leaf.	We've got next
6	your socks up.	Two months		12	someone down.	Night after

2 , 12 , 4 , ... , ... , ... , ... , ... , ... , ... , ... , ... ,

2 Complete the sentences with the correct adverb or preposition.

1 I didn't do much work, but I'm relieved that I scraped .... my exam.
2 My cousin's not likely to pass his exams, but it's not .... want of trying.
3 I frequently got told .... by my father for reading in bed late at night.
4 I'm delighted with Willie's progress; he's come .... extremely well this term.
5 If you could just cut .... all these little mistakes, you'd get a much higher mark.
6 He has a lot of problems with maths, and it's really holding him ....

Unit 17

1 Rewrite the sentences below using an idiom.

▶ Accept a difficult situation and deal with it. = Take it *in your stride* ....
1 Don't use your position in an aggressive way. = Don't throw ....
2 I heard about the job by chatting to people. = I heard about it on ....
3 Don't rely on only one thing for success. = Don't put all your ....
4 When I started the job, Bill looked after me. = When I started the job, Bill took me ....
5 He managed to get a start in the firm. = He got his ....
6 I was given the push. = They gave me ....
7 Make sure you hear about any new developments. = Keep your ear ....
8 He has a sensible and realistic attitude. = He keeps ....

Unit 18

1 Complete the crossword. The letters in the grey squares spell out an idiom. What is it, and what does it mean?

1 on the .... of happening = about to happen.

2 the gaining of control of a company by its managers.

3 .... aside = not get involved in something.

4 .... something up = support something that is weak or about to collapse.

5 .... into something = use up part of something, e.g. time or money.

6 catch somebody on the .... = surprise someone by doing something unexpected.

7 buck the .... = get different results from others in the same area.

8 .... sb/sth back = get or have again sth or sb that you used to have, e.g. customers.

9 make a .... = become popular and successful once more.

10 .... = the act of giving money to a company to rescue it from financial difficulties.

11 .... down = (of a company or an organization) reduce the number of jobs and become smaller.

The idiom in the grey squares is ....

Unit 19

1 Complete the texts.

My friend Josh had a café for a few years, and to start with, he was lucky: within a short (1) .... of time, it became a roaring (2) .... But then he got a bit greedy and started to cut (3) .... – first it was the quality of the coffee, then he cut back on staff. When the recession hit, his customers deserted him and he got into (4) .... water with the bank. In (5) ...., he should have maintained his standards because some customers might have remained loyal, even when times got tough.

I believe that in business, you can never rest on your (6) .... : you've got to be looking constantly at ways to improve. Some people get stuck in a rut, and when an opportunity comes along, they miss the (7) .... because they're not looking to the future. A good example is a friend of mine who manufactured wooden toys: they were beautiful and even won awards, but he was complacent. When an overseas manufacturer (8) .... the market with similar products at half the price, he had no alternative but to (9) .... up and move on. If you don't keep one (10) .... ahead of your rivals, you're never going to make it.

How do you organize a big family meal?

Ingrid

▶ Christmas is **a big deal** in my family – sometimes I think we **go over the top**! My sisters are all there in the kitchen the day before, cooking **like mad**, and it's great to see everyone **pitching in**. The important thing is to **clear up** the dirty things **as you go along**, otherwise the place **looks like a bomb has hit it**.

Cathy

▶ You're lucky, Ingrid! I **can't** cook **to save my life**, so I **buy in** loads of ready-made food – salads, smoked salmon, something **on those lines**. There are thirty of us so I just couldn't **pull off** a big meal like that on my own. One Christmas my sister **took over** because I was poorly, and it **was a** huge **weight off my shoulders**.

Dede

▶ We always **make a big thing of** Grandma's birthday – she's 92 this year. One year I **tried out** some new recipes, but our aunts **raised an eyebrow at** the chocolate fountain. I think I'll go back to the **tried and tested** recipes again this year!

Ken

▶ I get really **stressed out** with Christmas dinner. The turkey **takes up** so much space in the fridge, there's no room for the desserts. **There's no room to swing a cat** in my kitchen, so when it comes to **dishing up**, I'm balancing plates everywhere!

Glossary

go over the top	INF do sth in an exaggerated way (also **go OTT**).
like mad	INF a lot or to a great degree (also **like crazy**).
pitch in (with sb/sth)	INF join in and help other people with an activity.
clear (sth) up	make sth clean and neat.
as you go along	If you clear up **as you go along**, you tidy things while cooking the meal.
look like a bomb has hit it	INF look very untidy.
can't do sth to save your life	INF can't do sth at all, or only be able to do it very badly.
buy sth in	buy a large quantity of sth in preparation for an activity or event.
on those / the same lines	similar to sth or in a similar way (also **along those / the same lines**).
pull sth off	INF succeed in doing sth that is difficult.
take (sth) over (from sb)	do sth that sb else was doing.
be a weight off your shoulders	used to say that you are glad you no longer have to worry about a responsibility (also **be a weight off your mind**).
try sth out	test or use sth to see what it is like or whether it is suitable.
raise an eyebrow at sth	show by the expression on your face that you disapprove of sth or are surprised by it.
tried and tested	If sth is **tried and tested**, you have successfully used it in the past.
stressed out	INF too anxious to be able to relax. **stress sb out** v.
take up sth	fill or use an amount of space or time.
there's no room to swing a cat	INF = there's very little space to move around in.
dish (sth) up	serve food onto plates for a meal.

spotlight *a big deal, a big thing*

A big deal INF is something that is very important. If something isn't important, we say **it's no big deal** INF, e.g. *It's no big deal if you don't arrive at 6.00.* If you **make a big deal (out) of sth** INF or **make a big thing (out) of sth** INF, you behave as if it is very important.

1 Is the meaning similar or different? Write S or D.

1 It's a weight off my shoulders. / I'm glad I don't have to worry about it any more. ....
2 He can't swim to save his life. / He can't swim at all. ....
3 There isn't room to swing a cat. / We can't leave the cat in here. ....
4 She went a bit over the top. / She's on top of the world. ....
5 I expect people will pitch in. / I expect people will join in and help. ....
6 We didn't think you'd pull it off. / We didn't think you'd delay it. ....

2 Correct the mistake in each sentence.

1 We always do a big thing of my mum's birthday. ....
2 Thanks for your help – I really mustn't take out any more of your time. ....
3 What really stresses me up is driving around town in the rush hour. ....
4 I need some wallpaper or something down those lines. ....
5 My sister's bedroom looks like a bomb has exploded it. ....
6 She raised an eyelash when I ordered a chocolate pudding. ....

3 Rewrite the sentences, starting with the words given. Keep a similar meaning.

▶ I'm glad I don't have to worry about it.   It's a weight *off my shoulders.*
1 It really doesn't matter if you can't do it.   It's no ....
2 The office was unbelievably untidy.   The office looked ....
3 We need something similar to this.   We need something on ....
4 They behaved as if it was really important.   They made a ....
5 I used to do the cooking, but John does it now. John's taken ....
6 There isn't enough room for this table.   This table takes ....

4 One word is missing from each line. Where does it go? Write it at the end.

I'm the world's worst cook: I can't cook to ⟨ my life! So when I realized   ▶ *save*

I had to cook for a big family party, my first thought was to in a lot of   1 ....

ready-cooked food, but then I thought, 'Look – it's no deal! Be confident!'   2 ....

My sister kindly offered to pass on some of her and tested recipes – after   3 ....

all, this was no time for me to show off and start out new things – and she   4 ....

assured me that all the family would pitch and give me a hand on the day.   5 ....

I spent one whole day shopping mad, buying far too much food, and by   6 ....

the time I got home, I was so out I had to go and lie down. On the day of   7 ....

the party, I forced myself to be really organized and up the cooking stuff   8 ....

as I along. My sister arrived at midday and could see I was exhausted, so   9 ....

she took from me in the kitchen while I set the table. And in the end,   10 ....

when she and I had finally dished everything, it looked fabulous.   11 ....

5 ABOUT YOU AND YOUR FAMILY Complete the questions. Then write your answers in your notebook, or talk to another student.

1 For a big family meal, do you usually try .... new recipes, or do you usually stick to the .... and tested dishes?
2 Who in your family can't cook to .... their ....?
3 Do you usually tidy the kitchen up .... go along?
4 Does everyone in your family .... in and help?
5 Does your family go over the .... when preparing a big meal?
6 What about birthdays: do you .... big thing of them in your family?

A Preparations for an outdoor event

TIPS FOR FESTIVAL GOERS

• Find a good spot to **set up** camp, **put** your tent **up**, and then get to know your neighbours. That way, you can **keep an eye on** each other's stuff.

• Don't **roll up** with loads of equipment; try to **make do with** the minimum. If you take too much, the chances are you'll end up **leaving something behind**. But one thing that **will come in handy** is a torch – to help you find your way back to your tent after dark.

• You can **take the easy way out** by buying food and drinks on site, but it's not cheap.

• Don't **wear yourself out** by trying to see all the acts. Relax, and **go easy on** the alcohol.

Glossary

keep an eye on sth/sb	take care of sth/sb, so they are not stolen, damaged, or harmed.
roll up	INF arrive somewhere, often late or unexpectedly.
make do (**with sth**)	manage with sth that is not completely satisfactory.
leave sth/sb behind	not take sth/sb with you when you go somewhere.
come in handy/**useful**	INF be useful for a particular situation.
take the easy way out	end a difficult situation by choosing the simplest solution, even if it is not the best one.
wear yourself/sb out	make yourself/sb feel very tired. SYN **tire yourself/sb out**. **worn out** ADJ.
go easy on sth	INF used to tell sb to use or eat less of sth.

spotlight *put sth up, set sth up*

Both can mean to build or place something somewhere, but we say *set up camp* and *put up a tent*. **Set sth up** is not used for permanent things (NOT *set up a new car park*). You can use **put sth up** or **set sth up** for most temporary things, e.g. ***put/set up*** *a fence / road block / shelter*.

1 Form sentences using words from each column.

We set up	in	on the cakes.
They rolled	the easy	out.
Try not to tire	yourself	handy.
The cash came	camp	late as usual.
You should go	up	near a lake.
Don't take	easy	way out.

2 Complete the dialogues.

1 She came home completely exhausted. ~ Yes, she ....
2 Was the torch useful on the trip? ~ Yes, it ....
3 What time did your sister arrive? ~ She finally .... two hours late.
4 Do you want the tent here? ~ Yes, could you .... please?
5 Could you look after my bag, please? ~ Don't worry, I'll .... on it.
6 I've been drinking too much coffee. ~ You ought to go .... it for a while.
7 Can you manage with this small knife? ~ Yeah, we can .... with it.
8 You didn't take the bag? ~ No, we left ....

B A successful festival

Glastonbury memories

I'**d had my doubts about** the weather. Last year, it **tipped down** all weekend and we **got soaked to the skin**, and this year wasn't looking promising either; in the end, the rain **held off**. The festival **kicked off** with a short set by the Moogs, who **went down really well**. After that, I wandered around the different stages, at one point **stumbling on** an amazing performance of jazz dance. I'd heard that Joan Baez had had to **pull out**, but in fact, she turned up and **put on** a great show. For me, it was **the high point of** the weekend.

Glossary

have your doubts about sth/sb	have reasons why you do not feel certain about sth/sb.
tip down	INF (of rain) fall fast; rain a lot.
be/get soaked to the skin	(of a person) be/get very wet.
hold off	If rain **holds off**, it does not fall, although you thought it would.
kick off	INF (of an event) start in a particular way. OPP **wind up**.
stumble on/across sth	find sth by chance.
pull out (**of sth**)	stop being involved in an event or activity.
put sth on	produce or provide sth, especially for the benefit of other people or for a special purpose.
the high point of sth	the best, most enjoyable, etc. part of sth. OPP **the low point of sth**.

spotlight Describing successful events

Go down + ADJ, ADV, or N can mean to cause a particular reaction.
The band went down really well. = were very successful or popular.
They went down a bomb. INF = were very successful or popular. Also **go down a storm** INF.

---

3 Good news or bad news? Write G or B.

1 The rain held off for the evening. ....
2 The group went down a bomb. ....
3 I got soaked to the skin. ....
4 The band put on a real show. ....
5 Several bands had to pull out. ....
6 It tipped down all day. ....

4 One word is missing in each line of text. Where does it go? Write it at the end.

Last year at the Isle of Wight festival, I'd had my ⟨ about whether   *doubts*

to go or not, but in the end I did, and the rain held for the whole 1 ....

week. This summer, though, it just down the whole time and I got 2 ....

fed up with being to the skin all the time. I wandered around with 3 ....

a friend, and in one corner we suddenly stumbled an incredible band 4 ....

called 'Engine Room' who were going a storm. A guy next to us 5 ....

said that their performance had kicked with an amazing version of 6 ....

'Leila', and the high came when they were joined on stage by 7 ....

Paul McCartney, who went down pretty too. Watching someone like 8 ....

him putting a real show is a great experience; I forgot about the rain. 9 ....

5 ABOUT YOU Have you ever been to an open-air music festival or concert? If so, what was the weather like? Did it go down well? What was the high point for you? Write your answers in your notebook or talk to another student.

22 I can describe a date

Blind Date

A friend of both Luisa and David decided that they might like each other, so arranged for the two of them to meet and have dinner at a restaurant.

Luisa

Preparation: The dress I'd had in mind was perfect, but at the last minute I noticed it had a mark on it so I rushed around trying to find something else, getting all hot and bothered in the process. I was pretty wound up by the time the taxi called for me!

First impressions: David appeared to have bags of confidence and was good fun. And really handsome – I couldn't take my eyes off him.

What was the conversation like? Great. The waitress came several times to take our order – we were chatting away quite happily and it was a long time before we got round to looking at the menu.

Will you meet again? We swapped phone numbers. As far as I could tell, he seemed keen!

David

Preparation: This being a blind date, I wanted to make an impression, but I decided to keep it casual.

First impressions: When Luisa arrived at the restaurant she was a bundle of nerves, and she seemed unhappy about something. But she soon snapped out of it and started to enjoy herself.

What was the conversation like? Fine. Luisa was shy at first but gradually came out of her shell and we talked about our friends, travelling, and the like. In fact, the time just flew by.

Will you meet again? I've got her number, but I don't think romance is on the cards.

Glossary

have sth/sb in mind	know the type of thing/person you want for a particular purpose.
rush around/round	try to do sth or a lot of things in a short space of time.
(all) hot and bothered	INF feeling anxious and under pressure.
wound up	INF anxious and worried. If you **wind sb up** INF, you deliberately do or say sth to make them angry or upset.
call for sb	meet sb at their home in order to take them somewhere. If you **pick sb up**, you go in your car to collect sb from their home or another place.
bags of sth	INF a lot of sth.
chat away	talk in a relaxed way.
get round to (doing) sth	find the time to do sth.
as far as I can/could tell	used to say that you think sth may be true but there may be facts you do not know.
blind date	a meeting between two people who have never met to spend some time together and see if a romantic relationship develops.
make an impression (on sb)	make sb notice and admire you.
be a bundle/bag of nerves	be very nervous.
snap out of it	INF stop being unhappy, upset, etc.
come out of your shell	be less shy and more confident with people.
and the like	and similar things.
fly by	If a period of time **flies by**, it passes very quickly. SYN **flash by**.
be on the cards	INF be likely to happen.

spotlight *eye*

I couldn't take my eyes off him. = I found him so attractive that I watched him all the time.
I couldn't look her in the eye. = I couldn't look at her directly because I was embarrassed or ashamed.

1 **Are these good signs or bad signs on a date? Write G or B.**

1　They chatted away. ....
2　She wound him up. ....
3　Time just flew by. ....
4　He couldn't take his eyes off her. ....
5　She didn't come out of her shell. ....

6　They had bags of fun. ....
7　The taxi picked her up late. ....
8　She left feeling hot and bothered. ....
9　She made an impression on him. ....
10　Another date isn't on the cards. ....

2 **Change one wrong letter in each sentence.**

▶　I've been gushing around all day getting ready for my date tonight. *rushing* ....
1　How did your bland date go last night? ....
2　She seemed to enjoy herself, as far as I could sell. ....
3　It was fantastic; the time just blew by. It was midnight before we knew it. ....
4　What exactly do you have in mine for us to do this afternoon? ....
5　OK, I'll fall for you at about 5.00, so please be ready to leave. ....
6　I know you're upset, but it's time you slapped out of it and got on with your life. ....

3 **Complete the dialogues. You may need more than one word.**

▶　Did Isobel seem happy? ~ Yes, as far as I *could tell* ....
1　Did Anna realize you had lied to her? ~ Yes, I couldn't look her ....
2　Did the date go well? ~ Yeah, but I was a .... of nerves before meeting him.
3　Did you manage to write that email to Sam? ~ No, I just didn't get .... it.
4　Could you give me a lift to the airport? ~ OK, I'll .... in half an hour.
5　She was gorgeous, wasn't she? ~ Yes, Freddy couldn't take .... her.
6　Was he easy to talk to? ~ Oh, yeah, we .... quite happily for hours.

4 **Cross out one unnecessary word in each line.**

… I went on a blind ▶ ~~first~~ date last night with a guy called Eric. I don't know

what I had in the mind, but it certainly wasn't Eric. I was a bit shocked,

because when he picked me all up at the station, he looked a complete mess, and

as far as I could tell him, he was still wearing the clothes he'd been gardening

in and hadn't got him round to making himself look presentable. But I can

say that he had big bags of personality – a bit too much, in fact, because

by the time we got to the restaurant, he'd managed to get wind me up with his

extreme views on women's rights, equality, and the same like. I can't say that

the evening flew well by: time seemed to drag interminably, particularly as Eric

chatted himself away while I sat there like a fool. He took me to the station and said he'd

like to meet again. At that point I couldn't look at him in the eye because for me

another date was not on the playing cards. What a relief to get home!

5 **Complete the sentences using words from the box. There are more words than you need.**

> runs　dates　do　call　make　wound　in　pick　bundle　come

1　Do people often go on blind .... in your country?
2　If you went on one, would you be relaxed, a bit .... up or a .... of nerves?
3　If you go on a first date, what's the best way to .... an impression on the person?
4　Are you shy, and if so, what would make you .... out of your shell?
5　Should the man .... for the woman at her home, or just meet her somewhere?

6 **ABOUT YOU** Write your answers to the questions in Exercise 5 in your notebook, or talk to another student.

weddingblog.com

Marisa's wedding POSTED BY Shania on May 18th

When my sister's boyfriend, Glyn, finally **popped the question** – and she said 'yes' – the family decided that Marisa's **big day** would be one she would never forget. Dad said, '**the sky's the limit** – you're to have **nothing but** the best.' Marisa just wanted to get a wedding dress **off the peg**, but Mum **wouldn't hear of** it, and she ended up in a handmade gown which nearly **broke the bank**.

The ceremony was beautiful and **went off without a hitch**. Then, at the reception, it was Dad's big moment – he got up to **propose a toast to** Marisa and Glyn, and you could see he **was speaking from the heart**. Unfortunately, though, his emotions **got the better of him** and we couldn't **shut** him **up**. He **went on and on about** his beautiful little girl, then talked about Glyn **in glowing terms**, and ended up by saying how having grandchildren would be **the icing on the cake**! Poor Marisa had her head in her hands at this point. He finally had to stop when Mum **broke down in tears**, which was lucky because it was getting rather embarrassing! But actually, I think that speech really **made** Marisa's **day**.

Glossary

pop the question	INF ask sb to marry you.
the sky's the limit	INF there is no limit to what sb can spend, achieve, etc.
nothing but	only.
off the peg	(of clothes) made to a standard size and not made especially for you. (Sth that is **off the shelf**, e.g. computer software, can be bought immediately and is not designed or made especially for you.)
won't/wouldn't hear of sth	refuse to accept a suggestion or an offer.
break the bank	INF If sth **breaks the bank**, it costs a great deal of money.
go off	(of an organized event) happen in a particular way. (**It went off without a hitch** = it happened and nothing went wrong.)
propose a toast (**to sb**)	ask people to wish sb happiness and success by raising their glasses and drinking. (You **raise your glass to sb**.)
(**speak**) **from the heart**	(speak) in a very sincere way (also **from the bottom of your heart**).
get the better of sb	If your emotions **get the better of you**, they are too strong to control, and you behave in a way that you do not want to.
shut sb up	IMPOLITE make sb stop talking or making a noise.
go on and on (**about sth**)	talk about sth for a long time in a boring way.
in glowing terms	in a very positive way. (If you speak **in glowing terms** about sb, you **are singing their praises**.)
the icing on the cake	an additional thing that makes a good situation even better.
break down (**in tears**)	lose control of your emotions and start crying.

spotlight Idioms with *day*

It's Laura's big day tomorrow. = a very important day (often a wedding day).
Winning the cup made my day. = made me feel very happy.
It's not every day you go to a wedding. = it's a very unusual or special event.

1 Match the sentence halves.

1 Then he proposed a toast ....   a was just the icing on the cake.
2 It's not every day ....   b and spoke about her in glowing terms.
3 He went on and on about the food ....   c and he broke down in tears.
4 He sang her praises ....   d you go to a wedding with 500 guests.
5 The fact that the sun shone all day ....   e until eventually we shut him up.
6 He bought his suit off the peg ....   f she was thrilled and said 'yes'.
7 His emotions got the better of him ....   g and asked us to raise our glasses.
8 When he popped the question ....   h so it wouldn't break the bank.

2 Circle the correct word or phrase.

1 She's feeling very nervous because it's her *large* | *big* day tomorrow.
2 I bought some new software for my computer off the *shelf* | *peg*.
3 If you let your feelings get the *best* | *better* of you, you won't be able to finish the speech.
4 We had nothing *only* | *but* praise for the way the reception was organized.
5 We can spend whatever we feel like – the sky's the *top* | *limit*!
6 When Chris *popped* | *popped out* the question, did he give her the ring?
7 They had a rehearsal the day before the wedding, and it went *out* | *off* without a hitch.
8 I offered to help with the decorations, but they *wouldn't* | *didn't* hear of it.

3 Put the words in order and add one more word.

▶ for | nothing | we | best | kids | want | the | our We want nothing but the best for our kids.
1 heart | she | spoke | the | really ....
2 day | good | the | really | my | weather ....
3 shelf | medicine | get | the | you | can | this ....
4 room | on | tidying | on | mum | and | about | my ....
5 icing | on | winning | the | was | the ....
6 lottery | win | day | it's | every | you | the ....
7 happy | raise | please | glasses | the | to | couple ....
8 hitch | off | the | a | ceremony | without ....

4 Complete the sentences using a word from the left and a word from the right. You may need to change the form of the words.

bottom	sky	glow	big		bank	heart	up	of
break	hear	break	shut		tears	limit	day	terms

1 I didn't expect him to get upset, but he just .... down in ....
2 In the speech, she talked about her daughter in .... It was lovely.
3 I tried to .... them .... , but they wouldn't stop shouting; I was really annoyed.
4 It's a very nice restaurant, but it won't .... the .... The set menu's only €12.
5 I offered to help tidy up after the party, but they wouldn't .... it.
6 It rained a lot, but nothing was going to spoil Maxine and Gervase's ....
7 I would like to thank you from the .... of my .... for all your kindness.
8 After his success at the national games, the .... is the .... for this young athlete.

5 ABOUT YOU Think about a member of your family whose wedding you attended. Write your answers in your notebook, or talk to another student.

1 Whose big day was it?
2 Do you know who popped the question, and where?
3 Did anyone propose a toast? If so, who, and to whom?
4 Did they sing someone's praises? If so, whose?
5 Did anyone break down in tears? If so, who and why?
6 Did the wedding go off without a hitch? If not, what happened?

24　I can talk about reunions

A　School reunions

GEMMA ▶ It's my school reunion, twenty years on … should I go or not?

LOFTY ▶ **There's nothing worse than** a school reunion for reminding you of bad childhood memories. You're **under no obligation to** go, so if you're in any doubt, don't go. Personally, **I wouldn't be seen dead** at one; it would just **bring out the worst in** me.

CASS ▶ If you're nervous about **taking the plunge** and walking in on your own, why not **get in touch with** a few old friends and go together? Then **there's safety in numbers**.

LINA ▶ I went to one last year and **had a whale of a time**! It was a great chance for us all to **catch up**. **Go for it!** You**'ve got nothing to lose.**

Glossary

there's nothing worse / better / more exciting, etc. **than …**	used to emphasize how bad/good/exciting something is.
under an obligation to do sth	forced to do sth for legal or moral reasons. OPP **under no obligation to do sth**.
I wouldn't be seen dead …	INF used to say you wouldn't do a particular thing or go to a particular place because it would be embarrassing.
bring out the best/worst in sb	make sb show their best/worst qualities.
take the plunge	INF decide to do sth difficult or important after thinking about it for a long time.
get in touch (**with sb**)	speak or write to sb, especially after a long time.
there's safety in numbers	SAYING being in a group makes you safer or makes you feel more confident.
have a whale of a time	INF have a lot of fun.
catch up (**with sb or with/on sth**)	find out about things that have happened.
go for it!	EXCLAMATION used to encourage sb to do sth or try very hard.
have (got) nothing to lose	If you **have nothing to lose**, you should try something because even if it fails, it will not make your situation any worse.

1　Complete the sentences.

1　I haven't spoken to Damien for years; I must try and .... in touch with him.
2　Always walk home with someone else: remember that there's .... in numbers.
3　It's a dreadful club – I wouldn't be seen .... in there.
4　In the end I .... the plunge and asked her out; fortunately she said 'yes'.
5　After weeks of worrying, I did go to the reunion and had a whale of a ....
6　There's nothing .... than bumping into your old enemy at a school reunion.

2　One word is missing in each line. Where does it go? Write it at the end.

Ten years after I left school, Marco Tomasi got in ⋀ with me and said he　　*touch*

wanted to meet and up on what I'd been doing. I used to go out with　　1 ....

him, and something about him always out the worst in me, so I wasn't　　2 ....

keen. I knew that I was under obligation to see him again, especially after　　3 ....

the way he'd behaved. But in the end I decided that I had to lose, and my　　4 ....

sisters said, 'Look – what's the worst that can happen? Go it!' Thinking that　　5 ....

is safety in numbers, I invited them along, but they refused. In the end,　　6 ....

I met him for dinner one evening and to my surprise, we had a of a time.　　7 ....

B Overheard at the reunion

Look who's here! It's Gemma – wow, she **looks a million dollars**!

Look, I know we're all **pushing 40**, but that outfit Marilee's wearing **puts years on** her.

Don't look now, but that man over there is an ex-boyfriend of mine. I **was glad to see the back of** him, I can tell you.

Poor Clara – she used to be a model and now she's **all skin and bones**. I guess time just **catches up with** you!

Look at Marco – he obviously **keeps in trim**. I wonder if he's married? Oh, he seems to be with Gemma. Maybe they're more than **just good friends**!

Glossary

look who's here!	used when sb arrives and you are surprised.
look a million dollars	INF (of a person) look very good or very attractive.
be pushing 40, 50, etc.	INF be nearly 40, 50, etc.
put years on sb	INF used to say that sth makes sb seem much older than they are. OPP **take years off sb**.
don't look now	used to tell sb to look at sb else, but not immediately because you do not want that person to know you are discussing them.
be glad to see the back of sb	INF be happy when sb leaves because you do not like them.
be (all) skin and bones	INF be very thin in an unattractive or unhealthy way.
catch up with sb	begin to have an effect on sb. (Compare with page 64.)
keep in trim	stay in healthy physical condition. OPP **be out of shape**.
just (good) friends	used to emphasize that two people are not having a romantic relationship.

3 Circle the correct answer.

1 If someone looks a million dollars, they *are rich* | *look great*.
2 If your clothes put years on you, they make you look *older* | *younger*.
3 If you're glad to see the back of someone, you *enjoy* | *don't enjoy* their company.
4 If you're just good friends, you *are* | *aren't* in a romantic relationship with someone.
5 If someone is pushing fifty, they are *over* | *under* fifty.
6 If you're keeping in trim, you're *in good shape* | *out of shape*.
7 If your age is catching up with you, you're feeling *older* | *younger*.
8 If someone is all skin and bones, they look *attractive* | *terrible*.

4 Complete the dialogues with a word or phrase.

1 Well, _____ who's here! It's Olivia! ~ Wow, she obviously _____ in trim.
2 Don't look _____ , but Anna's looking awful. ~ Yeah, she's all skin and _____ .
3 Don's overweight and it's put _____ on him. ~ Yes, he really looks out of _____ .
4 Well, we're all _____ 50, aren't we? ~ Yeah, time is catching _____ with us all.
5 Suri's looking a _____ dollars. ~ I think that hair colour _____ years _____ her.
6 Is Martin going out with Naomi? ~ I don't think so. She says they're just good _____ .

5 ABOUT YOU Have you been to a school reunion? If so, what was it like? Or would you like to go to one in the future? Why / Why not? Write your answers in your notebook, or talk to another student.

25 I can describe a football match

A How the media saw it

The decision by the Liverpool manager to leave key players **on the bench** and **gamble on** youth didn't **pay off** at Stamford Bridge yesterday. Chelsea **brushed aside** a Liverpool team that was way **below par**, and should have won more easily than the 2-1 score suggests. Lampard and Ballack gave Chelsea a 2-0 lead, and although Liverpool **hit back** in the second half, they were never really **in contention**. With Manchester United's game **rained off** last night, this win means that Chelsea **have gained ground on** the league leaders, but there is still **a long way to go**.

Glossary

on the bench	A player who is **on the bench** for a match is a substitute.
gamble on sth/sb	take a risk with sth/sb, hoping you will be successful.
pay off	INF (of a plan or action) be successful and bring good results.
brush sb/sth aside	treat sb/sth as unimportant.
hit back	start to perform well against a team that has been in the lead.
in contention (**for sth**)	having a chance of success; in a position to win sth.
rained off	If an event is **rained off**, it is postponed because of rain.
gain ground (**on sb**)	gradually get closer to sb you are competing with.
a long way to go	a lot more to do before you are successful.

> **spotlight** Expressions with *par*
>
> *The team were* below par *today.* = less good than usual or expected.
> *We're* on a par with *Arsenal.* = about the same level/standard as Arsenal.

1 Circle the correct answer.

1 The game was rained *out* | *off* last night.
2 The team is still *in* | *on* contention.
3 We're gaining *ground* | *speed* on the leaders.
4 The team was *below* | *under* par today.
5 He brushed *away* | *aside* my comments.
6 We're on *par* | *a par* with the others.

2 Complete the dialogues.

1 Did they score first? ~ Yes, but we .... back ten minutes later.
2 Is he in the starting eleven? ~ No, he's on the ....
3 Do you think you'll win the title? ~ I don't know. There's still a long .... to go.
4 Did they play well? ~ No, I thought we were way below ....
5 Are they still playing tonight? ~ No, it's been rained ....
6 Why aren't Coles and Low playing? ~ The manager's gambling .... the younger players.

3 Rewrite the sentences using the word in capitals. Keep the meaning the same.

1 We're about the same standard as Everton. PAR ....
2 The coach treated the comments as unimportant. BRUSH ....
3 We have a chance of winning the title. CONTENTION ....
4 He's confident the strategy will work. PAY ....
5 We're catching the league leaders. GROUND ....
6 Is he going to risk Palmer tonight? GAMBLE ....

B How the fans saw it

Chelsea fans

'I thought we **eased off** and **let** them **off the hook** in the second half.'

'I'm disappointed we didn't **go all out for** a third goal.'

'A win's a win, and now we're **within striking distance of** Man United.'

Liverpool fans

'We had to **dig deep**, but we **fought back** well in the second half.'

'We **held our own** for half an hour, but we were always going to **come off worse** with that team.'

'We**'re out of the running** for the league now. I think our manager**'s lost the plot**.'

Glossary

let sb off the hook	INF allow sb to get out of a difficult situation.
go all out for sth	make a big effort to achieve sth.
within striking distance (of sb/sth)	near enough to reach or attack sb/sth or to achieve sth.
dig deep	use all your effort.
fight back	work hard to achieve or oppose sth, especially in a situation where you are losing.
hold your own (against sb)	compete equally against sb, especially sb stronger than you, in a competition or difficult situation.
come off worse	lose a fight, competition, etc., or suffer more compared with others.
be in / out of the running (for sth)	have some/no chance of being successful in sth.
lose the plot	INF no longer understand a situation or how to deal with it.

spotlight *ease off*

If a player or team **eases off**, it usually means they try less hard (as above). If something unpleasant or annoying **eases off**, it becomes less strong, e.g. *The rain is easing off*. *The pain will ease off soon*.

4 Are you pleased or unhappy with your team? Write P or U.

1 We dug deep. ....
2 We let them off the hook. ....
3 We lost the plot. ....
4 We're in the running. ....
5 We held our own. ....
6 We fought back. ....
7 We came off worse. ....
8 We're within striking distance. ....

5 Complete the text.

The conditions were terrible at the start of the game and they had a much bigger side, so we (1) .... off worse in the early exchanges. But the guys (2) .... deep and once the rain (3) .... off I felt we pretty much (4) .... our own. In fact, in the second half, we were the ones going all (5) .... for the winning goal. Unfortunately it never came, and some people may say we let them off the (6) .... in the end. But I still thought it was a good performance, and if we win on Saturday we'll be within (7) .... distance of second place, so we're definitely still in the (8) .... for the title.

26 I can describe a conference

Feedback from the 10th International Memory Conference, York

✚ A terrific conference. The time just **flashed by** and I **came away with** a wealth of ideas. You can give yourselves **a pat on the back**!

✚ I really enjoyed the weekend. I met some delegates[1] who I didn't **see eye to eye with**, but that's given me plenty of **food for thought**. Thanks from one very satisfied delegate!

✚ I was impressed with the standard of speakers – Jim Rose really **opened** my **eyes** with his talk, and he was brilliant at answering questions **off the cuff**. Plus I got the chance to hear about the latest research, which had been my aim **all along**.

[1]delegates

✚ Thank you. You **lined up** some great speakers. I really appreciated the way they **bridged the gap between** theory and practice, and managed to **cater for** all sorts of participants. And the accommodation on the university campus was **second to none**.

━ I was disappointed at the lack of opportunity to **bounce ideas off** one another. We needed more time to **feed** our ideas **back** to the organizers while the conference was still going on.

━ A couple of events were swapped but we were not told about it, so I **missed out on** Jim Rose's apparently excellent talk. Instead, I sat through a terrible talk in the Great Hall where the speaker really didn't **know his stuff**. And we needed wireless facility – it would be worth **bearing in mind** for next year.

Glossary

flash by	If time **flashes by**, it goes very quickly. SYN **fly by**.
come away with sth	leave a place with new knowledge or ideas or a particular impression.
a pat on the back	INF praise for something you have done well.
see eye to eye with sb	share the same views as sb about sth.
food for thought	an idea that makes you think about sth seriously and carefully.
open sb's eyes (to sth)	make sb realize the truth about sth.
all along	all the time; from the beginning.
line sb/sth up	arrange for sb to be available for an event or arrange for an event to happen.
bridge the gap/gulf/divide (between …)	reduce the differences between two things or groups of people.
cater for sb/sth	provide the things that a person or a situation requires.
second to none	as good as the best; excellent.
bounce ideas off sb	discuss ideas with other people to get their opinion and make a decision.
feed (sth) back (to sb)	give information or opinions about sth to sb, especially so that it can be improved. **feedback** N.
miss out (on sth)	lose the opportunity to have or to do sth.
know your stuff	INF know a lot about a particular subject or job.
bear sth in mind	remember an important piece of information that could be useful in the future.

spotlight Idioms with *off*

He speaks well off the cuff. = without planning it first; spontaneously.
She said a number off the top of her head. = without careful thought or checking the facts.
His talk was a bit off the wall. = INF unusual; slightly crazy.

1 Circle the correct word.

1 If you're speaking off the *cuff | wall*, you are speaking spontaneously.
2 If a school is second to none, it is *the best | second best*.
3 If you've known something all along, you've known it *for a while | from the beginning*.
4 If you bear something in mind, you remember some information to use *now | later*.
5 If you say something off the top of your head, you do it *without | after* thinking carefully.
6 If you don't get the chance to do something you enjoy, you *miss it out | miss out on it*.
7 If something gives you food for thought, you *eat | think about* it.
8 If someone makes you realize the truth about something, they open your *ears | eyes* to it.

2 Complete the sentences with a word or phrase that has the opposite meaning of the words in italics.

▶ Did she *criticize* you for your talk, or did she give you a pat on the back   ?
1 Was it a fairly *sensible* talk, or was it a bit _____ ?
2 Had she *planned* what she was going to say, or did she just speak _____ ?
3 Will you just *ignore what people said*, or will you bear _____ ?
4 Did they *say nothing* to you after your talk, or did they give you some _____ ?
5 Did the time pass *slowly* or did it _____ ?
6 Have you found out about it *recently*, or have you known about it _____ ?

3 Complete the dialogues.

1 A Do you get on well with your boss?
  B No, we don't really see _____ to _____ , unfortunately.
2 A I was sorry to _____ out on the chance to hear Professor Quentin.
  B Yes, he's a great speaker, and he really _____ his stuff.
3 A Do you know who they've got _____ up to open the conference?
  B Not yet. But it's hard to find someone who can _____ for the interests of everyone in the audience.
4 A How did the discussion go?
  B Fantastic! It was a great opportunity to _____ ideas off each other.
5 A I thought my talk went OK.
  B It was far better than that – you should give yourself a _____ on the back.
6 A When I fed _____ to the organizers, I told them I wasn't happy about the venue.
  B Let's hope they _____ that in mind for next time.

4 Order the words to make sentences.

1 and | between | the | must | rich | bridge | we | gap | poor _____
2 the | to | see | I | didn't | with | eye | eye | teacher _____
3 important | eyes | my | she | things | more | opened | to _____
4 new | a | away | lot | with | ideas | came | we | of _____
5 my | off | an | top| I | answer | head | gave | the | of _____
6 back | on | a | organizers | pat | the | the | deserve _____

5 ABOUT YOU Think about the last time you listened to a speaker giving a talk. Circle the correct word, then write your answers in your notebook, or talk to another student.

1 Did the time go slowly, or did it flash *back | by*?
2 Did the speaker *tell | know* his/her stuff?
3 Was the talk very conventional, or a bit off the *cuff | wall*?
4 Did the speaker cater *for | with* the whole audience?
5 Did it give you food for *thinking | thought*?
6 Did you come *away | along* afterwards with any new ideas?

Review: Events

Unit 20

1 Complete the dialogues. You may need more than one word.

▶ Is Milly a good cook? ~ No, she can't cook to save her life _____ .
1 Goodness, it was a mess. ~ Yes, it looked like a bomb _____ .
2 Who's going to carry on after you? ~ Edward said he would take _____ .
3 Have you tested it yet? ~ No, but we're going to try _____ next week.
4 I only made a little mistake. ~ Yes, it was stupid of Don to make a big thing _____ .
5 It's a tiny bathroom. ~ I know, there's no room to swing _____ .
6 Did anyone disapprove? ~ Yes, the managing director raised an _____ .
7 Will the new plans be similar? ~ Yes, something along _____ .
8 I expect you're pleased you don't have to go. ~ Yeah, it's a weight _____ .

2 Complete the idiom or phrasal verb being defined.

1 **like** _____ INF	a lot, e.g. *practise like* _____ .
2 **can't do sth to** _____ **your life** INF	can't do sth at all, or only very badly.
3 **pull sth** _____ INF	succeed in doing sth that is difficult.
4 _____ **out** INF	too anxious or tired to be able to relax.
5 **pitch** _____ **(with sb/sth)** INF	join in and help other people with an activity.
6 _____ **(sth) up**	serve food onto plates for a meal.
7 **a big** _____ INF	is something that is very important. If something isn't important, we say 'it's no big _____ '.
8 **tried and** _____	successfully used or relied on in the past.

Unit 21

1 Match 1–8 with a–h.

1	put up ____	a	your doubts about something
2	come ____	b	something behind
3	set up ____	c	a tent
4	have ____	d	the easy way out
5	leave ____	e	camp
6	make ____	f	an eye on something
7	keep ____	g	in handy
8	take ____	h	do with something

2 Rewrite the sentences using the words in capitals, in the correct form. Keep the meaning the same.

▶ Could you watch my bag for me? EYE Could you keep an eye on my bag for me?
1 It rained very heavily. TIP _____
2 I found the book by chance. STUMBLE _____
3 We got very wet. SKIN _____
4 We made good use of that tin opener. COME _____
5 I got very tired. WEAR _____
6 The band were very popular. BOMB _____
7 We can manage with two assistants instead of three. MAKE _____
8 I'm a bit uncertain about Jeremy. DOUBTS _____

Unit 22

1 Tick the correct ending.

1 She was lovely, and I (a) couldn't look her in the eye. ☐ (b) couldn't take my eyes off her. ☐
2 It was a very noisy place, which (a) wasn't what I had in mind. ☐ (b) wasn't on the cards. ☐
3 The date went well, (a) as far as I could tell. ☐ (b) as far as it goes. ☐
4 I should never have agreed to go with Luis because (a) he just snapped out of it. ☐ (b) he just winds me up. ☐
5 Mai was a bag of nerves at first, but later she a) came out of her shell. ☐ b) wound me up. ☐
6 I was so embarrassed when he mentioned his wife that (a) I couldn't take my eyes off him. ☐ (b) I couldn't look him in the eye. ☐
7 We were going for a meal, and Hari (a) called for me at the station. ☐ (b) picked me up at the station. ☐
8 It's been hectic – I've been (a) rushing round all day. ☐ (b) getting round to it all day. ☐

2 Complete the conversation about Anna's evening out.

tami So Anna, how did your (1) .... date go last night?
anna Well, I was a (2) .... of nerves for days beforehand. But anyway, Andy
      (3) .... me up at the station, and we went straight to the restaurant that he'd booked.
tami So what was he like to look at?
anna Not bad at all! He was quite attractive and had (4) .... of confidence too. He talked
      a lot to start with, but then he was good at asking questions, and I started to come out of my
      (5) .... In fact, he was very easy to talk to – we (6) .... away for hours
      and the time just (7) .... by.
tami So do you think you'll see him again?
anna I hope I (8) .... a good enough impression on him. We swapped mobile numbers and
      he said he'd ring. Yeah, I reckon a second date is on the (9) .... !

Unit 23

1 Complete the crossword.

1 Ask someone to marry you. (3,3,7)
2 You can spend, achieve, or do anything. (3,4,3,5)
3 Ask people to wish someone happiness or success by raising their glasses and drinking. (7,1,5)
4 Speak in a very sincere way. (5,4,3,5)
5 Cost a great deal of money. (5,3,4)
6 (Speak about someone) in a very positive way. (2,7,5)
7 Something that makes a good situation even better. (3,5,2,3,4)
8 If your emotions .... you, they are too strong to control. (3,3,6,2)

2 Complete the dialogues with a single word.

1 Did you have the suit specially made? ~ No, I got it off the _____ .
2 Did it all go smoothly? ~ Yes, it went off without a _____ .
3 Did you offer to help? ~ Yes, but she wouldn't _____ of it.
4 He went on and on. ~ I know, you just can't shut him _____ .
5 You must have been thrilled to win. ~ Yes, it really made my _____ .
6 Did she start crying? ~ Yes, she broke down in _____ .
7 Did her uncle say nice things about her? ~ Yes, he was singing her _____ .
8 Is it the wedding tomorrow? ~ Yes, it's the big _____ .

Unit 24

1 Complete the paraphrases. You may need more than one word.

1 If someone's nearly fifty, you could say that they're _____ fifty.
2 If someone's extremely thin, you might say that they're all skin _____ .
3 If someone's looking wonderful, you might say they look a _____ .
4 If an outfit makes someone look older, you might say it puts _____ them.
5 If you're trying to encourage someone to do something, you might say, 'Go _____ !'
6 If someone has become too fat, you might say they're out _____ .

2 Rewrite the sentences using the word in capitals. Keep a similar meaning.

▶ She's exceedingly thin. BONES *She's all skin and bones.*
1 We had a lot of fun. WHALE _____
2 I must contact Stephanie. TOUCH _____
3 They can't force you to do it. OBLIGATION _____
4 I'll be happy when he leaves. BACK _____
5 We're not in a romantic relationship. GOOD _____
6 I would never go to that place. DEAD _____
7 A day on the beach is as good as anything. NOTHING _____
8 I just want to find out the latest news. CATCH _____

Unit 25

1 Complete the definitions of these idioms and phrasal verbs with a single word.

1 If you *dig deep* in a game, you use all your _____ .
2 If you *hold your own*, you compete _____ .
3 If you *are out of the running*, you have _____ chance of being successful.
4 If you *brush someone aside*, you treat them as _____ .
5 If rain *eases off*, it becomes less _____ .
6 If you are *on a par* with someone, you are at the same _____ .
7 If you *gamble on* someone, you take a _____ with them.
8 If a player is *on the bench*, he or she is a _____ .

2 Complete the sentences on the right with a single word, so that they have the same meaning as the sentences on the left.

1 The game was postponed because of rain.   The game was rained ....
2 We still have a chance of winning.   We are still in ....
3 We're getting closer.   We're gaining ....
4 We weren't very good today.   Today we were below ....
5 We tried a new system but it didn't work.   We tried a new system but it didn't pay ....
6 We allowed them to get out of that situation.   We let them off the ....
7 In the second half, we didn't try as hard.   In the second half, we eased ....
8 He doesn't know what he's doing.   He's lost the ....

Unit 26

1 Complete the conversation.

tony   I thought it was a good conference, didn't you? City Hall was excellent.
sian   Yeah, as a venue it's (1) .... to none.
tony   And they'd (2) .... up some interesting speakers as well.
robin Yeah. My only criticism is that the sessions were a bit short and time just seemed to
       (3) .... by. I felt we (4) .... out on the opportunity to ask questions at the
       end of the sessions and (5) .... ideas off one another.
tony   Mmm. And one or two of the talks were maybe a bit academic; they didn't (6) .... the
       gap between theory and practice very successfully.
sian   I know, but it's difficult to (7) .... for everyone, and some people want the academic
       background. Still, I learnt a lot of new stuff – I just don't read enough these days.
robin No, me neither. I certainly (8) .... away with some interesting new ideas. So, all in all, a
       good conference.

2 Complete the idioms being defined. You will find one of the words for each idiom in the box.

| wall   pat   cuff   food   head   stuff   bear   come ✓   eye |

▶ come **away** with sth = leave somewhere with a particular impression or knowledge.
1 .... **something in** .... = remember an important piece of information that
                                                                       could be useful in the future.
2 **a** .... **on the** .... = praise for something you have done well.
3 **off the** .... **of your** .... = without careful thought or checking the facts.
4 .... **for** .... = an idea that makes you think seriously and carefully.
5 .... **your** .... = be well informed about a particular subject or job.
6 .... **the** .... = unusual; slightly crazy.
7 **see** .... **to** .... = share the same views as someone about something.
8 .... **the** .... = without planning it first.

A Scandal

BBC under pressure to sack presenter

Politicians **are putting pressure on** the BBC **to** remove chat-show host Bob Aldred, after a story **leaked out** that he uttered racist remarks following his Saturday show. The comments were made **off the record**, and colleagues feel they have **been blown out of proportion**. However, Aldred is **a household name**, and any comments that could **stir up** controversy and **cast doubt on** the integrity of the BBC would be very damaging. Friends hope the incident will quickly **blow over**, but critics argue that the BBC has been left with no option. 'This story won't **go away**,' said one MP. 'The BBC must act now to **stamp out** any possible accusation of racism, and **the sooner the better**.'

Glossary

put pressure on sb (**to do sth**)	force or try to persuade sb to do sth; that person is then **under pressure**.
leak out	(of secret information) become known to the public.
off the record	used for saying that a remark is not official or intended to be made public. OPP **on the record**.
blow sth (**up**) **out of** (**all**) **proportion**	make sth seem much worse or more dangerous than it really is.
a household name	a name known to everyone; a famous person.
stir sth up	try to cause arguments or problems.
cast doubt(s) on sth	make people feel less certain about sth.
blow over	If a difficult situation **blows over**, people stop talking about it and soon forget about it.
go away	disappear.
stamp sth out	get rid of sth that is wrong or dangerous, often with force.
the sooner the better	as soon as possible.

1 Circle the correct answer.

1 If you **cast doubt on something**, you make other people feel *more / less* certain about it.
2 If a situation **blows over**, people *start / stop* worrying about it.
3 If a comment is made **on the record**, it *is / isn't* intended to be made public.
4 If information **leaks out**, it becomes *known / official*.
5 If you **stamp something out**, you *put your foot on it / get rid of it*.
6 If a problem **goes away**, it *disappears / moves somewhere else*.

2 Rewrite the sentences using the correct form of the word in capitals. Keep the same meaning.

▶ We need to get rid of prejudice. STAMP *We need to stamp out prejudice.*
1 He tried to make her change her mind. PRESSURE
2 His comments weren't intended to be made public. RECORD
3 We need to do this, and as soon as possible. SOONER
4 He's known to everyone. HOUSEHOLD
5 The secrets have become known recently. LEAK
6 People will soon forget about the incident. BLOW
7 She made it seem much worse than it was. PROPORTION
8 His comments have caused a lot of anger. STIR

B Opinions about the press

'Newspapers print all sorts of allegations, many of then untrue, but **mud sticks**, and the unfortunate victims **bear the brunt of** it.'

'Some newspaper stories may **not ring true**, but generally journalists **go to great lengths to** check their facts and ensure their stories are accurate.'

'**If it weren't for** the press, a lot of things would **be swept under the carpet** and might never **come out into the open**.'

'Newspapers sometimes **overstep the mark**, but they also **speak out against** social injustice, so I tend to **have mixed feelings** about them.'

Glossary

bear the brunt of sth	suffer the worst part of sth unpleasant.
not ring true	If sth **doesn't ring true**, you don't believe it, even though you cannot explain why.
go to great lengths (**to do sth**)	try in a determined way to achieve sth. (If you will **go to any lengths** (**to do sth**), you are so determined to achieve sth that you would act in an extreme way if necessary.)
if it weren't/**wasn't for sb**/**sth**	used to say who or what is preventing sth from happening (**If it weren't for** the press, … = Without the press, …).
sweep sth under the carpet	try to keep sth a secret, especially sth you have done wrong.
come out in/**into the open**	(of sth that was previously secret) become known. SYN **come to light**.
overstep the mark	upset sb by doing or saying more than you should. SYN **go too far**.
speak out (**against sth**)	state your opinions in public, especially in order to protest against or defend sth.
have mixed feelings about sth/**sb**	feel both positive and negative about sth/sb.

spotlight Sayings about truth

Two contradictory sayings are often used when discussing the press:
Mud sticks. = People remember the bad things they hear about someone, even if they are later shown to be false.
There's no smoke without fire. = If something bad is said about something, it usually has some truth in it.

3 Same or different? Write S or D.

1 They'll go to great lengths to find out.   They'll go to any lengths to find out. ....
2 They've gone too far.   They've overstepped the mark. ....
3 I have mixed feelings about it.   I have bad feelings about it. ....
4 There's no smoke without fire.   Mud sticks. ....
5 The facts will come out in the open.   The facts will come to light. ....
6 We know it because of John.   If it weren't for John, we wouldn't know it. ....

4 Complete the dialogues.

1 Is the information still secret? ~ No, it's all out in the .... now.
2 Are you sure it's the right thing to do? ~ No, I've got .... feelings, actually.
3 Will you support the protest? ~ Yes, we have to .... out against the government.
4 Do you believe the story? ~ You know what they say: there's no smoke ....
5 Will the government tell us? ~ No, they'll sweep it ....
6 Do you believe what they're saying? ~ No, it doesn't ring ....
7 Who has suffered the most criticism? ~ Well, Amelia's borne the .... of it.
8 Did he try to find out? ~ Yes, he went to great .... to discover the truth.

28 I can talk about crime

A Robbery

Robbery **in broad daylight** leaves shop owner stunned

Police **are on the lookout for** two men who **held up** a shop in Weston yesterday and stole £2,000. The two **were lying in wait for** the owner, Rob Hadley, when he returned to the shop shortly after 2 p.m. Mr Hadley was held **at gunpoint** while the men took money from the till and the flat above the shop. They **made off with** the money along Ship Street and escaped across the common. Mr Hadley said he was stunned by the attack. A police spokesperson, Ann Tandy, said they **were stepping up** their campaign to get guns off the streets **in the wake of** the robbery. 'We **will crack down** hard **on** anyone caught **in possession of** firearms,' said Tandy. 'We need to **nip** this **in the bud**.'

Glossary

in broad daylight	at a time of day when it is not dark or beginning to get dark (often used when you are surprised to see sth at this time of day).
be on the lookout for sb/sth	INF be looking carefully for sb/sth in order to find them.
hold sth up	use violence to steal from a shop, bank, etc.
lie in wait (for sb)	hide while waiting to surprise, attack, or catch sb.
at gunpoint	while being threatened with a gun.
make off with sth	steal sth and hurry away with it in order to escape.
step sth up	increase the amount or speed of sth.
in the wake of sth	coming soon after or following sth.
crack down (on sth/sb)	INF try harder to prevent an illegal activity and deal severely with those caught doing the activity. **crackdown** N.
in possession of sth	FML having or owning sth, often sth that is illegal or important.
nip sth in the bud	INF stop a bad situation from becoming worse by taking action at an early stage of its development.

1 **Circle the logical answer(s). Sometimes both answers may be logical.**

  1 The police were lying in wait for *the robbers | their colleagues*.
  2 We want to nip *roller skating | under-age drinking* in the bud.
  3 They made off with the *money | jewels*.
  4 She was in possession of *her clothes | secret information*.
  5 They're having a crackdown on *shopping | gambling*.
  6 The company want to step up their *idea | production*.

2 **Write in the missing prepositions.**

  1 lie _____ wait _____ somebody
  2 be _____ the lookout _____ somebody
  3 _____ broad daylight
  4 _____ gunpoint

  5 _____ the wake _____ something
  6 make off _____ something
  7 _____ possession _____ something
  8 nip something _____ the bud

3 **Complete the text. Then circle the full idioms and phrasal verbs.**

Early yesterday morning the police received a tip-off about a robbery at the post office in Denton. They were (1) _____ in wait for the robbers when they arrived on the scene, and caught them as they attempted to (2) _____ off with the money. Both men were charged with robbery and being in (3) _____ of an illegal firearm. One of the police officers said that in the (4) _____ of several robberies in the area, they had been on the (5) _____ for these two men, and their arrest was a further success in their campaign to (6) _____ down on armed robbery in the area.

B Crime stories in the news

Police **press charges against** MP

Duke vows to **clear** his **name**

GOVERNMENT TO **TIGHTEN UP** GAMBLING LAWS

Police **go on the offensive**

YOUNGSTERS
BEING LED ASTRAY

Reporter **goes under cover**

Plan to **phase out**
complicated police forms

POLICE **TIPPED OFF**
BY GANG MEMBER

Knife crime **on the up**

Accused athlete
in the clear

POLITICIANS MUST **CLEAN UP**
THEIR ACT SAY PUBLIC

Glossary

press charges (against sb)	officially accuse sb of committing a crime.
clear sb's name	prove that sb did not do sth that they were accused of.
tighten sth up	make a law, rule, or system more strict.
go on the offensive	begin to take action against sb who is attacking or criticizing you, or sth you think is undesirable.
lead sb astray	be a bad influence on sb and make them do sth silly or criminal.
go/be under cover	pretend to be sb else in order to find out secret information.
phase sth out	gradually stop using sth over time. OPP **phase sth in**.
tip sb off	give sb a warning or secret information. **tip-off** N.
on the up	increasing (as above), or improving, e.g. *Business is on the up*.
in the clear	no longer believed to be guilty of sth bad or illegal.
clean up your act	INF start behaving in a more moral and responsible way.

4 Match 1–6 with a–f.

1 tip ....
2 lead ....
3 press ....
4 clear ....
5 go ....
6 clean ....

a your name
b on the offensive
c up your act
d somebody off
e charges
f somebody astray

5 Circle the correct answer.

1 If you **phase something in**, you introduce something *immediately / gradually*.
2 If somebody is **in the clear**, they *are found innocent / have escaped*.
3 If crime is **on the up**, it is *increasing / at its highest point*.
4 It you **tighten up** a law, you *change it / make it stricter*.
5 If you **tip somebody off**, you give them *money / a warning*.
6 If you **clean up your act**, you behave *more responsibly / in a more organized way*.

6 Rewrite the sentences using the word in capitals. Keep the meaning the same.

1 They're going to gradually discontinue the scheme. PHASE ....
2 The policeman pretended to be a criminal. COVER ....
3 He was a bad influence on the boy. ASTRAY ....
4 She wants to prove that she's innocent. CLEAR ....
5 The police have accused him of committing the crime. PRESS ....
6 They are beginning to take action against him. OFFENSIVE ....

29 I can describe a demonstration

A A news report

An estimated **turnout** of 50,000 demonstrators **from all walks of life joined forces** yesterday in the capital for an anti-government rally. The protesters **made their way** along the river to St John's Square, **calling on** the government **to bring an end to** poverty and injustice. Many local businesses **had boarded up** their premises amid fears of attack. Despite threats of violence beforehand, however, the march was allowed to **go ahead. In the event**, it **passed off** quite peacefully, although a smaller protest by about fifty demonstrators **was broken up** by the police, and a number of arrests were made.

Glossary

turnout	the number of people who attend an event. **turn out** V.
from all walks of life	A crowd **from all walks of life** consists of many different types of people (your **walk of life** is your background, job, etc.).
join/combine forces	work together to achieve sth.
make your way	(with adverbial phrase) move or get to a particular place.
call on sb to do sth	officially ask sb or an organization to do sth.
bring/put an end to sth	stop sth happening.
board sth up	cover the windows or door of a building with wooden boards to protect it or stop sb entering.
go ahead	happen; take place. **go-ahead** N (*The march was given the **go-ahead***).
in the event	as it actually happened (used especially when things did not happen as expected).
pass off	take place and be completed in a particular way (*The protest **passed off** peacefully / smoothly / without incident*). SYN **go off**.
break sth up	make a group of people leave a place or stop doing sth.

1 Complete the paraphrase on the right with one or two words.

1	How many were at the march?	What was the .... ?
2	Let's work together on this.	Let's .... forces on this.
3	They moved towards the square.	They .... their way towards the square.
4	The windows were covered in boards.	The windows were ....
5	Will the protest still take place?	Will the protest still .... ?
6	As it happened, we lost.	In the .... , we lost.
7	The protest was stopped and we had to leave.	The police .... up the protest.
8	They were from many different backgrounds.	They were from all .... of ....

2 Complete the dialogues.

1 What do the protesters want? ~ They're .... on the government to stop imports.
2 Were there any problems at the meeting? ~ No, it was fine; it .... peacefully.
3 Will the march take place? ~ Oh, yes, they've been given the .... from the police.
4 What are the people's demands? ~ They want the leaders to .... an .... to the war.
5 Was the turnout as you expected? ~ No. .... event, there were a lot more people.
6 Did you work in isolation? ~ No, we joined .... with another team, which was great.
7 How did you get to the demonstration? ~ We made .... on foot.
8 Did the weather affect the march? ~ Yes, fewer people .... than we'd hoped.

B The protesters' views

People need to **stand up for** what they believe in – and today we did. We definitely **got our message across**; we can't **back down** now. We'**re pressing ahead with** plans for further marches, which could **pave the way for** a coordinated international campaign.

We organized a **sit-in** in front of the embassy, but the police broke it up.

The police **cordoned off** part of the square and ordered us to stay there for reasons of safety. In fact, we were just **being fenced in** so that the press couldn't talk to us.

The authorities **shut down** our website, but we managed to **spread the word** by phone.

Glossary

stand up for sb/sth	support and defend sb/sth.
back down (**on sth**)	admit that you are wrong or have lost an argument.
press ahead (**with sth**)	continue doing sth in a determined way.
pave the way (**for sth**)	create a situation which makes it easier for sth to happen.
sit-in	a protest in which people sit down and refuse to leave a place until their demands are listened to. **sit in** v.
cordon sth off	stop people from getting into an area by surrounding it with the police or by putting a barrier round it.
fence sb in	(often passive) 1 surround sb with a fence. 2 restrict sb's freedom. SYN **hem sb in**.
shut sth down	stop a machine, business, etc. from operating. **shutdown** N.

spotlight Communicating information

If you **get your message across** (**to sb**), you succeed in communicating with other people. You may need to **spread the word**, i.e. tell a lot of people about something, or **put the word out about sth** INF. The opposite is to **keep sth to yourself**, i.e. keep it secret.

3 Circle the correct answer. Both answers may be possible, but have a different meaning.

1 The demonstrators organized *a sit-in | a fence-in* to protest about students' fees.
2 The government is trying to *spread | put* the word about climate change.
3 This is secret information: please keep it *for | to* yourself for the time being.
4 I don't know why the police *cordoned off | fenced in* that particular area.
5 I don't think the protesters can *back down on | press ahead with* this issue.
6 The company was trading illegally, so the police shut it *off | down*.

4 Rewrite the sentences using the word in capitals. Keep the meaning the same.

1 They will never admit they were wrong. BACK
2 Don't tell anyone about it. KEEP
3 We will certainly proceed with our plans. PRESS
4 He always defended his beliefs. STAND
5 Why did they put a barrier round the café? CORDON
6 How will we tell everyone? SPREAD
7 The talks made the reforms possible. PAVE
8 It's very hard to explain what we mean. MESSAGE

A Forthcoming election

PM under fire

The prime minister **has come under fire** during this election campaign for being slow to respond to events, but he was **quick off the mark** this morning. In a speech in Dover, he claimed that the Opposition's tax policies didn't **add up**, and that they **were plucking** numbers **out of the air**. Meanwhile, the Opposition were trying to **capitalize on** the latest bad unemployment figures, which clearly illustrated, in their view, that the only thing which could **stop the rot** was a change of government. They also **talked up** the latest opinion-poll figures, which now put them **neck and neck** with the government. **In the final analysis** it **will** just **boil down to** who the voters choose to believe.

Glossary

come/be under fire	be criticized severely for sth you have done.
quick/slow off the mark	fast/slow in reacting to a situation. (👁 See page 162.)
add up	INF seem reasonable or logical (used mainly in a negative sense, e.g. *His story doesn't add up*).
pluck sth out of the air	say a name, number, etc. without giving it any thought.
capitalize on sth	gain a further advantage for yourself from a situation.
stop the rot	stop a bad situation from getting worse.
talk sth up	describe or discuss sth in a way that makes it sound better than it is.
neck and neck	(of two people or groups) level with each other in a race or competition.
in the final analysis	used to state a basic truth after everything has been discussed and considered.
boil down to sth	If a situation or problem **boils down to** one thing, that thing is the main point in the situation, or the main cause of the problem.

1 Cover the glossary, then complete the definitions.

1 If you are *neck and neck* with somebody, you are .... with them.
2 If you *capitalize on* something, you gain an .... for yourself.
3 If someone's ideas don't *add up*, they don't seem ....
4 If you *stop the rot*, you stop a .... situation from continuing.
5 If you are *slow off the mark*, you are slow in .... to something.
6 If you *come under fire*, you are being .... for something you've done.
7 If you *pluck* a figure *out of the air*, you say a figure without ....
8 If you *talk something up*, you make it sound .... than it is.

2 Write one word in each space.

The government came under (1) .... once again this morning, this time from doctors who feel it has been (2) .... off the mark in reacting to the recent outbreak of swine flu. One doctor summed up the feelings of many when he said that the government was good at talking (3) .... its response and making it sound fine, but the truth was somewhat different. 'The solution for this problem requires time, effort, and money. But in the (4) .... analysis, it all (5) .... down to money. The figures given by the government are just (6) .... out of the air, and it isn't ready to spend the necessary amount.'

B Political scandal

WAR OF WORDS CONTINUES

Last night, politicians from all sides were still engaging in **a war of words** over the scandal surrounding MPs' expenses. Some were claiming the newspaper revelations had been **a** long overdue **wake-up call**, and several MPs were quoted as saying it was an opportunity for parliament to **put its house in order**. However, one senior government figure **was not giving an inch**. He said journalists had been too quick to **jump on the bandwagon**, and that MPs who had not broken any rules deserved to **be given the benefit of the doubt**. But with the press **having a field day**, this story is likely to **run and run**, and it doesn't **bode well for** parliament's languishing reputation.

Glossary

a war of words	a bitter argument between groups over a period of time.
put your house in order	make necessary changes or improvements in your business, way of life, etc.
not give/budge/move an inch	INF refuse to change an opinion, decision, etc.
jump/climb on the bandwagon	INF, DISAPPROVING join others in doing or saying sth that is popular and fashionable in order to make yourself popular.
give sb the benefit of the doubt	treat sb as if their behaviour is honest or correct, even though you are not certain that it is.
have a field day	(often used of the media) be given the opportunity to do sth you enjoy, especially when it causes trouble for sb else.
run and run	If sth is likely to **run and run**, it is likely to continue for a long time. (We often say sth *looks set **to run and run*** = looks likely to.)
bode well/ill for sb/sth	FML be a good/bad sign for sb/sth.

spotlight *wake-up call*

The literal meaning of **a wake-up call** is an arranged telephone call to wake you up at a particular time. Metaphorically, it is an event that makes you realize there is a problem that must be tackled (as above).

3 Circle the correct answer(s). Both answers may be correct.

1 We need to *put | settle* our own house in order first.
2 Too many people are waiting to *climb | jump* on the bandwagon.
3 The journalists are *making | having* a field day with this.
4 I think we should *leave | give* her the benefit of the doubt.
5 They want him to change his mind but he won't *move | give* an inch.
6 The newspapers are still having a war of *ideas | words* over this issue.
7 After the latest problems, this should be a wake-up *call | ring* for parliament.
8 This new scandal looks set to *run and run | race and race*.

4 Complete the sentences. You will find one of the words for each idiom or phrasal verb in the box.

> field   benefit   jump   bode   set ✓   wake-up   inch   war   house

▶ The row about pensions _looks set_ to run and run.
1 We should put our own _____ in _____ before we criticize others.
2 I don't know if it's true, but we'll give him the _____ of the _____ for now.
3 You're just like a politician: you'll _____ on the _____ at the first opportunity.
4 Journalists will _____ a _____ day when they get hold of this story.
5 The attack was a _____ for us to take the terrorists seriously.
6 There's been criticism of the policy, but the prime minister won't _____ an _____ .
7 We had the usual _____ of _____ in parliament today, mostly about nothing.
8 The opinion poll is disastrous for the government, and doesn't _____ for their future.

31 I can talk about conflict

A A community in conflict

Fate of Charmy Wood **hangs in the balance**

Environmental groups **are locked in battle** with the council over the proposed new bypass through parts of Charmy Wood. Opponents of the scheme believe the town **can ill afford to** lose an area of natural beauty, and a bypass will just **open the floodgates to** further development. The council remain adamant that there is **a crying need for** the bypass to keep traffic out of the town centre, and they say they cannot **free up** any other land. Council leader Val Moran believes the protesters are **out of step with** the majority, and says the council **will stand firm** and **press on with** the new road. It seems that both sides **are poles apart**, and it is highly unlikely that the council can **meet** the protesters **halfway**.

Glossary

hang in the balance	If sth **hangs in the balance**, its future is uncertain.
be locked in battle/ dispute, etc.	(of two people or groups) be involved in a dispute or argument to which there is no obvious solution. SYN **be at loggerheads**.
can ill afford (to do) sth	used to say that sb should not do sth because it will cause problems.
open the floodgates (to sth)	If an action or decision **opens the floodgates**, it allows a lot of things to happen that weren't previously possible.
a crying need for sth	a great and urgent need for sth.
free (sb/sth) up	make sb/sth available for a particular purpose.
out of step (with sb)	having ideas that are different from other people's.
stand firm	refuse to change your opinion.
press on (with sth)	continue doing sth in a determined way. SYN **press ahead (with sth)**.
be poles apart	(of two people or groups) be widely separated in interests and ideas.
meet sb halfway	reach partial agreement with sb, or give sb part of what they want.

1 Cover the glossary and complete the definitions.

1 If you are *out of step* with others, you have _____ ideas from them.
2 If you are *at loggerheads* with someone, you are involved in a _____ with them.
3 *A crying need* for something is an _____ need for something.
4 If you *open the floodgates* to something, you make it _____ for it to happen.
5 If you *press ahead* with something, you _____ with it.
6 If you *meet someone halfway*, you give them _____ .

2 Replace the underlined parts of the text in a way that keeps a similar meaning.

Residents of Denway Lane ▶ are currently involved in a battle with Paul Hobbs, head teacher of Denway School. Mr Locke wants to (1) make available a large part of the playing fields for development in order to fund a new laboratory. Residents say schools (2) cannot afford to give up valuable green space in a built-up area, and (3) are refusing to change their opinions, despite pressure from Mr Locke, who has vowed to (4) continue with his plans. With the two sides (5) having such different views, it is hard to see how they can (6) find a compromise. The future of the playing fields may (7) be uncertain for some time.

▶ *are locked in* _____
1 _____   4 _____   7 _____
2 _____   5 _____
3 _____   6 _____

B War metaphors

Some phrases with military origins are used figuratively to talk about conflict situations.

> The government has been engaged in **a running battle** over the introduction of identity cards, and now ministers are threatening to **break ranks** and **side with** the Opposition.

> Council leader Bryn Jones **will be** directly **in the firing line** now the council has finally decided to **bite the bullet** and raise car parking charges in the town by as much as 15 per cent.

> The Union **is sticking to its guns** in demanding a 7 per cent pay rise, but in the current economic climate it could **be fighting a losing battle**.

> **Having a foot in both camps** has not helped my supervisor: he has recently been attacked by both shop-floor workers and senior management.

Glossary

a running battle	an argument that continues over a long period of time.
break ranks	(of a member or members of a group) stop supporting the group of which you are a member. (If you **close ranks**, you join together closely to defend yourselves, especially when being criticized by others.)
side with sb	agree with sb and support them in an argument.
be in the firing line	be in a position where people can criticize or blame you.
bite the bullet	INF force yourself to do sth difficult or unpleasant that you have been avoiding.
stick to your guns	INF continue to have a particular opinion about sth even though others are saying that you are wrong.
fight a losing battle	try to do sth that will probably fail.
have/keep a foot in both camps	be involved with two different or opposing groups.

spotlight Literal meanings

In the past, soldiers were given a bullet to bite on during a medical operation without an anaesthetic; from this we get **bite the bullet**. When soldiers **close ranks**, they move closer together to defend themselves. A soldier or gunner is required to keep in position – **stick to his guns** – and not surrender.

---

3 Cover the glossary. Then complete the idioms with words associated with war.

1 a running ....
2 bite the ....
3 stick to your ....
4 have a foot ....
5 fight a losing ....
6 be in the firing ....

4 Rewrite the sentences using a suitable idiom or phrasal verb, without changing the meaning.

1 One councillor won't support his own party. One councillor has ....
2 He's involved with both parties. He's got a ....
3 They've had an argument over this for ages. They've had a ....
4 He'll make the tough decision and raise taxes. He'll ....
5 The minister is supporting the Opposition. The minister is ....
6 She's not going to change her mind on this. She's ....
7 He's trying but it won't be successful. He's fighting ....
8 The minister is likely to be criticized. The minister is in ....

A Instant fame

Britain's got talent – but should it remain hidden?

Large TV audiences prove that talent shows are compulsive viewing. Who will **rise to the occasion**? Who will **go to pieces**? But whilst these shows are an opportunity for instant fame, it can **come at a price**. When people are plucked from obscurity and acquire fame **beyond their wildest dreams**, it can **go to their head**. Many of these 'instant stars' quickly **fall by the wayside**, and the public can be very fickle: **building somebody up** one minute, then **knocking them down** the next. Perhaps we should **tread** more **carefully** rather than allow a single audience reaction to **make or break** a young performer.

Glossary

rise to the occasion	do well in a difficult situation.
go to pieces	become so upset or nervous that you cannot do sth as well as you should.
at a price	involving an unpleasant consequence (**come at a price**).
beyond your wildest dreams	better than anything you could have imagined.
go to sb's head	If success or praise **goes to sb's head**, it makes them feel more important than they really are, and they usually suffer as a result.
fall by the wayside	not be successful or effective any longer.
tread carefully	be very careful about what you do or say.
make or break sb/sth	be the thing which makes sb/sth either a great success or a complete failure. (Also as ADJ *a **make-or-break** situation*.)

spotlight *build up*

If you **build sb up**, you talk about them in a positive way so that people are impressed by them. If you then **knock sb down**, you are negative about them. If you **build up sb's hopes**, you make them think something good is going to happen when in fact it is very unlikely.

1 Is the speaker sounding positive or negative about Mel? Write P or N.

1 Success went to Mel's head. ....
2 Mel went to pieces. ....
3 This is beyond Mel's wildest dreams. ....
4 Mel rose to the occasion. ....
5 Mel's fallen by the wayside. ....
6 They built up Mel's hopes. ....

2 Complete the sentences.

1 This could be a make-or- .... performance for Jessica.
2 Winning the competition was beyond my .... dreams.
3 It's a big challenge for Connie, but I'm sure she'll .... to the occasion.
4 Ravi was too young to cope with fame, and the money went to his ....
5 As soon as I got up on stage I just went to .... and couldn't sing. It was horrible.
6 The press built him up, and then .... him down; that happens so often.

3 Rewrite the sentences using the word in capitals. Keep the meaning the same.

1 A lot of actors fail and give up. WAYSIDE ....
2 We must be very careful what we say. TREAD ....
3 He was successful but it wasn't all pleasant. PRICE ....
4 It was better than anything I could've imagined. DREAMS ....
5 Holly was too nervous and she performed badly. PIECES ....
6 I'm sure Jason will perform very well on the night. RISE ....

B In the public eye

Jodie separation shock

Jodie Webb faced the press last night after news **got out** that her four-year marriage to actor Des Miles **had reached the end of the line**. In an emotional statement, Jodie said they **had done their utmost** to keep the marriage alive, but being **in the public eye coupled with** long periods of separation **had taken its toll**. Despite the news, her agent predicted that Jodie would **bounce back from** this current **setback**, and was determined it shouldn't **cast a shadow over** the release of her latest film. Jodie made a plea for fans to leave her in peace, before **fighting her way through** the crowd and into the back of a waiting car.

Glossary

get out	(of secrets or information) become known to the public. SYN **leak out**.
(**reach**) **the end of the line/road**	(reach) the point at which sth can no longer continue in the same way.
do/try your utmost	try as hard as you possibly can.
in the public eye	well known to many people through the media.
couple sth with sth	(usually passive) combine sth with sth (**coupled with sth** = combined with sth).
take its toll (**on sb/sth**) / **take a heavy toll** (**on sb/sth**)	have a bad effect on sb/sth; cause damage, suffering, etc.
bounce back (**from sth**)	become confident, healthy, or successful again after having problems.
setback	a difficulty or disappointment that prevents progress or makes a situation worse. **set sb back** v.
cast a shadow (**over sth**)	make sb feel less happy or hopeful about sth.
fight your way (**through/ past sb/sth**)	move with difficulty through a crowd of people or through/past an obstacle.

4 Tick the correct answer(s). One, two, or three may be correct.

1 He always .... his utmost to help.
   tries ☐ makes ☐ does ☐
2 The injury has cast a .... over her future.
   shadow ☐ shade ☐ spell ☐
3 She fought her way .... the crowd.
   along ☐ past ☐ through ☐

4 The accident has taken .... on him.
   its toll ☐ a heavy toll ☐ a long toll ☐
5 This disappointment has really .... her back.
   settled ☐ driven ☐ set ☐
6 I think they've reached the end of the ....
   line ☐ road ☐ path ☐

5 One word is missing in each line of the text. Where does it go? Write it at the end.

Although actress Corinne Black had tried her ⟨ to keep it secret, the ▸ utmost

news out last night that she was being treated for a form of skin cancer. 1 ....

As she struggled to fight her through the crowds at a charity gala, 2 ....

she admitted to waiting reporters that being in the public had 3 ....

made life difficult for her recently, and coupled the birth of her second 4 ....

child only eleven months ago, the illness had her back quite 5 ....

considerably, and taken a heavy on her. Despite this, she said 6 ....

she was determined to back as soon as possible, and her condition 7 ....

would certainly not a shadow over her son's first birthday next month. 8 ....

A   Disaster headlines

HURRICANE **RIPS THROUGH** WESTERN FLORIDA

Thousands evacuated as fire **takes hold** in Alicante province

HOUSES **SWEPT AWAY** BY FLOOD WATERS

Climate change **wreaks havoc on** coral reefs worldwide

Survivors **caught up in** north Indian floods **come to terms with** loss of homes

ETHIOPIA **IN THE GRIP OF** SEVERE DROUGHT

Coal mine **caves in** following flood, but no **lives lost**

BUSH FIRES IN SOUTHERN AUSTRALIA **WIPE OUT** WHOLE TOWNS

Glossary

rip through sth	move forcefully and rapidly through sth.
take (a) hold	become very strong and difficult to remove or stop.
sweep sth away	(often passive) (of floods, a tornado, etc.) completely destroy sth.
wreak havoc (on sth)	cause a lot of damage, destruction, or confusion.
be/get caught up in sth	become involved in sth undesirable.
come to terms with sth	gradually accept a difficult or unpleasant situation.
in the grip of sth	experiencing sth unpleasant that cannot be stopped.
cave in (on sb/sth)	(of a roof, wall, etc.) collapse and fall.
lose your life	be killed. **loss of life** N.
wipe sth/sb out	(often passive) destroy or get rid of sth/sb completely.

1   One word is wrong in each sentence. Cross it out and write the correct word at the end.

▶ My grandfather lost ~~the~~ life during the great storm of 1987.   *his*
1   It's hard to get to terms with the loss of whole communities.   ....
2   A South American civilization was wiped off by earthquakes 3,800 years ago.   ....
3   The tornado is wreaking damage on all parts of the region.   ....
4   The roof caved down, and the people below were lucky to survive.   ....
5   Many tourists have been caught up on the forest fires in California.   ....
6   As the fire started to make hold, people ran to escape the flames.   ....

2   Complete the text with an idiom or phrasal verb from the box in the correct form.

caught up	come to terms ✓	sweep sth away	wreak havoc
rip through	cave in	loss of life	in the grip

Texans are counting the cost and beginning to ▶ *come to terms* .... with the devastation caused by bad weather: the state of Texas is (1) .... of the worst winter for twenty years. Fierce winds have (2) .... central Texas this week, and several tornadoes have (3) .... on a line of small towns in their path. Local resident Clint Vaughn saw his home (4) .... by rising floodwater. 'It came so fast, we barely had time to get out; we almost got (5) .... in the destruction; I stood with my mouth open as the roof of the house just (6) .... It was terrifying,' Vaughn said. 'Astonishingly, there has been no (7) .... , but many have been injured and the hospitals are full to overflowing.'

B Heavy snow

The heavy and unexpected snowfall in recent days has had serious consequences.

Motorists **heading for** the city centre on the A36 **were caught unawares** as traffic **came to a standstill**. Trapped in their cars for hours, they were finally rescued and **towed away**.

Supplies of salt and grit for the roads **are running low**, which may **put lives at risk**.

Some rural areas **have been** completely **snowed in** and villages temporarily **cut off**.

Children **have been turned away** from schools due to teacher shortages, and workplaces have been closed **for the foreseeable future**.

Snow is still falling **thick and fast**, so the Met Office is advising people to stay at home.

Glossary

head for sth	move towards a place. SYN **make for sth**.
catch sb unawares	happen in a way that sb was not expecting and was not prepared for.
come to a standstill/halt	slowly stop completely. SYN **grind to a standstill/halt**.
tow sb/sth away	(of a driver or car) pull another car using a rope or chain.
run low	If your supply of sth **is running low** or you **are running low on** sth, you only have a little left.
at risk (**of/from sth**)	in danger of sth unpleasant or harmful happening (**put lives at risk**).
be snowed in	be unable to leave a place because of heavy snow.
be cut off	be unable to leave a place or receive visitors or services from outside.
turn sb away	refuse to allow sb to enter a place.
for the foreseeable future	for the period of time when you can predict what is going to happen, based on present circumstances.
thick and fast	happening very quickly and in large amounts or numbers.

3 Write in the missing preposition or adverb.

1 We were turned .... from the factory.
2 They were snowed .... for days.
3 The cottage was cut ....
4 Make .... the nearest exit quickly.
5 Luckily, no lives were put .... risk.
6 Traffic ground .... a standstill.
7 The cars were towed ....
8 It will last .... the foreseeable future.

4 Rewrite the sentences using the word in capitals. Keep the meaning the same.

▶ The snow is falling heavily. FAST *The snow is falling thick and fast.*
1 The train gradually stopped. STANDSTILL ....
2 We couldn't contact anyone. CUT ....
3 They removed the car and took it to the police station. TOW ....
4 I went towards the hospital. HEAD ....
5 They refused to let us in the building. TURN ....
6 There is hardly any food left. LOW ....
7 We'll be cut off for some time. FORESEEABLE ....
8 I didn't expect so much snow. UNAWARES ....

Review: What's in the news?

Unit 27

1 Put the dominoes in the correct order to make a joined sequence of idioms. Write the correct order of dominoes below.

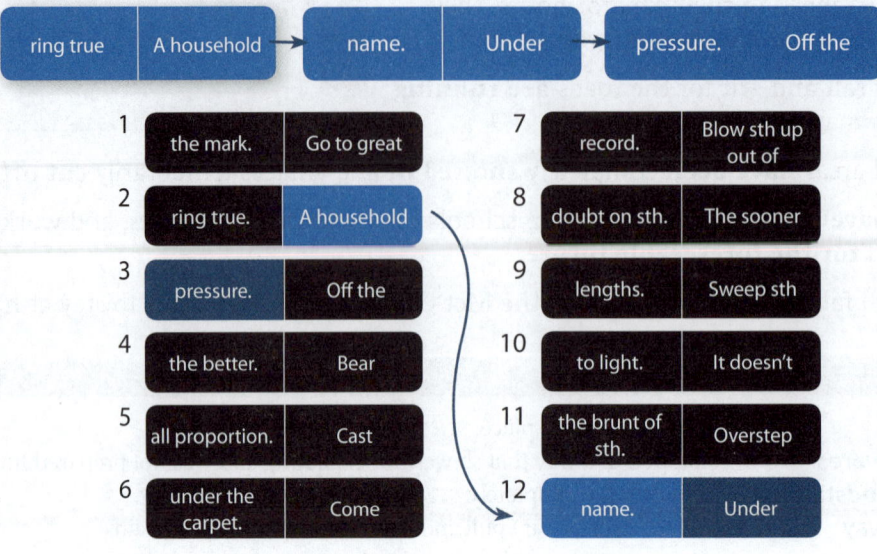

ring true	A household	name. → Under → pressure. Off the

1	the mark.	Go to great
2	ring true.	A household
3	pressure.	Off the
4	the better.	Bear
5	all proportion.	Cast
6	under the carpet.	Come
7	record.	Blow sth up out of
8	doubt on sth.	The sooner
9	lengths.	Sweep sth
10	to light.	It doesn't
11	the brunt of sth.	Overstep
12	name.	Under

2 , 12 , 3 , ... , ... , ... , ... , ... , ... , ... , ... , ...

2 Complete these opinions about stories in the press.

1 'I think the protesters are just .... up trouble; things are perfectly all right as they are.'
2 'This is a huge scandal for the government, and it won't just blow .... if the Prime Minister takes no action. He's hoping it will all .... away, but it won't.'
3 'Every day new information leaks ...., and if it .... for the press, we wouldn't know any of it. It's a disgrace.'
4 'We've known for years that things were bad, but now everything is out in the ...., it's even more shocking than expected. The politicians have really .... the mark.'
5 'It's time we put .... on our leaders to reform the laws on privacy, and the .... the better as far as I'm concerned.'
6 'I used to have mixed .... about the government, but now I'm sure they've been covering things up. I voted for them because I thought they would .... out corruption, but we now see that quite the reverse has happened. I'm very shocked.'

Unit 28

1 A word is missing in each sentence. Where does it go? Write it at the end.

▶ Police are ⟨ up the search for the missing teenager. _stepping_
1 The thief was arrested in of a considerable amount of jewellery. ....
2 Certain companies need to clean up act with regard to tax evasion. ....
3 When journalists go cover, they can put themselves in considerable danger. ....
4 The gang were just in wait for Richards; he didn't stand a chance. ....
5 The opposition party is going the offensive over European legislation. ....
6 Police in Leeds are the lookout for a gang of bicycle thieves. ....
7 The manager was held up gunpoint and forced to hand over the cash. ....
8 An enquiry has been ordered in the of the explosion at the power plant. ....

2 Complete the dialogues. You will find one of the words for each idiom or phrasal verb in the box.

> crack   up   name ✓   tip   clear   astray   bud   daylight

▶ Did he prove he was innocent? ~ Yes, he was able to _clear his name_ .
1 Who gave the police the information? ~ They were _____ _____ by a shopkeeper.
2 The older boys are a bad influence on Sam. ~ Yes, they're _____ him _____ .
3 Was the burglary at night? ~ No, it was in _____ _____ , but no one saw anything.
4 The police won't press charges. ~ That's right. He's completely _____ _____ .
5 Is the crime rate rising? ~ Yes, it's _____ _____ .
6 They should stop it before it gets worse. ~ Yes, they should _____ it _____ _____ .
7 We need to deal with burglary more severely. ~ Yes, we need to _____ _____ on it.

Unit 29

1 Using the verbs in the box in the correct form, complete the texts about an anti-war demonstration seen from different perspectives.

> turn out   pave   stand up   bring   pass off   spread   cordon off   call on
> board up   make   break up

DEMONSTRATOR The demonstration was an opportunity for us to (1) _____ for what we believe in and (2) _____ the word to as many people as possible. We hope this will (3) _____ the way for further demonstrations in the future.

POLICE The protesters (4) _____ their way along Prince Street, but we (5) _____ part of Parliament Square for security reasons.

ANTI-WAR POLITICIAN The protesters were exercising their democratic right to protest by (6) _____ the government to (7) _____ an end to this pointless war.

PRO-WAR POLITICIAN The protesters claimed there would be massive support for this demonstration, but fewer than 5,000 (8) _____ , so it was both a failure and a huge waste of police resources.

ONLOOKER The police had to (9) _____ one or two fights between pro- and anti-war demonstrators, but in general it seemed to (10) _____ quite peacefully.

SHOPKEEPER If they want to demonstrate, why don't they go to a public park? I lost money because I had to close my shop and (11) _____ the windows.

Unit 30

1 One word is missing in each sentence. Where does it go? Write it at the end.

> ▶ They're talking ⟨ the latest opinion-poll results, but in fact they're terrible. _up_
1 The truth about politics is that it all boils to a matter of trust. _____
2 I'm prepared to give them the of the doubt – but it's the last time. _____
3 I thought they would compromise, but they wouldn't an inch. _____
4 In the analysis, we have no choice but to vote against the government. _____
5 It's high time the party put its own in order. _____
6 The minister just the figures out of the air; it was obviously nonsense. _____
7 I wanted to believe her, but her story just didn't up. _____
8 We definitely need to capitalize this success while we can. _____

2 Complete the sentences, using idioms from the table in the correct form. You can move horizontally or vertically, backwards or forwards.

COME	UNDER	QUICK	MARK	HAVE
A	FIRE	OFF	THE	A
WAR	OF	WORDS	DAY	FIELD
NECK	AND	CLIMB	ON	THE
STOP	NECK	WELL ←	BODE	BANDWAGON
THE	ROT	A	WAKE-UP	CALL

▶ The results of the opinion polls don't *bode well* .... for the government.
1 The press have heard rumours about illegal activities in the Independent Party; they will ....
.... with that.
2 The results of these local elections should act as .... for the government.
3 The results were incredibly close: the two candidates are running ....
4 Car manufacturers will .... in the press today for continuing to ignore
government calls for better safety.
5 Tensions have been heightened between the two countries because of ....
.... over territorial disputes.
6 To regain its global status, the city must try to .... which has set in over
the last few years.
7 The candidate saw that voters were increasingly interested in green issues, and as a result, we saw him
.... It's deeply cynical of him.
8 The government has been surprisingly .... in introducing new
climate change legislation.

Unit 31

1 Is the meaning the same or different? Write S or D.

1 We can ill afford to do nothing.   Our best solution would be to do nothing.   ....
2 Shall we meet them halfway?   Shall we accept some of their demands?   ....
3 I'm sure they'll close ranks on this.   I'm sure they won't support their party on this.   ....
4 I think they'll bite the bullet.   I think they'll break ranks.   ....
5 We need to stand firm on this.   We need to stick to our guns on this.   ....
6 Our future hangs in the balance.   Our future is looking more secure.   ....
7 They're at loggerheads over this.   They're locked in dispute over this.   ....
8 We're in the firing line.   We're fighting a losing battle.   ....

2 Circle the correct word.

1 If the law is passed, it will *release | open* the floodgates for thousands of people to request
compensation.
2 They've been locked in battle for months, and they're still poles *apart | away*.
3 On this issue, the government is out of *pass | step* with the voters.
4 There is a *running | crying* need for improvement in train services.
5 If we can get extra staff, it will free us *up | out* to concentrate on the key problems.
6 I didn't expect him to *side | keep* with the director. I feel very let down.
7 We have no choice but to press *ahead | over* with the scheme, despite the protests.
8 He's trying to keep a foot in both *camps | sides*, but it won't work.

Unit 32

1 Complete the crossword. The letters in the grey squares spell out a word. What is it?

1 Most people don't realize that fame comes at a .... : a complete lack of privacy.

2 One TV appearance alone has the power to make or .... a new performer.

3 The press is happy to .... young people up, but just as happy to knock them down.

4 When people are fragile, we need to .... carefully and handle them sensitively.

5 The group are remarkably resilient, and after this setback I'm sure they will .... back.

6 Let's hope that she overcomes her nerves and can .... to the occasion on Saturday.

7 Anyone who is in the .... eye will tell you that it's not all fun and games.

8 The scandal described in the magazine will .... a shadow over his career.

9 Winning the competition would be .... my wildest dreams.

The word in the grey squares is ....

2 There is one word too many in each line. Cross it out.

▶ As the money disappeared, all their promises fell ~~down~~ by the wayside.

1 Having so many children has taken its heavy toll on her health. She's exhausted.

2 Smoking is coupled with obesity greatly increases heart problems.

3 Winning the competition has clearly gone up to her head. She's unbearable.

4 We had to fight for our way past the hundreds of people outside the theatre.

5 I can't promise anything, but I will certainly try to my utmost to do it by tonight.

6 My sister went to the pieces when I told her the cat had died. She really loved it.

Unit 33

1 Complete the idiom or phrasal verb in each sentence.

1 The train slowed down and eventually ground to a ....

2 Another earthquake will put more lives at ....

3 The road will remain closed for the foreseeable ....

4 The hurricane will wreak .... when it hits the coast.

5 Once the forest fires take a ...., they are almost impossible to stop.

6 The people are still coming to .... with the loss of their homes.

2 Read the text, then replace the underlined phrases with idioms and phrasal verbs.

▶ coming to terms with

1 ....

2 ....

3 ....

4 ....

5 ....

6 ....

7 ....

People are still ▶ accepting the idea of the heaviest snowfall in the United Kingdom for many years. Thousands of motorists driving home yesterday afternoon were (1) very surprised to find themselves in difficulty as the snow fell (2) quickly and heavily, and traffic on several motorways (3) stopped completely. Many cars had to be (4) pulled away by trucks, and the emergency services have warned that conditions could get worse. In the countryside, many people were (5) unable to leave their homes because of the snow this morning and couldn't get to work, and in parts of Wales, whole villages are (6) isolated by the snow. The meteorological office say we are now (7) experiencing the coldest winter on record.

34 I can talk about communicators

A Good communicators

Good communicators are people who:

- are first of all good listeners, and really **take in** what others have to say.
- make sure their body language **isn't at odds with** what they are saying.
- **pick up on** little things that are important to people, such as important names or dates.
- **keep** people **in the picture** about things.
- know when to distribute information **on a need-to-know basis**.
- don't **get** people's **backs up** by being rude, aggressive, dismissive, etc.
- **win** people **over** rather than make demands.
- are prepared to **open up to** people, so that others will open up to them.

Glossary

take sth in	understand, absorb, and remember new facts and information.
be at odds with sth	be in conflict with sth; contradict sth.
pick up on sth	notice sth and perhaps react to it.
on a need-to-know basis	so that sb is told only what they need to know and only when they need to know it.
get sb's back up	INF annoy sb.
win sb over/round (**to sth**)	get sb's support or approval by persuading them you are right or sth is right.
open up (**to sb**)	talk about what you really feel and think.

spotlight Giving people information

If you **put sb in the picture**, you give them the information they need to understand a situation. If you **keep sb in the picture**, you continue to give them the necessary information. SYN **keep sb posted** (**about/on sth**). If you **get the picture**, you understand a situation that somebody is describing to you.

1 Cover the glossary, then answer the questions.

1 If someone puts you in the picture, what do they do? ....
2 Are you pleased if someone keeps you posted? ....
3 If someone gets your back up, how do you feel? ....
4 If you win someone over, what does that involve? ....
5 If you say to someone that you get the picture, what does it tell them? ....
6 If you've picked up on something, what have you done? ....
7 If you open up to someone, what do you do? ....
8 If what someone says is at odds with what they do, are you pleased? ....

2 Complete the final word in each dialogue.

1 Did you understand everything? ~ No, I couldn't take it all ....
2 Do you want to know what's happening? ~ Yes, could you keep me .... ?
3 Do you find him annoying as well? ~ Yes, he really gets my back ....
4 Do you have all the details? ~ No, but Jane will put me in the ....
5 Do you give them much information? ~ Only on a need-to-know ....
6 They will need persuading. ~ Don't worry. Pete will soon win them ....

3 ABOUT YOU What are the three most important points at the top of the page? Which are you good at or bad at? Write your answers in your notebook, or talk to another student.

B A poor communicator

HOLLY Do you think Jonathan will use our ideas in the advertising campaign?

JAKE I think he's **mulling** them **over**, but **reading between the lines** I'd say 'maybe'.

HOLLY He doesn't **give** much **away**, does he?

JAKE No. He doesn't **let** anyone **in on** what he's thinking. He prefers to **keep things to himself**, which is probably why we end up **getting the wrong end of the stick** so often.

HOLLY Doesn't it **occur to** him that it's very frustrating to **be kept in the dark** like this?

JAKE No. **It makes no odds** to him what people think. Or if he does care, he doesn't **let on**.

Glossary

mull sth over	spend time thinking carefully about a plan or proposal.
read between the lines	look for or discover a meaning that is suggested rather than actually stated.
give sth/sb away	make known sth that sb wants to keep secret.
let sb in on sth	INF allow sb to share a secret, or know what only a few people know.
get (hold of) the wrong end of the stick	INF understand sth in the wrong way.
occur to sb	(of an idea or a thought) come into sb's mind.
it makes no odds	INF used to say that sth makes no difference or is not important.
let on (to sb about sth)	INF tell sb sth, especially sth you have been keeping secret.

spotlight Keeping information back

If you **keep sth to yourself**, you don't tell others about it. If you **play/hold/keep your cards close to your chest**, you keep your plans or ideas secret. If you **keep sb in the dark**, you don't tell them something because you want to keep it secret from them.

4 Do you know? Write 'yes', or 'perhaps', or 'no'.

1 He plays his cards close to his chest. ....
2 He gave it away. ....
3 I'm reading between the lines. ....
4 He let on. ....

5 It didn't occur to him to tell me. ....
6 He let me in on it. ....
7 He kept me in the dark. ....
8 I got the wrong end of the stick. ....

5 Rewrite the sentences starting with the words given.

▶ I haven't told people about the project.   I've *kept the project to myself.*
1 I don't tell other people my ideas.   I keep my cards ....
2 I completely misunderstood what he meant.   I got ....
3 It should've stayed a secret but I told someone.   I gave ....
4 I wanted to think about it.   I wanted to mull ....
5 I didn't tell her because I didn't want her to know.   I kept ....
6 He didn't tell me exactly but I knew what he meant.   I read ....
7 I don't realize that I'm being secretive.   It doesn't ....
8 I don't care what people think.   It makes ....

35 I can use the language of discussion

A Winning the argument

In a heated discussion, how annoyed are you by people who:	very/quite/not at all
• want to win the argument **at all costs**?	
• **play devil's advocate** all the time?	
• constantly **butt in** when you're trying to speak?	
• **beat about the bush** all the time instead of **getting to the point**?	
• always seem to **miss the point** of what people are saying?	
• always want to **have the last word**?	
• just want to argue **for the sake of it**?	
• refuse to **back down** and admit they are wrong?	

Glossary

at all costs	used to say that something must be done, however difficult it is. SYN **at any cost**/**price**.
play devil's advocate	pretend to disagree with sb in order to start an argument or discussion.
butt in	interrupt sb.
beat about the bush	discuss sth in an indirect way, without saying what you really want to say. (👁 See page 162.)
get to the point	stop talking about unimportant details and say what is most important.
miss the point	not understand the main thing that sb is trying to say.
have the last/**final word (on sth)**	win an argument by making the last statement or final decision on sth.
for the sake of it	If you do sth **for the sake of it**, you do it because you enjoy it, not because you want to achieve anything else.
back down (on sth)	admit that you are wrong or have lost an argument.

1 Is the meaning similar or different? Write S or D.

1	She always has the final word.	She always butts in.
2	He wants to win at all costs.	He wants to win at any price.
3	She never gets to the point.	She always misses the point.
4	He keeps butting in when I'm talking.	He keeps interrupting when I'm talking.
5	He loves to play devil's advocate.	He often argues for the sake of it.
6	She doesn't beat about the bush.	She never backs down.

2 Complete the sentences.

1 I never get a chance to finish what I'm saying, because he keeps _____ in.
2 Mr Ellis explained it carefully, but Anya still completely _____ the point.
3 Stop _____ about the bush and get to the _____ of what you're trying to say.
4 However much you argue with her, she always has to have the final _____ .
5 Even if you prove he's wrong, he still won't _____ down.
6 I don't think she disagreed with you. She was just playing _____ advocate because she enjoys arguing for the _____ of it.

3 ABOUT YOU Write your answers in the questionnaire at the top of the page, or talk to another student. Do you do any of these things?

B Discussion topics

Do you believe in **life after death**?

Are exams **a necessary evil**?

In life, **we get what we deserve**. Discuss.

Does **the end** ever **justify the means**?

We all have to **play a part in** the fight against crime. Do you agree?

Giving women equal pay may be **politically correct**, but is it **going too far?**

Why do some teenagers **go off the rails**, while others don't?

We still haven't **got to grips with** traffic congestion and pollution. Why not?

Is it true that **you can't teach an old dog new tricks**?

Glossary

life after death	a state of existence that some people believe continues after death.
a necessary evil	an unwelcome thing that we have to accept.
you get what you deserve	used to say you think sb has earned the bad things that happen to them.
the end justifies the means	SAYING bad or unfair methods of doing sth are acceptable if the result of the action is good or positive.
play a part in sth	be actively involved in sth.
politically correct	(abbreviated to **PC**) used to describe carefully chosen language or behaviour that won't upset or offend anybody. **political correctness** N.
go too far	say or do sth which is considered too extreme.
go off the rails	INF start behaving in an unacceptable way that shocks or upsets people.
get to grips with sth	start to deal with a difficult task, problem, or situation.
you can't teach an old dog new tricks	SAYING you can't make people change their methods and ideas when they have used or held them for a long time.

4 Complete the text.

We have CCTV (closed circuit television) everywhere these days. Has it (1) .... too far? I believe the increase in the number of cameras is simply a symptom of the dangerous society we live in. If cameras help to reduce crime, then as far as I'm concerned, we have to get to (2) .... with the idea and accept that the end (3) .... the means. Basically, we get what we (4) .... I know that's not the (5) .... correct view, as CCTV is seen as an infringement of our personal liberty, but we all have to play a (6) .... in reducing crime, and if CCTV helps us to do that, then it's a necessary (7) ....

5 Respond to each situation with a suitable idiom.

▶ It seems an extreme solution. ~ Yes, but the end *justifies the means* .

1 Can he change his ways after all this time? ~ No, you ....

2 Is it right for us to suffer for these mistakes? ~ Yes, we ....

3 I don't like prisons, but we can't do without them. ~ Yes, they're ....

4 Do people live on after they die? ~ No, I don't believe in ....

5 Their response was excessive. ~ Yes, they've ....

6 We're not supposed to say, 'she's only a housewife'. ~ No, it's not ....

7 Traffic congestion is a really urgent problem. ~ Yes, we'll have to ....

8 His son's started missing school and hanging around in a gang. ~ Yes, he's really ....

6 ABOUT YOU What's your opinion on the discussion topics at the top of the page? And CCTV? Write your answers in your notebook, or talk to another student.

36 I can talk about presentations

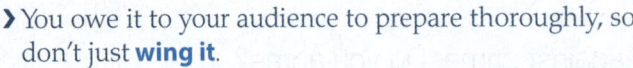

A Advice on giving a presentation

> You owe it to your audience to prepare thoroughly, so don't just **wing it**.

> Decide on just two or three main messages that you want them to **come away with**.

> **Draw on** your own experience: this will give the talk greater credibility.

> If you're worried about anything in the talk, **run** it **by** someone you know first.

> Arrive with plenty of **time to spare** and make sure all the equipment **is set up** and in good working order. This will help to **put** your **mind at rest** before you start.

> Start with something to **make** people **sit up and take notice**; laughter often helps to **loosen up** an audience. They want the talk to succeed, and they will be **rooting for** you.

Glossary

wing it	INF do sth without preparation or plans.
come away with sth	leave a place with new knowledge or ideas or a particular impression.
draw on sth	use experience, knowledge, or a supply of sth that you have gained over time.
run sth by sb	tell sb your ideas so that they can give their opinion.
time/money/room, etc. **to spare**	more than enough time/money/room, etc.
set sth up	make a piece of equipment ready to use.
put sb's mind at rest/ease	stop sb feeling worried.
make sb sit up (and take notice)	do sth surprising or impressive that makes sb pay attention to you.
loosen sb up	make sb more relaxed (also **loosen up** become more relaxed).
root for sb	(usually in progressive tenses) support and encourage sb in a competition or a difficult situation. (Also **cheer sb on** shout encouragement at sb in a competition.)

---

1 Tick the words in italics which are possible. One, two, or three may be correct.

1 I don't have a great deal of *help* ☐ *time* ☐ *money* ☐ to spare.
2 Did you come away from the talk with any *ideas* ☐ *thoughts* ☐ *advice* ☐?
3 It would be wise to run your *speech* ☐ *idea* ☐ *plan* ☐ by your boss first.
4 Could you help me set up this *PC* ☐ *car* ☐ *armchair* ☐?
5 This time I had to draw on my *savings* ☐ *experience* ☐ *friends* ☐.
6 If you talk to your sister, it'll put her mind at *ease* ☐ *safety* ☐ *rest* ☐.

2 Complete the questions.

1 If you had to give a speech, would you prepare thoroughly, or just try to .... it?
2 Would you start with something that would make the audience .... up and take ...., or begin in a more low-key way?
3 Is it advisable to .... your speech by someone else to see what they think?
4 Do you agree that you should always try to .... up the audience with humour?
5 If you were giving a talk, would you want your friends/colleagues in the audience, rooting .... you?
6 What kinds of things can you do to set your .... at rest before you get up to speak?

3 ABOUT YOU Write your answers to Exercise 2 in your notebook, or talk to another student.

B How not to give a presentation

We had to **sit through** Rob's disastrous presentation to the group today. We were overloaded with information, and he completely **lost sight of** the main points; he should **have pared** it **down**. He thought a good powerpoint would compensate for poor presentation skills, but **nothing could have been further from the truth**. Most of the time he spoke too slowly (one or two people **were nodding off**). Then Dr Eisner asked him a tricky question and you could see the panic **set in**. When Elaine asked about projected sales, he **jumped in** before she'd finished, and they ended up **at cross purposes**. He was hoping it would be the presentation **of his life**, but instead, he ended up **a nervous wreck**.

Glossary

sit through sth	stay till the end of a speech, performance, etc. that you think is boring or too long.
lose sight of sth	stop considering sth and forget about it.
pare sth down	reduce the size or amount of sth, especially with lots of small reductions.
nothing could be further from the truth	used to emphasize that sth is definitely not true.
nod off	INF fall asleep for a short time while sitting in a chair.
set in	If sth unpleasant **sets in**, it starts to have an effect which could continue for a long time. (*Panic/The rain/The winter set in.*)
jump in	interrupt sb while they are talking. SYN **butt in**.
(talk) at cross purposes	If two people are (**talking**) **at cross purposes** they think they are talking about the same thing, but in fact they are not.
a nervous wreck	INF a person who is very upset and worried.

spotlight *of your life*

The phrase **of your life** is used to emphasize that something is the best or worst that you have experienced. It follows a noun or a noun phrase.
*He gave the speech **of his life**. = the best speech he has given.*
*I had the fright **of my life**. = the most frightening experience ever.*

4 Positive or negative? Write P or N.

1 They're talking at cross purposes. ......
2 No one nodded off. ......
3 She gave the talk of her life. ......
4 Her nerves started to set in. ......
5 We had to sit through the presentation. ......
6 He didn't lose sight of his aims. ......

5 Complete the conversations. Then underline the full phrasal verbs and idioms.

1 A I got the shock of my .... today.
   B Why? What happened?
   A Well, I had to sit .... a dreadful meeting on government borrowing this morning, and unfortunately I happened to .... off for a few minutes. But this afternoon I discovered that someone had posted a video of me snoring on YouTube!

2 A I thought the new accountant was OK, but nothing could be further from the ....
   B What do you mean?
   A Well, he dominated the meeting and .... in every time I tried to speak.

3 A How did your talk go?
   B Well, I was a nervous .... beforehand, but I'd run it by my boss, and he'd helped me to .... it down so it was a lot clearer and shorter. He reminded me not to lose .... of my main points, and I think in the end it went quite well.

37 I can talk about meetings

A First meetings

How did your first meeting go?

OLGA When I met my new boss, it wasn't exactly **a meeting of minds**. I didn't know what to **make of** him really, and **to start with**, I just had to **play it by ear**. But we're OK now.

JACEK My new host family are fantastic! We got on really well **right from the word go**. They welcomed me **with open arms**, and I **felt at home** almost immediately.

KARIN I met my boyfriend on the Internet and I reckoned we'd **be on the same wavelength**. But as I was driving to meet him in person, **my heart was in my mouth**. He was lovely, though, and I **was** immediately **struck by** his quirky sense of fun.

Glossary

a meeting of minds	a situation in which people have similar ideas and opinions.
make sth of sb/sth	understand or regard sb/sth in a particular way.
play it by ear	deal with a situation by reacting as things happen, rather than having a plan.
(right) from the word go	(right) from the beginning.
with open arms	If you welcome or greet sb **with open arms**, you welcome them in a very affectionate and enthusiastic way.
(feel) at home	(feel) comfortable and relaxed.
be on the same wavelength	INF (of two or more people) think in a similar way about sth.
my heart was in my mouth	used to say you felt very nervous or frightened about sth.
be struck by sb/sth	INF be impressed by or interested in sth.

spotlight *to start with*

To start/begin with can mean 'at the beginning' (as above), but it can also be used to emphasize a list of points to support an argument e.g. *The hotel was awful.* **To start with**, *the room was dirty, then the service … .* SYN **for a start**.

1 True or false? Write T or F.

1 If you *play it by ear*, you start out with a clear plan of what you want to do. ......
2 If there's *a meeting of minds* between you and your boss, you understand each other. ......
3 If you liked your job *from the word go*, it means you liked it from the beginning. ......
4 If you're *on the same wavelength* as a colleague, you think in a similar way. ......
5 If you*'re struck by* a new colleague's personality, you don't like them. ......
6 If *your heart is in your mouth*, you're feeling very worried about something. ......

2 Complete the dialogues. You may need more than one word.

1 Did you feel relaxed with them? ~ Yes, they really made me feel ....
2 Were they pleased to see you? ~ Yeah, they welcomed me ....
3 Did you know what she meant? ~ Well, to .... I didn't, but then I got it in the end.
4 Mrs Esposito was very odd, wasn't she? ~ Hmm, I didn't know what to make ....
5 I bet he was nervous before the presentation. ~ Yes, his heart ....
6 Will you just see how things go? ~ I think that's best. I'll just play ....
7 Why were you fed up? ~ Well, for ...., the room was cold, then I couldn't hear what anyone was saying. In the end, I just sat and doodled.
8 Did you have a good rapport with them? ~ Yes, we got on from ....

3 ABOUT YOU Can you remember any first meetings with people? Who were they with, and how did they go? Write your answer in your notebook, or talk to another student.

B Badly run meetings

The chairperson may be responsible when a meeting goes badly. Here's why:

- Participants are allowed to arrive **in dribs and drabs**.

- They don't know what's happening because the chairperson **has thrown together** the agenda at the last minute, and **has**n't **laid down** clear rules for the conduct of the meeting.

- Without firm guidance from the chair, one or two people may **hold the floor** and **ramble on** for ages, and as a result, the meeting **runs over** with nothing achieved.

- Poor time management may mean people **rush into** decisions, or that decisions **are left hanging**.

- One person at the meeting (often the chairperson) **forges ahead with** their own agenda, **to the detriment of** the meeting and the other participants.

Glossary

in dribs and drabs	gradually and in small amounts or numbers.
throw sth together	make or produce sth in a hurry.
lay sth down	officially state rules, principles, etc. that people must obey or follow.
hold the floor	speak during a discussion, especially for a long time so that nobody else can speak.
ramble on	INF speak about sth for a long time in a boring or confusing way.
run over	continue for longer than planned.
rush into sth	do sth without thinking carefully about it first.
leave sth hanging	fail to make a definite decision or statement about sth.
forge ahead (**with sth**)	make strong and steady progress with sth.
to the detriment of sth/sb	resulting in harm or damage to sth/sb.

4 Write sentences using words from each column.

I threw ✓	on	and drabs
They arrived	was left	so others can't speak
Don't rush	ran	some lunch ✓
We're forging	together ✓	a decision
The situation	into	with the plans
She rambled	in dribs	for hours
The meeting	the floor	hanging for days
Don't hold	ahead	over by half an hour

I threw together some lunch.

5 Rewrite the sentences using the word in capitals. Keep the same meaning.

▶ The meeting went on longer than it should have. RUN *The meeting ran over.*
1 The measures will harm patient care. DETRIMENT
2 The chairperson informed us of the rules of the meeting. LAY
3 Dad wouldn't stop talking about the wedding. ON
4 Don't make your mind up too quickly. RUSH
5 The money was released very gradually. DRIBS
6 They produced a video in a hurry. THROW
7 We're making excellent progress with the project. AHEAD
8 I don't want to leave the situation unresolved. HANG

38 I can use idioms for commenting

A Commenting on a situation

Mrs Aswad told me **in no uncertain terms** what she thought of Amina Baba.

It**'s common knowledge** Dima's a member of the Communist party. **Contrary to popular belief**, however, his wife isn't.

It's my car **in name only**. **To all intents and purposes**, it belongs to my son.

He agreed to consider an operation on his eye, but only **as a last resort**.

Mac said we'd get fourteen in the minibus **at a push**, but **strictly speaking** it's only supposed to hold twelve.

All things being equal, I'd rather go to university near where I live.

Glossary	
in no uncertain terms	clearly and directly.
be common knowledge	be sth that everyone knows.
contrary to popular belief	used to emphasize that what you are saying is the opposite of what many people think.
in name only	If sth exists **in name only**, it is officially described in a particular way, but the description is not really true.
to all intents and purposes	used to say that although sth is not exactly true or accurate, the effect is the same as if it were true or accurate.
as a last resort	used to say you will do sth only after trying everything else to solve a problem. SYN **if all else fails**.
at a push/pinch	INF If you can do sth **at a push/pinch**, you can do it, but only with difficulty.
strictly speaking	= being completely correct and accurate.
all (other) things being equal	used when saying what you would normally choose unless there were special facts to consider.

1 **Cover the glossary, then complete the last word of each idiom.**

▶ as a last *resort*

1 in no uncertain ....
2 to all intents and ....

3 all other things being ....
4 contrary to popular ....
5 strictly ....

2 **Complete the dialogues.**

1 Is it your flat? ~ In .... only. My brother lives there most of the time.
2 Would you rather give the job to a woman? ~ Yes, all other things being ....
3 Can we get three in the back of the car? ~ Yes, at a ....
4 Are you retired? ~ No, I'm still working, ... to popular belief.
5 Do people know about their engagement? ~ Yes, it's common .... now.
6 Are they living separately? ~ Yes, to all .... and purposes.

3 **Rewrite the sentences using idioms from above. Keep the meaning the same.**

▶ If there's no reason not to, I'll vote for Cal. *All things being equal, I'll vote for Cal.*

1 He told me very clearly what he thought of me. ....
2 Everyone knows they're married. ....
3 We can only just get six people round the table. ....
4 I'll sell the car if there's no other solution. ....
5 To be completely accurate, a tomato is a fruit. ....
6 Most people think he's Welsh, but it's not true. ....

B Expressing an attitude

They'll be lucky to find a restaurant open at this time of night.

She's clever, **I'll give you that**, but I don't trust her.

I think we should help Grandad – **it's the very least we can do**.

I have to work this weekend, **worse luck**! Still, I'm on holiday next week, **thank goodness**.

They all filed in, and **last but not least** came John.

I thought it was **a bit late in the day** for the woman to complain about the shoes: she's worn them for two months!

He can go and live in Las Vegas **for all** I **care**.

It's all very well for him **to** say it's not important, but I've worked hard on this project.

Glossary

you'll/they'll, etc. **be lucky**	INF used to tell sb/others that what they want probably will not happen.
I'll give you that	INF used to admit that sth is true, even though you do not like it, or do not agree with things related to it.
it's the (very) least I can do	INF used to say you are willing to do sth, and feel you should probably do more.
worse luck!	INF used to show that you are disappointed or annoyed about sth.
thank goodness	used to say that you are relieved and pleased about sth.
last but not least	used when mentioning the last person or thing in a group in order to say that they are as important as the others.
(a bit) late in the day	too late to take action. (The speaker is usually annoyed.)
for all sb cares	INF used to say that a person is not worried about or interested in what happens to sb/sth.
it's/that's all very well (for sb) (to do sth)	used to show your irritation with a comment that sb has made.

4 Cross out the wrong answer, then underline the full idiom in each sentence.

1 I'll give you a hand tomorrow – it's the *least | little* I can do.
2 They all got here – last *and | but* not least was Tom.
3 I won't be able to see them, *worse | worst* luck.
4 They were better than us. ~ Yeah, *I | I'll* give you that.
5 I felt it was a bit *late | later* in the day for her to call off the party.
6 I'm hoping to leave work early today. ~ You'll *have | be* lucky.
7 It's all *quite | very* well for the teacher to say the test was easy - she didn't have to do it.
8 I could be seriously ill for *all | everything* she cares.

5 Express the ideas on the left starting with the words given.

▶ Say it's now too late for Bill to cancel.
It's a *bit late in the day for Bill to cancel.*

1 Say you're disappointed you have to stay in.
I have to ....
2 Say you're relieved that Kara arrived safely.
Kara arrived ....
3 Tell Ken you'll help him, and wish you could do more.
I'll help you – ....
4 Say you're not bothered if Miles decides to live abroad.
Miles can live ....
5 Admit that the weather is better in Spain.
The weather ....
6 Tell someone they probably won't find a taxi.
You'll ....

39 I can use idioms for emphasis

A Adding emphasis

These idioms go within a sentence, or are added at the end, to emphasize what is being said.

It's **by far** the best film Almodovar has made.

My brother sometimes leaves his bike in the hall **for weeks on end**.

I think we are **well and truly** lost.

Dartmouth is the best place to stay **without a doubt**.

Max was here a minute ago, then he disappeared – **just like that**.

The owner of the shop was very helpful, and gave us a free map **into the bargain**.

My next-door neighbour is **ever such a** kind woman.

He's **not just any** doctor – he's a top surgeon.

He hasn't eaten all day, so **no wonder** he's hungry.

I've spent £200 this week **as it is**.

Glossary

by far	(used with comparative and superlative adjectives or adverbs) by a large amount. SYN **far and away**.
for hours/days/weeks on end	used for emphasizing how long sth continues.
well and truly	INF completely.
without (a) doubt	used to emphasize an opinion.
just like that	INF suddenly, without warning or explanation.
into the bargain	in addition to the things already mentioned.
ever such (a) / ever so	INF (used before adjectives/adverbs) very; really.
not just any	used to say that sb or sth is not ordinary, but is especially good or important.
no wonder	used to emphasize the fact that sth is not surprising.
as it is	already (used to express concern that an amount or number will increase further).

1 Replace the word(s) in italics with an idiom that keeps a similar meaning.

1 He recommended a place to stay, and gave me a lift there *as well*. ....
2 Happily the war is now *completely* over. ....
3 They were *very* grateful for our help. ....
4 She is *easily* the best student in the class. ....
5 He didn't sleep well, so *it's not surprising* he's tired now. ....
6 They kept me waiting for a reply for days *and days*. ....

2 Add an idiom to emphasize what is being said. Rewrite the sentence with the idiom in the correct place.

▶ He said he had a problem, and left. *He said he had a problem and left, just like that.*
1 It's the best part of town. ....
2 He gave me a discount, and wrapped it up nicely. ....
3 Karoly's a generous guy. ....
4 Unfortunately the party was over when we arrived. ....
5 I think it's her most interesting novel. ....
6 I've been back there three times today; I don't want to go again. ....
7 She ate some seafood that was off, so she's feeling ill. ....
8 It's silk. It's the finest silk you can buy. ....

B Exaggeration

Some idioms give a more colourful and emphatic description of a situation or someone's state. They are often informal, and more commonly used in spoken English.

Neutral message	Exaggerated message
Rodney is better than the rest of us at maths.	Rodney is **streets ahead of** the rest of us at maths. INF = much better than the rest. SYN **head and shoulders above sb** INF.
My cousin is lazy.	My cousin **doesn't do a stroke of work**. INF = does no work at all.
The two boys get on well.	The two boys **get on like a house on fire**. INF = like each other very much.
I didn't know what to say.	I **was lost for words**. = was so surprised or shocked that I didn't know what to say.
There was some trouble at the party.	**All hell broke loose** at the party. INF = sth happened which caused people to get angry and start fighting or arguing.
I stayed out of his way.	I **avoided him like the plague**. = INF was determined to keep away from him completely.
I was surprised when he said he was going abroad.	I **couldn't believe my ears** when he said he was going abroad. INF = was extremely surprised.
Transport groups are angry about the increased fares.	Transport groups are **up in arms about** the increased fares. INF = extremely angry. Also **up in arms over sth**.
We'll have to work hard to get the show ready on time.	We'll have to **pull out all the stops** to get the show ready on time. INF = make the greatest effort possible.
I'd like to be in his position.	I**'d give my right arm to** be in his position. INF = would do anything.
Dad was angry about me staying out late and told me off.	My dad **came down on me like a ton of bricks**. INF = was extremely angry with me and told me off severely. (It could also mean to punish sb severely.)
She talks a lot.	She **doesn't half** talk a lot! INF **not half** is used to emphasize a statement or opinion.

3 Cover the table above. Match 1–8 with a–h.

1 I avoided them like the ....
2 I couldn't believe my ....
3 She was lost for ....
4 We'll have to pull out all the ....
5 They get on like a house on ....
6 He came down on her like a ton of ....
7 All hell broke ....
8 He doesn't do a stroke of ....

a work.
b stops.
c plague.
d loose.
e words.
f fire.
g ears.
h bricks.

4 Rewrite the sentences using the word in capitals to emphasize what is being said.

▶ They get on well. FIRE *They get on like a house on fire.*
1 She'd love to go waterskiing. ARM ....
2 They'll have to work hard. PULL ....
3 They're very angry over it. ARMS ....
4 I was surprised when I heard the news. EARS ....
5 They're much better than me. STREETS ....
6 That boy does nothing. STROKE ....
7 She really told him off. BRICKS ....
8 I didn't go anywhere near her. PLAGUE ....
9 These guys work hard. HALF ....
10 There was a lot of trouble. HELL ....

Review: Communication

Unit 34

1 The same word is missing from each pair of sentences. Write it in.

1 a Could you .... me posted, please?
   b They wanted to .... us in the dark about the results.
2 a She knew I was getting married, but she didn't .... on to Jimmy.
   b I wish they'd .... me in on the secret; it's very frustrating!
3 a I'd like a couple of days to mull .... their offer.
   b She tried hard to win him .... , but he refused to be persuaded.
4 a He got .... of the wrong end of the stick.
   b I tend to .... my cards close to my chest.
5 a His actions are at .... with what he says.
   b It makes no .... to me when we leave.
6 a That woman really puts my back .... !
   b I'd like you to open .... to me and tell me what's wrong.
7 a You'll be told .... a need-to-know basis.
   b She's very observant; she picked up .... a tiny detail in the painting.
8 a I decided it was time to put him in the .... about the new plans.
   b I'd be grateful if you could keep me in the .... as things develop.

2 Put the words in order and add one more word.

▶ the | stick | we | the | got | wrong |of *We got the wrong end of the stick.*
1 it | take | can't | all | I ....
2 idea | the | like | our | lines | he | doesn't | reading ....
3 could | me | it | occurred | she | that | wrong | be ....
4 we | odds | it | him | makes | to | lose | if ....
5 her | she | chest | to | her | plays | close ....
6 to | a | it's | so | secret | it | yourself ....

Unit 35

1 Correct the mistakes where necessary. Be careful: some sentences are correct.

1 If you vote for that party, you'll take what you deserve. ....
2 I agreed with the speaker, but it took him ages to get round the point. ....
3 He used to be a model citizen, but for some reason, he got off the rails. ....
4 That's all very well, but I think you're missing the point completely. ....
5 Look, stop beating about the bushes and tell me what you know! ....
6 It's a hard lesson to learn, but the ending justifies the means. ....
7 I've come to realize that stress at work is a necessary devil. ....
8 That woman complains just for the sake of it. ....
9 I have several friends who believe in live after death. ....
10 Nobody has really got to grips with the problems of the national football team. ....
11 It's no good trying to persuade her; you can't teach an old cat new tricks. ....
12 Why do you always try to save the last word? ....

2 Read the text, then replace phrases in the text with the items below.

My sister Alicia hates arguing, especially with our brother Freddie; she will avoid it <u>wherever possible</u> ✓. What she finds most irritating is that Freddie likes to disagree with her just for the sake of it, and when he gets very animated, she tells him his behaviour is excessive. She also uses language which is meant to avoid offending anyone, and that really annoys Freddie. Another thing she hates is his habit of interrupting when she's speaking, and the fact that he always wants to win the argument. Still, Alicia is also quite determined, and if she thinks she's making a valid point, she won't accept that she has lost the argument.

▶ at all costs *wherever possible* ....
1 play devil's advocate ....
2 he's gone too far ....
3 politically correct ....
4 butting in ....
5 have the last word ....
6 back down ....

Unit 36

1 Choose the best ending to follow each phrasal verb on the left.

1 draw on	a some equipment
2 set up	b before someone has finished speaking
3 come away with	c what you are going to say
4 sit through	d for a few minutes
5 nod off	e all your experience
6 butt in	f some good ideas
7 loosen up	g a dull talk
8 pare down	h the audience

2 Complete the dialogues. You may need more than one word.

1 It's definitely not true, is it? ~ No, nothing could be further ....
2 Was there some misunderstanding? ~ Yes, we were at .... purposes.
3 Has Jim's advice stopped them worrying? ~ Yes, it's put their minds ....
4 You must've been very worried. ~ Yes, I was a nervous ....
5 He didn't prepare the talk at all, did he? ~ No, he just .... it, as usual.
6 Did you get there early? ~ Yes, I had about fifteen minutes to ....
7 That car nearly hit him. ~ Yes, it must have given him the fright ....
8 Did they come to support you? ~ Oh yes, they were all .... for me.

Unit 37

1 Rewrite the sentences, starting with the words given. Keep a similar meaning.

▶ The situation was not resolved. The situation was left *hanging* ....
1 We have the same way of thinking. We're on ....
2 They were very happy to see me. They welcomed me with ....
3 I'll react to things as they happen. I'll play ....
4 I felt incredibly nervous. My heart was ....
5 We had exactly the same ideas. It was a meeting ....
6 He just made the dish in a hurry. He just threw ....

2 Complete the crossword. Which phrasal verb is spelt out in the grey squares?

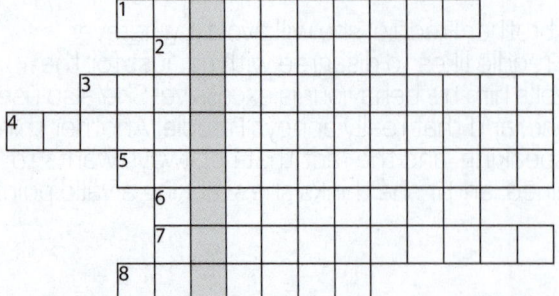

1 Make strong and steady progress with something. (5,5)
2 If you state officially that people must obey rules/principles, you .... rules/principles. (3,4)
3 If something happens from the very beginning, you can also say it happens .... (4,3,4,2)
4 Gradually, or in small amounts or numbers. (2,5,3,5)
5 Speak during a discussion, especially for a long time so that nobody else can speak. (4,3,5)
6 If something results in harm or damage to something, we can also say it happens to the .... of something. (9)
7 at the beginning. (2,5,4)
8 continue for longer than planned. (3,4)
   The phrasal verb in the grey squares is ....

Unit 38

1 Complete the definitions with one or two words.

1 If you do something *as a last resort*, you do it because all other methods or solutions have ....
2 If you say something has happened '*a bit late in the day*', you probably feel ....
3 If you say '*thank goodness*' when someone arrives, it means that you are .... they have got there.
4 If a country is a democracy *in name only*, it means that country is .... democratic.
5 If someone says what they think of you *in no uncertain terms*, they tell you ....
6 If you say '*that's all very well for her to say*', you are expressing .... at what she has said.
7 If someone says, '*you can leave for all I care*', it means he is .... in what you do next.
8 If someone says, 'I'm meeting Bernard later, *worse luck*', it means they are .... about meeting him.

2 Complete the sentences with the most suitable idiom from the box.

> I'll give you that   thank goodness   in no uncertain terms   at a push   it's the least I can do
> worse luck   to all intents and purposes   contrary to popular belief

1 He wasn't happy, and he told us so ....
2 I'd like to go with you, but I've got to go to the dentist's, ...
3 There's not much space, but we could put the sofa in that corner ....
4 You were right about the food being poor, ...
5 I can't drive you home, but I'll take you to the bus station – ....
6 His name is Falcone, but .... , he isn't Italian, and has never been to Italy in his life.
7 It was a terrible journey, but we got there in the end, ...
8 Originally it was my brother who bought the flat, but I'm living there and paying the mortgage and all the bills, so .... , it's mine.

Unit 39

1 One word is missing in each sentence. Where does it go? Write it at the end.

▶ He's ever ⟨ a nice man. _such_
1 I hadn't expected him to say that, and I was just lost words. ....
2 It's far the best DVD player you can buy. ....
3 I made a mistake, and she came on me like a ton of bricks. ....
4 They're giving away free drinks, so wonder the bar is full. ....
5 A digital radio is the best one for you to get a doubt. ....
6 My sister doesn't phone me for weeks end. ....
7 They sent me a new printer, and a replacement cartridge the bargain. ....
8 This is just any champagne; this is the best. ....

2 Complete the dialogues. The second speaker uses more exaggeration.

▶ A Their relationship is over, isn't it?
   B Yes, it's _well and truly_ .... over.

1 A He's terribly lazy.
   B Yes, he never .... of work.
2 A She seemed annoyed about the contract.
   B Yeah, she was up in .... it.
3 A I like Milos.
   B Yes, he's .... so nice.
4 A They're good friends, aren't they?
   B Yes, they get on like .... fire.
5 A Martin's a much better candidate.
   B I agree, he's .... above the rest.
6 A So you'd really like to meet her?
   B You bet. I'd give .... just to speak to her.
7 A It's astonishing news, isn't it?
   B I know – I .... ears.
8 A He's made a big effort with this contract.
   B Yes, he's .... stops.

A   Why do people tell lies?

❝ I was **scared to death** of telling the truth about my past; I knew people would disapprove. ❞

❝ I decided to **keep** the truth **from** my mum to **spare her feelings**. ❞

❝ I didn't **let on to** my friends that I'd lost my job; I didn't want to **lose face**, I guess. ❞

❝ In retrospect, I realize that I just couldn't **face up to** the truth about my addiction: that's why I lied. ❞

❝ I made a terrible decision at work, and then tried to **cover** it **up** and prevent the facts from **coming to light**. It was stupid of me. ❞

Glossary	
scared to death	INF very frightened. (Also **scare sb to death** make sb very frightened. SYN **scare the life/the living daylights out of sb** INF.)
keep sth from sb	avoid telling sb sth.
spare sb's feelings	be careful not to do or say anything that may upset sb.
let on (to sb / about sth)	INF talk about sth that is intended to be secret.
lose face	be regarded by others as stupid or wrong as a result of sth you have said or done. (If you **save face**, you avoid being regarded as stupid or wrong.)
face up to sth	accept and deal with sth that is difficult or unpleasant.
come to light	become known to people.

spotlight Hiding information

These phrasal verbs refer to action taken to hide the truth about something bad, illegal, embarrassing, etc.
Politicians tried to cover up *the scandal.* **cover-up** N.
The boy stole the chocolates but his parents hushed it up.

1   Complete the sentences.

1 I didn't tell her the truth because I wanted to _____ her feelings.
2 People will be very angry if this information comes to _____ .
3 I knew they were getting married but I didn't let _____ to anyone.
4 I didn't tell him what actually happened because I was scared to _____ .
5 It was a scandal in the village. They tried to _____ it up, but everyone knew.
6 My grandfather was very ill, but the rest of the family _____ the truth from him.
7 I think she lied because it was easier than _____ up to the truth.

2   Use an idiom or phrasal verb to explain why the underlined people lied in these situations. Use a different idiom or phrasal verb in each answer.

▶ The boy was very ill, but <u>his parents</u> didn't tell him. *They wanted to keep it from him.*
1 Ann had a bruise on her face, but her <u>best friend</u> told her it looked OK. _____
2 <u>Mary</u> knew her best friend was pregnant, but she kept it secret. _____
3 <u>A young boy</u> lost his strict father's expensive watch, but denied it. _____
4 <u>Joe</u> couldn't read or write, but he told people he'd forgotten his glasses. _____
5 Doctors said she wouldn't walk again, but <u>she</u> refused to believe it. _____

B Who are more honest?

Men or Women?

'My wife Marcia **goes red as a beetroot** whenever she tells a lie, and that **gives the game away**. She's worried that if she tells a lie, she'll **have** it **on her conscience**, and she can't **live with** that. But **when it comes to glossing over** the truth, she's pretty good at that!'

'When my husband Jeremy comes home late after a football match, he often tells me **a pack of lies** about why he's late. He thinks he can **pull the wool over** my **eyes**, but I **see through** him immediately (I know he's been to the pub). And if I dare to say, 'Oh, come on – **I wasn't born yesterday**!' he gets quite upset.'

Glossary

go (**as**) **red as a beetroot**	have red cheeks because you are embarrassed.
give the game away	reveal sth that is intended to be a secret (often by accident).
have sth on your conscience	feel guilty because of sth you did or didn't do.
live with sth	accept sth unpleasant that you cannot change.
when it comes to (**doing**) **sth**	on the subject of sth.
gloss over sth	ignore sth or avoid saying sth, or treat it as unimportant.
a pack of lies	INF a story that is completely untrue.
pull the wool over sb's eyes	INF trick sb by giving them the wrong information.
see through sb/sth	realize that sb is not telling the truth, or that sth is not true; understand the truth about a situation.
I wasn't born yesterday	INF = I'm not stupid enough to believe what you say. SYN **pull the other one** INF.

4 One word is either missing or wrong in these sentences. Add the missing word or correct the mistake.

1 He wouldn't lie because he'd have it in his conscience. ....
2 When it comes helping others, my parents are fantastic. ....
3 It was a ridiculous story – look, I wasn't yesterday. ....
4 Of course, as soon as she mentioned your name, she gave the game up. ....
5 That girl told me packs of lies. ....
6 He's always trying to pull the wool over my ears. ....
7 His wife will never come back, and he finds that very difficult to live. ....
8 Unfortunately, when I made up the story, my aunt looked through it immediately. ....

5 Replace the words in italics with an idiom or phrasal verb that keeps the same meaning.

1 It's a horrible situation, but we'll just have to *accept* it. ....
2 Mark's story was *completely untrue*. ....
3 If I don't tell them the truth, I'll *feel guilty*. ....
4 When I mentioned Claude's name, Pam *looked very embarrassed*. ....
5 It's not very sensible to *ignore or avoid* the facts. ....
6 *On the subject of* lying, the headmaster takes it very seriously. ....

6 ABOUT YOU Do you think men are more honest than women? Do you think men are better liars? Write your answer in your notebook, or talk to another student.

41   I can talk about competition

A   Who will win 'Dancing Stars'?

Corinne and Jason **set the pace** from week one, and **forged ahead** of the rest. They **slipped up** a bit in their first dance last week, but they're still going to **take some beating**.

Pam and Mike are the **dark horses** in this competition. They**'ve been gaining ground** week by week, and I think they might **be keeping something up their sleeve**.

Alex and Sylvia are **neck and neck** with Pam and Mike. Now the competition **is hotting up**, the smallest thing could **tip the balance in** one couple's **favour**. It's impossible to say who**'ll come out on top**.

Glossary

set the pace	establish a standard or rate that others have to try to achieve.
forge ahead (**with sth**)	make strong and steady progress with sth.
slip up	INF make a careless mistake. **slip-up** N.
take some beating	INF If sb **will take some beating**, it means they are very good and it will be hard for sb else to do better. SYN **be hard to beat**.
gain ground (**on sb**)	gradually get closer to people you are competing with. SYN **catch up** (**with sb**).
keep/have sth up your sleeve	keep a plan or idea secret until you need it.
hot up	INF become more exciting or show an increase in activity.
tip the balance (**in sb's favour**)	give a slight advantage to sb.
come out on top	be more successful than the others.

spotlight Idioms from horse racing

A dark horse was a racehorse that nobody knew anything about. Now it refers to a person who other people know very little about, especially one who might achieve something that you don't expect. Two horses that are **neck and neck** in a race are level with each other. Now we also use it about two people or two teams in a race or competition.

1   Are the meanings similar or different? Write S or D.

1	They're setting the pace.	They're neck and neck.
2	They'll take some beating.	They'll be hard to beat.
3	They're gaining ground.	They're catching up.
4	The competition is hotting up.	The competition is slipping up.
5	They're forging ahead.	They're gaining ground.

2   Rewrite the sentences using the correct form of the word in capitals. Keep the same meaning.

▶ They're making great progress. FORGE *They're forging ahead.*
1   They're level with each other. NECK
2   They're catching up. GROUND
3   It could give you a slight advantage. BALANCE
4   The race is getting more exciting. HOT
5   She'll take some beating. HARD
6   He could surprise us. HORSE
7   She made a mistake. SLIP
8   I think he has a secret plan he's holding back. SLEEVE

B And the winner is….

I think the result was **in the balance** right up to that last dance, but we **gave it our all** and in the end it just **came down to** the judges' decision. The whole competition has been brilliant, and winning it is just **a dream come true**.

Well, we **gave** it **our best shot**, but it wasn't quite good enough. I thought we could **pull** it **off** with that last dance, but it wasn't to be. Maybe we **paid the price for playing it safe** – I don't know. Anyway, it was **a close thing**, and when I **look back on** the competition as a whole, I'm proud of what we've achieved.

Glossary

in the balance	If the result of sth is **in the balance**, it is uncertain.
give it your all	make the maximum possible effort.
come down to sth/sb	If a situation **comes down to sth**, that thing is the most important factor.
a dream come true	INF sth that happens which you have wanted for a long time.
give sth your best shot	INF try as hard as you possibly can in doing sth.
pull sth off	INF succeed in doing sth that is difficult.
pay the price for (doing) sth	suffer as a result of bad luck, a mistake, or sth you have done.
play (it) safe	not take any big risks.
look back (on sth)	think about a past event.

spotlight *a close thing/shave/call*

A close thing is a situation in which success or failure is equally possible.
A close shave/call is when you just manage to avoid a dangerous situation or accident.

3 Complete the last word in each dialogue.

1 You did everything you could. ~ Yes, I gave it my best ....
2 You didn't take too many risks? ~ No, we decided to play it ....
3 How much do you want to win? ~ It would be a dream come ....
4 You nearly had an accident then. ~ Yes, it was a close ....
5 Are you confident about the result? ~ Yes, I still think we can pull it ....
6 Could either of them win? ~ Yes, I think it's still in the ....

4 Complete the text.

I remember when Federer played Nadal at Wimbledon. They (1) .... it their all for over three hours of brilliant tennis and it all came (2) .... to the final fifth set. In the end Nadal (3) .... off an incredible victory, but (4) .... back on it, I think Federer will feel he paid the (5) .... for only succeeding with one of the thirteen break points that he had. For Nadal, it was his first Wimbledon title, and a (6) .... come true.

5 ABOUT YOU Have the sentences been true for you in a competition, or for a team you support? Write your answers, or talk to another student.

Winning it was a dream come true. *Winning the championship was a dream come true. I'd been practising for months.*
I gave it my best shot but it wasn't quite good enough. ....
I was amazed I pulled it off. ....
Looking back on it, I paid the price for … ....

I can talk about humour

A Funny or not funny?

You're **pulling** my **leg**!

He's **having** you **on**!

I **laughed my head off**.

The joke **fell flat**.

TYPES OF HUMOUR

FUNNY

We **were in stitches**.

NOT FUNNY

She said it **tongue in cheek**.

She loves **practical jokes**.

They **had a good laugh about** it.

A broken leg is **no laughing matter**.

It **got beyond a joke**.

Glossary

pull sb's leg	INF tell sb sth which is not true, as a joke. SYN **have sb on** INF.
a practical joke	a trick which is intended to surprise sb or make them look silly, often involving physical actions (you **play a practical joke on sb**).
tongue in cheek	If you say sth (**with**) **tongue in cheek** or **with your tongue in your cheek**, you are not being serious and mean it as a joke.
laugh your head off	INF laugh loudly and for a long time. SYN **be in stitches** INF.
have a good laugh (**about sth**)	find sth very funny and amusing.
fall flat	If a joke **falls flat**, no one laughs at it.
be/get/go beyond a joke	If a situation **has got beyond a joke**, it has become annoying or worrying.
no laughing matter	sth which is too serious to make jokes about.

1 Answer the questions with 'yes' or 'no'.

1 If someone is pulling your leg, should you believe them? ....
2 If something is beyond a joke, is it very funny? ....
3 If someone puts a frog in your bed, is that a practical joke? ....
4 If someone says something tongue in cheek, are they being serious? ....
5 If someone is having you on, are they telling you something which is true? ....
6 If you are in stitches, are you laughing? ....

2 Rewrite the sentences on the left starting with the words given. Keep the meaning the same.

1 They all found it very amusing.   They all had a good ....
2 You're having me on.   You're pulling ....
3 No one laughed at her jokes.   Her jokes fell ....
4 She was saying it as a joke.   She was saying it tongue ....
5 It's no longer a laughing matter.   It's gone ....
6 He laughed his head off.   He was in ....

3 ABOUT YOU Write answers to the questions in your notebook, or talk to another student.

1 Do you ever play practical jokes on people? If so, what kind?
2 Do you often have people on? If so, what about?
3 Do you often say things tongue in cheek? If so, who to?
4 Do you ever tell jokes that fall flat? Can you remember any?
5 When was the last time you had a good laugh?

B Humorous idioms

Idioms are quite often used for ironic or humorous effect.

Idiom and example	Meaning
Where did he get those CDs? *~ I think they **fell off the back of a lorry**.*	If you say sth **has fallen off the back of a lorry**, you mean it is probably stolen.
I can jump over that gate. *~ **Famous last words**.*	**famous last words** SAYING used when you think sb is being too confident about sth that is going to happen or that they are going to do.
Is he always that silly? *~ Yes. I'm afraid **the lights are on but no one's home**.*	**the lights are on but no one's / nobody's home** used to say that sb is stupid.
When was the last time he had a bath? *~ **I dread to think**.*	**I dread to think** = I'm afraid to think about that question as the answer might be too terrible or unpleasant.
***For reasons best known to himself**, my father's bought a house next door to a zoo.*	**for reasons best known to himself/herself** etc. used to say that you don't know or understand why sb has done sth.
*I'm off to bed. I need my **beauty sleep**.*	**beauty sleep** sleep that you need in order to feel healthy and look attractive.
Did Dr Fellows explain what to do? *~ Yes. But it was **as clear as mud**.*	**(as) clear as mud** = very hard to understand.
Matthew said he would help us. *~ Oh dear. That's **the kiss of death**, then.*	**the kiss of death** an action or situation that will bring bad luck or spoil an activity.
Where's Alfie? *~ **A call of nature**, I think.*	**(a/the) call of nature** a need to go to the toilet.
My sister thinks she can paint the whole house in a weekend. *~ Goodness. **What planet is she on?***	**What planet is he/she on?** used to say that sb's ideas are not realistic or practical (also **sb is (living) on another planet**).

4 Correct the mistake in each sentence, and write the correct word at the end.

1 I can do it. ~ Yeah, famous lost words. ....
2 Where did you get that? ~ It fell off the back of a train. ....
3 He's a bit stupid, isn't he? ~ Yeah, the lights are on but no one's here. ....
4 I need to get my beautiful sleep. See you in the morning. ....
5 Marty doesn't think we'll have to pay for drinks. ~ Gosh. What plane is he on? ....
6 That explanation was as clean as mud. ....
7 Marcel walked home in bare feet – for reasons better known to himself. ....
8 Where's your mum? ~ A cry of nature, I think. ....

5 Respond to the first speaker. Include a suitable idiom in your answer.

▶ He's taking ages to fill in that form. ~ *Yeah, the lights are on but no one's home.*
1 His flat's always dirty. How often does he clean it? ~ ....
2 I didn't understand a word of that explanation, did you? ~ ....
3 Why do you always go to bed so early? ~ ....
4 My brother is bringing boring old Malcolm to my party. ~ ....
5 Why are those radios so cheap? ~ ....
6 The boss told me he thinks we all like working late. ~ .... ?
7 He thinks he can beat all the girls easily. ~ ....
8 Where has Cathy gone? ~ ....

43 I can express criticism

A Online complaints blog

I hate Cheap Air!

ANTON ▶ I'm **sick to death of** being treated like a second class citizen. At check-in, they managed to **squeeze** a cool €130 **out of** me just to board the plane – it was **daylight robbery**. And frankly, the attitude of the staff **is beyond me**, but I reckon they're badly treated so they just **take** it **out on** the passengers.

JEZEBEL ▶ It said in the paper they're going to start charging for hand luggage!! If that isn't **a rip-off**, I don't know what is … but I **wouldn't put it past** them!

RUDY ▶ All those adverts of smiling passengers – why do we all **fall for** it every time? Listen, people, if you're so fed up with them, why don't you **vote with your feet**?

Glossary

sick to death of sth/sb	INF very annoyed or unhappy about sth that has lasted a long time. SYN **sick to the back teeth of sth/sb**.
squeeze sth out of sb	get sth by putting pressure on sb.
daylight robbery	INF used to say you think sth is much too expensive.
be beyond sb	INF be impossible for sb to understand or imagine.
take sth out on sb	be unpleasant to sb or punish them for sth that is not their fault, often because you are angry or upset.
a rip-off	INF If sth is **a rip-off**, it is more expensive than it should be. **rip sb off** v.
I wouldn't put it past sb (to do sth)	INF used to say you wouldn't be surprised if sb did sth bad or unusual because it would be typical of them.
fall for sth	be tricked into believing sth that is not true. SYN **be taken in by sth/sb**.
vote with your feet	show that you do not support or agree with sth/sb by not going somewhere or by walking away.

1 Circle the correct answer(s). Both answers may be correct.

1 The plane ticket's gone up by 3 per cent – it's *daytime* | *daylight* robbery.
2 Did you manage to *squeeze* | *squash* the truth out of Jake?
3 The students voted with their *feet* | *legs* and abandoned the lecture hall.
4 I'm just sick to *death* | *the back teeth* of working sixty hours a week.
5 Jenny may not invite either of us – I wouldn't put it *beyond* | *past* her.
6 Did you really believe I would fall *to* | *for* that old trick?

2 Complete the dialogues.

▶ They refused to come to the meeting. ~ That's right, they *voted with their feet*   .
1 I know she's capable of stealing. ~ Yeah, I wouldn't   .
2 It was a ridiculous price to charge. ~ I know, it was a   .
3 How can they charge so much? ~ I know, it's daylight   .
4 It's shocking that she lied about it. ~ Yeah, it's   why she would do that.
5 I'm amazed that he fooled you. ~ I know, I can't believe that I   it.
6 You must be tired of all the travelling. ~ Too right; I'm sick   .
7 So they made you pay another €20. ~ Yeah, they   me.
8 He shouted at me but I'd done nothing wrong. ~ Yeah, he was fed up and took it   you.

3 ABOUT YOU Have you ever had any problems with bad companies? Write your answers in your notebook, or talk to another student.

B Is criticism acceptable?

SONIA So how did the interview go, David?

DAVID Well, **no disrespect to** the interviewers, but I found them quite aggressive **to put it mildly**.

SONIA **To be fair**, that's their job, isn't it? You say what you think, and they **pull** it **to pieces**. That's what interviews are like – you shouldn't **take it personally**.

DAVID OK, that's **fair enough**, but I didn't expect the chairman to **jump down** my **throat** every time I opened my mouth. The thing is, I'**m all for** healthy discussion, but he just seemed to **have a bee in his bonnet** about expenses claims.

SONIA Well, it probably isn't very wise to **argue the toss** with any interviewer, **let alone** the company chairman. Better luck with your next interview!

Glossary

no disrespect (**to sb**)	used when you are going to criticize sb and do not want to seem rude or offend them.
to put it mildly / **and that's putting it mildly**	used to say that you could have used much stronger words to describe sth.
to be fair	used when you are defending yourself or sb/sth against criticism. SYN **let's be fair**.
pull/**tear sb**/**sth to pieces**	INF criticize sb or their ideas very severely. SYN **pull**/**tear sb**/**sth to shreds**.
take sth personally	let yourself get upset about sth that sb has said or done.
fair enough	INF used to say that something seems reasonable, but you do not agree with it completely.
jump down sb's throat	INF react very angrily to sb in an unfair way.
be all for sth / **for doing sth**	believe strongly that sth should be done. OPP **be dead set against sth**.
have a bee in your bonnet	INF think or talk about sth all the time and think that it is very important.
argue the toss	INF continue to argue against a decision, especially when it is too late to change it or it is not very important.
let alone	used to say that sth is even less suitable or possible than another unsuitable or unlikely thing.

4 Cross out one word in each sentence which is not necessary.

1 There isn't enough food for the four of us, let us alone the rest of the class.
2 If you want to leave school, be fair enough, but don't expect any help from me.
3 She didn't mean to upset you; don't take it out personally.
4 I'm all in for people contributing ideas, but we've got to make a decision very soon.
5 Mum is all dead set against us moving to the country, and I can understand why.
6 I only said I thought he could do better, but he jumped in down my throat!

5 One word is missing in each line of text. Where does it go? Write it at the end.

My dad has a ⟨ in his bonnet about me and my studies. I want to become   ▶ bee

a musician, but he's set against that. We had a row about it last night –   1 ....

it was my fault, I should know better than to argue the with him late at   2 ....

night. The thing is, disrespect to Dad, but I feel that I should give it a go,   3 ....

and be fair, it is my life! I gave him a couple of reasons why I should   4 ....

leave college, and of course he completely pulled my arguments to,   5 ....

and that's it mildly! He wants me to study law, just as he did, but it   6 ....

really doesn't interest me, and I think he takes that. And if I don't make it   7 ....

as a musician, I still won't get a job in the City, alone become a lawyer.   8 ....

A How to survive a plane crash

- Watch the flight attendant's safety demonstration: ignore it, and you could **be missing out on** vital information about how to brace yourself should the plane crash. And read the safety card in front of your seat; even if you fly often, **it does no harm to** be reminded.

- It **makes sense to** keep your seat belt on **at all times**, especially if you fall asleep.

- **Take note of** the nearest emergency exits. Count the rows between them and your seat.

- **In the event of** a crash, speed is **of the essence**. Stay calm and don't **get swept along** with the hysteria. **Keep your wits about you**; you**'ll stand a better chance of** surviving.

Glossary

miss out (**on sth**)	lose the opportunity to have or do sth.
make sense (**to do sth**)	be a sensible thing to do.
at all times	(used especially in instructions, announcements, etc.) always.
take note (**of sth**)	pay attention to sth and be sure to remember it.
in the event of sth	if sth happens.
of the essence	necessary and very important.
sweep sb along	If a situation or feeling **sweeps you along**, you are so involved in it that you forget about other things.
keep your wits about you	be aware of what is happening around you and ready to act and think quickly (also **keep your head**).
stand a chance of (**doing**) **sth**	have the possibility of succeeding in sth.

spotlight Advice

These phrases are used to suggest that someone should do something:
It does/would do no harm to ask for help.
There's no harm in asking for more time to finish the work.
It wouldn't hurt to take an umbrella with you.

1 Correct one word which is wrong in each sentence.

1 Keep your wit about you. ....
2 In an event of fire, leave quickly. ....
3 Don't miss out of this opportunity. ....
4 You stay a good chance of winning. ....
5 There's no hurt in asking her. ....
6 It makes sensible to do it now. ....
7 Take note for what he says. ....
8 It wouldn't harm to try it. ....

2 Complete the advice for nervous fliers.

Fear of flying is surprisingly common. The important thing is not to let yourself get (1) .... along by your own fear, and to (2) .... your head while on the plane at all (3) .... When you step onto the plane, it would do (4) .... to let the air crew know you are feeling nervous; they may help to reassure you. Be sure to listen and take (5) .... of the safety tips they give before take-off. Whenever you start to feel panicky, positive thinking is of the (6) .... : calm yourself by imagining that rather than being in the air, you are in a crowded living room. In the (7) .... of turbulence during the flight, bear in mind that this is very common and not dangerous. And lastly, don't avoid air travel – you could be (8) .... on some wonderful adventures!

B Advice on sleeping

COFFEEGEEK ▶ I can't sleep at night; I just lie there looking at the moon. ☹ HEEELP!

JOJO ▶ Hi. I'm no expert **by any stretch of the imagination**, but **it stands to reason that** sleeping in complete darkness promotes better sleep. Shut your curtains or blinds!

ALI ▶ I**'ve been in the same boat** as you, so I **feel for** you. My dad says that **if all else fails**, read the most boring book you can find. And don't **get worked up about** not sleeping – it only makes things worse.

YI ▶ My advice – **for what it's worth**! If you're lying there for hours, **you could do worse than** put on a relaxation CD, with the sounds of the ocean.

GINNIE23 ▶ **Your best bet** is to avoid caffeine and alcohol – especially alcohol, because it **keeps** you **from** falling into a deep sleep. Hope this helps.

Glossary

(**not**) **by any stretch of the imagination**	used to say strongly that sth is not true, even if you try to imagine it.
it stands to reason (**that …**)	= it is obvious or logical (that …).
be in the same boat	INF be in the same difficult situation.
feel for sb	have sympathy for sb.
if all else fails	used to say that if other methods do not succeed, there is one last thing you can try. SYN **as a last resort**.
get worked up (**about sth**)	INF get very excited, angry, or upset about sth (also **work yourself up** (**about sth**)).
for what it's worth	INF used to emphasize that sth is only your opinion or suggestion, and you are not sure how helpful it is.
you could do worse than	used to advise sb to do or try sth.
your best bet	INF the thing that gives the best chance of success.
keep sb from doing sth	prevent sb from doing sth.

3 **One word is missing in each line. Where does it go? Write it at the end.**

1 We've both just had pay cuts, so really we're in the boat. ....
2 OK, the plates are dirty, but don't get so up about it. I'll wash them later. ....
3 What it's worth, I don't share your views on child rearing. ....
4 I find that taking these pills me from feeling nervous. ....
5 Look, it stands to that no sensible person would buy that car. ....
6 You couldn't describe him as clever by any of the imagination. ....
7 You know that if all fails, you can always stay in my house. ....
8 If you're eating out, you do worse than the North China restaurant. ....

4 **Rewrite the sentences using the words in capitals. The meaning must stay the same.**

▶ If you want my opinion, he's useless. WORTH *For what it's worth, he's useless.*
1 I have great sympathy for her at this time. FEEL ....
2 We're both in a difficult situation. BOAT ....
3 The best thing you can do is to say nothing. BET ....
4 Try not to become over-excited about the plan. WORKED ....
5 It's not a bad idea to stay in a B and B. WORSE ....
6 As a last resort, you can refuse to work. FAIL ....

5 **ABOUT YOU** Write your own advice about getting a good night's sleep in your notebook, or talk to another student. Use *for what it's worth, your best bet, you could do worse than, if all else fails.*

A Problem solving

Thinking through a problem

• Is it a genuine problem, or just **a storm in a teacup**?

• If it's real, what's the root cause? Is it a person? Someone who **has a chip on their shoulder** for example, or someone **digging their heels in** and refusing to compromise?

• How big is the problem? Can you **sort** it **out** easily, or will you **have your work cut out**?

• How will you solve it? **Take the bull by the horns**, or **sit tight** for the moment?

Whatever you do, be clear about your course of action. Don't **fall into the trap of** doing neither one thing nor the other. Consider all the options, make your decision, and then **act on** it.

Glossary

think sth through	consider everything that could happen in a situation.
a storm in a teacup	a lot of anger and worry about sth unimportant.
have a chip on your shoulder	INF be sensitive about or feel offended by sth, as a result of sth that happened in your past. (See Unit 2.)
dig your heels in / dig in your heels	refuse to do sth or change your mind about sth.
have your work cut out	INF have a very difficult task or job to do.
take the bull by the horns	face a difficult situation in a very direct and confident way.
sit tight	stay where you are, without taking any action.
fall into the trap (of doing sth)	make a mistake that many people make.
act on/upon sth	take action as a result of a decision, advice, or information.

> **spotlight** Meanings of *sort sth out*
>
> *I'll sort out the problem.* = deal with it and solve it (as above).
> *The study's a mess. Could you sort it out?* = tidy it.
> *I need to sort out the insurance.* = arrange it successfully.

1 **Form six idioms using words from the box. You need to add more words to most of them.**

dig	storm	horns	fall	chip	sit	bull	teacup	tight	heels	shoulder	trap

....

....

2 **Rewrite the sentences using the words in capitals. Keep the meaning the same.**

▶ I spent the day tidying up the office. OUT *I spent the day sorting out the office.*
1 He made the mistake of doing everything himself. TRAP ....
2 She's made her choice; she must do something about it. ACT ....
3 He thinks the world is against him. CHIP ....
4 I would stay where you are and do nothing. SIT ....
5 He's refusing to change his mind. HEELS ....
6 She has to consider what might happen. THINK ....
7 It will be a difficult task for you. CUT OUT ....
8 I was asked to deal with the problem. SORT ....
9 It's a lot of fuss about nothing. STORM ....
10 He's going to confront the situation directly. HORNS ....

B A teenage problem

ELLE Jonathan's got important exams **coming up**, and his girlfriend**'s** just **finished with** him. He**'s in a terrible state** – I don't know what to do. He**'s** even **off his food**.

SIAN Come on, it's **not the end of the world**; he'll **get over** it.

ELLE But with these exams **hanging over** his **head**! In his present **frame of mind**, he'll fail.

SIAN I don't think so. Jonathan's a bright boy. **At the end of the day** I'm sure he**'ll pull himself together** and **sail through** his exams.

ELLE I don't know. Teenage relationships and school exams: what **a recipe for disaster**!

Glossary

finish with sb	end a romantic relationship with sb.
be in a (terrible) state (about sth)	be very anxious (about sth).
be off your food	not want to eat, usually because you are ill or upset.
not the end of the world	INF not the worst thing that could happen.
get over sth	recover from sth such as a disappointment or illness.
hang over sb / sb's head	If sth difficult or unpleasant **is hanging over you** / **your head**, you are thinking and worrying about it.
frame of mind	the way you think or feel about sth at a particular time.
at the end of the day	INF used to introduce a fact that remains true when everything else has been considered.
pull yourself together	regain control of your feelings and behave calmly.
sail through sth	pass an exam, test, etc. without any difficulty.
a recipe for disaster	a thing that is likely to cause sth bad to happen.

spotlight Meanings of *come up*

The race is coming up at 6 p.m. = is going to happen in the near future (as above).
The subject came up in conversation. = was mentioned or discussed.
Your number came up, so you've won. = was chosen.

3 Complete the dialogues. You may need more than one word.

▶ Will she be upset if she fails? ~ Yes, but it's not the end *of the world* .
1 Won't he eat anything? ~ No, he's .... food.
2 Do you think he'll pass the exam easily? ~ Oh yes, he'll .... it.
3 Is she very anxious about the tests? ~ Yes, she's .... about them.
4 The disappointment won't last. ~ I know. He'll .... it.
5 This will cause all sorts of problems. ~ I know. It's a .... disaster.
6 Has Lisa ended the relationship? ~ Yes, she's .... him.
7 Did they discuss the new bus route? ~ Yes, the subject .... up.
8 He must control his feelings and stay calm. ~ Hmm, he needs to .... together.

4 Complete the text.

Charlotte hasn't been in the most positive (1) .... of mind recently. She's got an interview (2) .... up next week for a job at the BBC. She's had it (3) .... over her for almost a month and she's in a real (4) .... about it. It's silly really, because I'm sure she'll (5) .... through the interview. And even if she doesn't, it's not the end of the (6) .... I know Charlotte's a very talented girl, and at the end of the (7) .... , that's what matters.

A A positive attitude

My brother's always loved surfing; he **lives and breathes** it. When he's out on the waves, he**'s** really **in his element**. Mum thinks he spends too much time surfing and not enough studying, but he just says, 'life's too short to waste time worrying'.

I took Martin skiing a couple of years ago and he absolutely **threw himself into** it and **took to** it **like a duck to water**. When we're on the slopes **there's no stopping** him till the sun goes down. He **gets** a bit **carried away** at times!

Lia's take on life is that good things generally **come her way**; she **writes off** any bad events **as** isolated incidents. It seems that **luck is on her side**.

Glossary	
live and breathe sth	spend much of your time doing sth you love.
be in your element	be very happy and comfortable in a situation.
throw yourself into sth	begin to do sth with energy and enthusiasm.
take to sth like a duck to water	learn a new skill quickly and easily.
there's no stopping sb	used to say that it is impossible to prevent sb from doing sth.
get carried away	INF become so excited or involved in sth that you lose control of your feelings or actions.
come your way	happen to you or become available to you.
write sth off (**as sth**)	decide that sth is a failure and not worth doing anything about.
luck is on your side	If **luck is on your side**, things happen the way you want them to.

spotlight Sayings about life

Life's too short. INF = Don't waste time doing unimportant things.
Life goes on. INF = Even though sb has had a bad experience, the rest of life goes on unchanged.
That's life! INF = You have to accept disappointments as part of life.

1 Correct the mistake in each sentence.

1 They said my eyesight will never be the same. Well, this is life, I guess. ....
2 If you don't get the job, write the experience out as bad luck. ....
3 Once she starts work in the garden, she's no stopping her. ....
4 He's obsessive about work and throws him into it. ....
5 She'd never played chess before, but she looked to it like a duck to water. ....
6 He got the job easily; I'd say that luck's by his side. ....

2 Complete the dialogues.

1 You've made far too much food for us! ~ Sorry, I just got ....
2 I've got to read through 200 emails on my computer. ~ Leave them! Life ....!
3 How did Hari's skiing lesson go? ~ Great! He took to it ....
4 I had my chances in the game. ~ Yeah, but you lost. I guess luck ....
5 Mark's obsessive about fishing, isn't he? ~ Yes, he lives .... it.
6 So you've put your disappointment behind you. ~ Yeah, life ...., doesn't it.
7 Would you want the job? ~ Well, if the chance .... my ...., I'd take it.
8 Was she happy doing the cooking? ~ Yes. She's in her .... in the kitchen.

B Negative thinking

Avoid these types of negative thinking!

• DON'T **dwell on** the negatives when something goes wrong in your life.

• DON'T **put yourself down** for minor **slip-ups**. Just accept them and move on.

• DON'T **jump to** negative **conclusions**. Wait and see how things **pan out**.

• DON'T **bury your head in the sand**. **Face up to** your problems; it helps in the long run.

• DON'T allow negative thoughts to **run through your mind**, or you will start to see everything **in a bad light**. Stay POSITIVE.

• DON'T set yourself goals which you can't **live up to**, such as 'I must get 100 per cent in the test'.

Glossary

dwell on/upon sth	spend time thinking about sth difficult or unpleasant.
put yourself down	criticize yourself in front of other people.
slip-up	a small mistake. **slip up** V.
jump to conclusions	make a decision about sth too quickly, before having all the facts. SYN **leap to conclusions**.
pan out	INF (of events or a situation) develop in a particular way.
bury your head in the sand	refuse to admit that a problem exists, or refuse to deal with it.
face up to sth	accept and deal with sth that is difficult or unpleasant.
run through sth	pass quickly through sth. (Sth can **run through your mind**.)
in a good/bad light	If you see sth **in a good/bad light**, it seems good/bad to you.
live up to sth	do as well as other people expect you to.

3 Is the meaning similar or different? Write S or D.

1	Don't bury your head in the sand.	Face up to the problem.
2	Let's see how the situation pans out.	Let's see how the situation develops.
3	She dwells on her mistakes.	She ignores her mistakes.
4	I can't live up to their expectations.	I can't be as good as they expect.
5	It was just a silly slip-up.	It was just a silly fall.
6	He always leaps to conclusions.	He always gets to the end.
7	Try not to see it in a negative way.	Try not to see it in a bad light.
8	Don't put yourself down.	Don't be so self-critical.

4 Complete the texts.

BILL I don't know why, but I have a habit of always seeing things in a bad (1) _____ . It's awful at night: I keep waking up with all these negative thoughts (2) _____ _____ my mind. Most of my worries are to do with work. At last week's meeting, for example, I (3) _____ up with some sales figures – only a tiny mistake, but I spent the rest of the meeting (4) _____ on it, so I didn't really contribute anything at all. I think my boss has very high expectations of me, and I just can't (5) _____ up to them.

MONICA I saw Derek with that blonde girl again today. Maybe I'm just (6) _____ to conclusions, but he seems really keen on her. I guess I'll just have to (7) _____ up to the fact I'm not his special one – let's face it, I'm no great beauty. Delia says I'm always (8) _____ myself down and that's why Derek isn't interested. She says I should cheer up, and just see how things pan (9) _____ . Easier said than done.

5 ABOUT YOU What advice would you give Bill and Monica in Exercise 4? Write your answers in your notebook, or talk to another student. Use language from the glossary.

A Decision-making styles

People make decisions in different ways. Some **weigh up** their options carefully, which is sensible as long as you don't **lose sight of** what's important. Others, **rightly or wrongly**, just follow their **gut feeling**. A surprising number **go for** the first available option and **rush into** a decision, regardless of its importance. People who don't trust their own judgement may **turn to** others, or **go with** the majority view, while those who **have a mind of their own** may not consult anyone at all. Then, of course, there are people who either **lack the courage of their convictions,** or worry so much about making the 'wrong' decision, that they can't make any decision.

Glossary

weigh sth up	consider the good and bad aspects of sth before reaching a decision about it.
lose sight of sth	stop considering sth; forget about sth.
rightly or wrongly	used to say that sth is true, whether people think it is a good thing or bad thing.
gut feeling/reaction/instinct	INF a feeling that sth is right, even if you cannot explain why.
rush into sth	do sth quickly without thinking about it first (also **rush headlong into sth**).
turn to sb/sth	go to sb/sth for help and advice.
go with sth	accept or agree to a decision, a plan, or an offer.
have a mind of your own	have your own opinions and make your own decisions without being influenced by others.
have/lack the courage of your convictions	be / not be brave enough to do what you feel is right.

spotlight *go for sth*

I always go for fish in a restaurant. INF = choose fish ('choose sth' as above).
The painting went for £100. = was sold for £100.
There were three people going for the job. INF = trying to get the job.

1 Write 'yes' or 'no'.

1 If you say something is true rightly or wrongly, is it true? ....
2 If you are weighing something up, have you already made a decision? ....
3 If something went for a large amount, has it been stolen? ....
4 If you lack the courage of your convictions, are you able to do what you feel is right? ....
5 If you have a mind of your own, are you easily influenced by other people? ....
6 If you lose sight of something, have you stopped thinking about it? ....

2 Complete the sentences.

1 When you have to make a decision, do you usually .... things up carefully, or are you in the habit of .... headlong into a decision without giving it much thought?
2 Do you think you often .... for the easiest option when making a decision?
3 Do you base a lot of your decisions on your own .... feeling or instinct?
4 Who do usually .... to when you need advice?
5 If you asked five people for their opinion before making a decision, would you normally .... with the consensus?
6 If you think something is the right thing to do, do you usually have the courage ....
.... ?

3 ABOUT YOU Write your own answers to Exercise 2 in your notebook, or talk to another student.

B Individual decisions

I once saw a boy steal some chocolate from a shop, and I **turned a blind eye**. Now I **draw the line at** any kind of stealing. If it happened again, I would **step in** and do something.

Yesterday it **was a toss-up** between a noisy crowded train journey, or driving for two hours on a boring motorway. I chose the train as **the lesser of two evils**.

I **was in two minds about** a holiday. I normally go away, but I really needed the money for some new furniture. In the end I decided to **give** the holiday **a miss**.

I **put up with** the fact that my girlfriend was a bit unreliable, but when she arrived an hour late for dinner on my birthday, that was **the final straw**. I finished with her.

Glossary

turn a blind eye (**to sth**)	pretend not to see or notice sth, usually sth bad.
step in	become involved in a difficult situation to help or make it stop.
be a toss-up	INF used for saying that you do not know which of two things to choose, or which of two things will happen. **toss up** V.
the lesser of two evils	the less unpleasant of two unpleasant choices.
be in two minds (**about sth / doing sth**)	be unable to decide (about sth / doing sth).
give sth a miss	INF decide not to do sth that you usually do.
put up with sth/**sb**	accept sth/sb unpleasant in a patient way.
the final/**last straw**	the last in a series of bad actions or events that makes it impossible for you to accept a situation any longer.

spotlight Idioms with *draw*

If you **draw the line** (**at sth**), you set a limit on what you will allow or accept. If you **draw a line under sth**, you decide that something is finished and you stop thinking about it. If you **draw lots**, you make a decision by writing the choices on pieces of paper, putting these into a container, and selecting one at random.

4 Match 1–6 with a–f.

1 I decided to give it ....
2 She turned a blind ....
3 We decided to draw ....
4 It was the final ....
5 I decided to draw a line ....
6 It was the lesser ....

a straw.
b of two evils.
c under it and move on.
d a miss.
e eye to it.
f lots to see who would go.

5 Complete the sentences.

1 If I had a cold, I would probably .... my English class a miss.
2 If I saw someone dropping litter, I would probably turn a .... to it.
3 If I saw a mother hitting a child, I would .... in and say something.
4 I couldn't .... up with a boyfriend/girlfriend/partner who smoked.
5 If it was a .... -up between going for a walk and having a swim, I'd go for a walk.
6 When I'm in two .... about buying something, I usually don't buy it.
7 If it's a choice between cleaning or ironing, I'd say ironing is the lesser of ....
8 I agree that people can protest, but I would .... the line at any form of violent protest.

6 ABOUT YOU Would you make the same decisions as the speakers at the top of the page and in Exercise 5? Why / why not? Write your answers in your notebook, or talk to another student.

A   What kind of risks do you take?

Are you one of life's gamblers?	Yes / No / Not sure
I never **put money on** a horse, a race, or anything like that.	_____
If I was investing money, I'd probably **hedge my bets** and **split** it **up**.	_____
There's no excuse for taking risks when you're driving.	_____
I'm always prepared to **stick my neck out** if someone asks my opinion.	_____
When people threaten to do things, I rarely **call their bluff**.	_____
I'm not the kind of person to **get myself into** difficult situations.	_____
In life, I think I tend to **play it safe** most of the time.	_____
Would I **risk my neck** to save someone else? That's a difficult one.	_____

Glossary

put money on sth	bet money on a horse, team, etc. in a race or game.
hedge your bets	reduce the risk of losing by choosing several possibilities instead of just one.
split sth up	divide sth into smaller parts.
there's no excuse for (doing) sth	= there's no acceptable reason for doing sth (used in reference to behaviour which you think is very bad).
stick your neck out	INF take a risk by doing or saying sth that may be criticized or proved to be wrong.
call sb's bluff	tell sb to do what they are threatening to do because you don't believe they intend to do it or are brave enough to do it.
get yourself into sth	become involved in a difficult situation, often without intending to.
play (it) safe	avoid taking any big risks.
risk your neck	risk being killed or injured in order to do sth. SYN **risk life and limb**.

1   Match the verbs on the left with the endings on the right.

1	stick	a	someone's bluff
2	risk	b	your bets
3	call	c	it safe
4	split	d	your neck
5	hedge	e	your neck out
6	play	f	something up

2   Complete the sentences.

1   Most people would say nothing in that situation, but my brother is always prepared to _____ his neck _____ and say what he thinks.
2   I'm always very careful not to _____ myself _____ debt. To be honest, there's _____ _____ for people spending money they haven't actually got.
3   I wanted a photo of the shark, but I wouldn't risk _____ and _____ trying to get it.
4   He threatened me saying he had a gun, but I called his _____ and he had nothing.
5   I wasn't sure who would win, so I _____ my bets and _____ money on two of them.
6   If you have money to invest, accountants often advise you to _____ it safe and _____ the money up into different investments such as shares, property, and a pension.

3   ABOUT YOU   How would you respond to the statements at the top of the page? Write your answers in your notebook, or talk to another student.

B Risk-takers

Why do people take risks?

Recent research **sheds** some **light on** this and suggests it may **be down to** the psychological **make-up** of a person. It seems that 60 per cent of risk-takers are 'sensation seekers': people who **seek out** and **thrive on** novel and exciting experiences. This does **not necessarily** involve risk, but it is a common by-product. Sensation-seekers are more **at risk from** drink or drugs, and more likely to **take a chance on a long shot**; they are less likely to **err on the side of caution**. However, not all risk-taking is bad. Mankind has only evolved by taking risks; without it we would stagnate.

Glossary

shed/**cast**/**throw light on sth**	help to explain sth by providing new information about it.
be down to sb/**sth**	be caused by a particular person or thing.
make-up	the different qualities or things that combine together to form sth. **make sth up** v.
seek out sth/**sb**	try to find sth/sb.
thrive on sth	enjoy sth so much that it makes you a happier or healthier person.
not necessarily	used to say that sth is possibly true but not definitely true.
take a chance (**on sth**)	decide to do sth knowing it may be the wrong choice.
a long shot	an attempt that is unlikely to succeed, but may be worth trying.
err on the side of caution	be prepared to miss an opportunity rather than take a risk.

spotlight Idioms with *risk*

If you are **at risk from**/**of sth**, you are in danger of something unpleasant or harmful happening.
If you **run the risk of sth**, you put yourself in a situation in which something bad could happen.
If you **do sth at your own risk**, you do it even though you have been warned of the dangers.

4 Replace the word(s) in italics with an idiom or phrasal verb that keeps a similar meaning. The first letter has been given to help you.

1 She *loves* work.   t ....
2 It's *composed* of four parts.   m ....
3 The mistake was *caused by* Jim.   d ....
4 Does he *actively look for* adventure?   s ....
5 I would *be careful rather than take a risk*.   e ....
6 Can you *help by explaining* any of this?   s ....
7 It's *unlikely to succeed but we can try it*.   a l ....
8 Is it a big problem? ~ *It could be, but that's not certain*. N ....

5 Complete the sentences.

1 Do you think you .... out novel and exciting experiences?
2 Do you .... on new challenges or do you prefer familiar things?
3 Is being a 'sensation seeker' part of your psychological .... - .... ?
4 Would you normally .... a chance on a .... shot?
5 Are you at .... from anything dangerous in your daily life?
6 Would you .... the risk of losing a lot of money in order to win a lot?

6 ABOUT YOU Write your own answers to Exercise 5 in your notebook, with your reasons, or talk to another student.

Review: Human behaviour

Unit 40

1 The same word is missing in each pair of sentences. Write it in.

1 a The information was hushed _____ to protect the doctor.
   b She tried to cover it _____ , but we found out.
2 a You nearly scared me _____ death!
   b It's hard to face up _____ the truth.
3 a It was clearly untrue about the money, but I didn't let _____ that I knew.
   b I told a lie, but I don't want to have that _____ my conscience.
4 a She couldn't gloss _____ the truth any longer.
   b You can't pull the wool _____ my eyes!
5 a The government announcement was an attempt to save _____ .
   b Neither side is prepared to lose _____ in the dispute.
6 a When it _____ to looking after children, she's brilliant.
   b We'll have to hope this information never _____ to light.

2 Complete the dialogues.

1 Why didn't you tell her the truth? ~ It was wrong not to, but I wanted to _____ her feelings.
2 Did he know his father was in prison? ~ No, his mother _____ it from him for years.
3 It's always difficult to give bad news. ~ Yes, it's tempting just to _____ over the truth.
4 Don't mention the surprise party to Alice. ~ No, we mustn't give the _____ away.
5 Why did she scream? ~ Well, you scared the living _____ out of her!
6 Do you feel responsible for the job losses? ~ Of course I do; it's very hard to _____ with.

Unit 41

1 Complete the definitions.

1 If something is *a close shave*, you manage to _____ a dangerous situation.
2 If you *slip up*, you make a _____ .
3 If you are *forging ahead*, you are making _____ quickly.
4 If you *play it safe*, you don't take _____ .
5 If you *pull something off*, you _____ in doing something _____ .
6 If something *tips the balance in your favour*, it gives you a slight _____ over somebody.
7 If the result is *in the balance*, it is not yet _____ .
8 If you *look back on something*, you think about a _____ .
9 If you are *neck and neck* with someone, you are _____ with them.
10 If you are *gaining ground on* someone, you are _____ with them.
11 If you *give something your all*, you _____ as much as possible.
12 If a game or race starts *hotting up*, it becomes more _____ .

Unit 42

1 Find answers to the clues by moving horizontally or vertically, backwards or forwards.

THE	A	NATURE	LAST	FAMOUS
KISS	CALL	OF	WORDS	THINK
OF	DEATH	I	DREAD	TO
TONGUE	IN	CHEEK	LAUGH	YOUR
PULL	FALLS	FLAT	MUD	HEAD
SOMEONE'S	LEG	CLEAR	AS	OFF

▶ Used for saying you think someone is too confident about something. = *famous last words.*
1 Very hard to understand. = ...
2 A need to use the toilet. = ...
3 Tell someone something that isn't true as a joke. = ...
4 Saying something in a way that is intended to be a joke. = ...
5 Laugh loudly and for a long time. = ...
6 If a joke does this, no one laughs at it. = ...
7 Something that will bring bad luck or spoil an activity. = ...
8 I don't want to think about that question, because the answer might be horrible. = ...

Unit 43

1 Complete the dialogue.

A I've heard the council is thinking of stopping people parking near the station.
B Well, I wouldn't (1) .... it past them, given what they've done to parking charges.
A Why, what's happened to them?
B It's not just 8 a.m. to 6 p.m. You have to pay in the evenings now as well.
A But that's a (2) .... -off!
B Well, I think it's probably (3) .... enough to make motorists pay a bit more, and I'm
   (4) .... for reducing the number of cars coming into town.
A But there aren't that many cars coming into town in the evening. It just seems as though they want to
   (5) .... it out on motorists.
B Well that's because they're an easy target. People prefer to use their cars, so the council thinks it can
   always (6) .... more money out of them.
A Well, I think it's daylight (7) ....
B You can argue the (8) .... for as long as you like, but it won't change things.

Unit 44

1 Complete this website advice page for young people travelling abroad.

HAVE A GREAT TRIP!

FOOD: Don't get paranoid about food poisoning or you will (1) .... out on some great food experiences. However, it (2) .... sense to drink bottled water at all times, and in some places, it does no (3) .... to remember the old adage, 'boil it, cook it, peel it, or forget it'.

CRIME: As a tourist you may be a target for pickpockets, so be alert and keep your (4) .... about you. Keep your valuables in a money belt – you'll (5) .... a better chance of not being robbed.

TRANSPORT: For what it's (6) ...., I don't think overnight buses are a great idea. You generally sleep badly and feel awful the next day. For overnight travel, your best (7) .... is to travel by train.

REMEMBER: In the (8) .... of anything unpleasant happening – and if all else
(9) .... – you can always consult your embassy and consulate 24-7.

Unit 45

1 One word is wrong in each sentence. Find the mistake and correct it.

1 I don't know why he's so aggressive; he's got a real fish on his shoulder. ....

2 This problem could get worse, so we'd better take the cow by the horns. ....

3 I'm afraid he's not going to compromise now; he's digging his toes in. ....

4 She's very bright, so I'm sure she'll fly through this exam. ....

5 He's getting very worked up about it, but it's just a storm in a saucer. ....

6 He won't change his mind easily; you'll have your job cut out to persuade him. ....

7 They've stepped into the trap of thinking it would be easy. ....

8 If we just sit loose, this problem might blow over. ....

2 Replace the words in italics with an idiom or phrasal verb, using the words in the box in the correct form. Keep a similar meaning.

> sort   food   dig ✓   pull   come   get   act   world   sail

▶ She's stubborn; I think she'll *refuse to change her mind*. *dig her heels in* ....

1 He made a decision but then didn't *do anything about* it. ....

2 It was a big disappointment and she still hasn't *recovered from* it. ....

3 You've got to *control your feelings and act more calmly*. ....

4 *It's not the worst thing that could happen.* ....

5 She'll *pass* the exam *easily*. ....

6 He *hasn't felt like eating* for a few days. ....

7 I'm sure the subject *was discussed* at the meeting. ....

8 We've got to *deal with* this problem. ....

Unit 46

1 Is the speaker feeling positive, or being critical of herself? Write P or C.

1 I get carried away. ....

2 I dwell on things. ....

3 I took to it like a duck to water. ....

4 I buried my head in the sand. ....

5 I threw myself into it. ....

6 I faced up to it. ....

7 I put myself down. ....

8 I was in my element. ....

9 I couldn't live up to it. ....

10 Luck's always on my side. ....

2 Complete each sentence in two different ways, starting with the words given.

1 He doesn't let these things worry him because { life's too ....
   life goes ....

2 She doesn't think about things carefully enough. { She jumps to ....
   She gets carried ....

3 Once he's got an idea, { there's no ....
   he throws ....

4 When she has a problem, { she buries ....
   she faces ....

Unit 47

1 Complete the texts. You will find one of the words for each idiom or phrasal verb in the box.

> rush   step   minds   rightly   courage   draw   turn   sight   straw   put ✓   weigh   toss

Some decisions I've had to make in the last year:

- I couldn't ▶ put _____ up _____ with _____ the flat I was living in any longer – it was really horrible, but I had to (1) _____ whether a move would be wise, given that I might be changing my job at the same time. I was in (2) _____ about whether to start looking around when, one day, the flat was broken into and my laptop was stolen. That was the (3) _____ , so that same day, I went and found a new place to rent.

- There was this problem with my job, as I said. I'd been working all hours of the day and night, admittedly for a lot of money, but I'd completely (4) _____ of the important things in life: family, friends, personal happiness. (5) _____ wrongly, I (6) _____ a decision and got a job providing support for elderly people in their homes. I'd always wanted to do something for the community, and you have to have the (7) _____ . I don't regret it at all.

- In the summer, my brother was in trouble over some small debts, and eventually he (8) _____ me for help. I worried about it for days; it was a (9) _____ as to whether I should get Dad to (10) _____ and sort him out financially, but in the end, I lent him the money myself. Hopefully he'll be able to (11) _____ under his problems and keep better track of his finances in future.

Unit 48

1 Read the definitions and complete the idioms and phrasal verbs.

▶ something that probably won't succeed, but is worth trying:	a _long_ _____ shot
1 make a problem easier to understand:	shed _____ on sth
2 decide to do something, knowing that it might be the wrong thing to do:	take a _____ on sth
3 not take any risks at all:	play it _____
4 ask someone to do what they are threatening to do, because you believe they don't intend to do it:	call sb's _____
5 become involved in a tricky situation without intending to do so:	get yourself _____ sth
6 do something very dangerous, especially something that might injure or kill you:	risk your _____
7 bet on a horse, race, etc:	_____ money on sth
8 be caused by a particular person or thing:	be _____ to sb/sth

2 Write in the missing prepositions or adverbs.

1 My brother's a real risk-taker: he thrives _____ dangerous sports like hang-gliding.
2 Personally I'm a very cautious person, and I always err _____ the side _____ caution.
3 Parking is allowed here, but purely _____ the customer's own risk.
4 I'm sticking my neck _____ here, but I think Barton will win the next election.
5 Millions of people around the world will be _____ risk from extreme weather in the future.
6 My sister is not the kind of person to seek _____ adventure; on the contrary.
7 The conference aims to throw light _____ how to manage financial risk.
8 The advisory committee is made _____ of experts in risk management.

49 I can use informal spoken idioms

A A range of opinions

The majority of idioms range from neutral to informal. The examples here are all informal, and used mostly in spoken English.

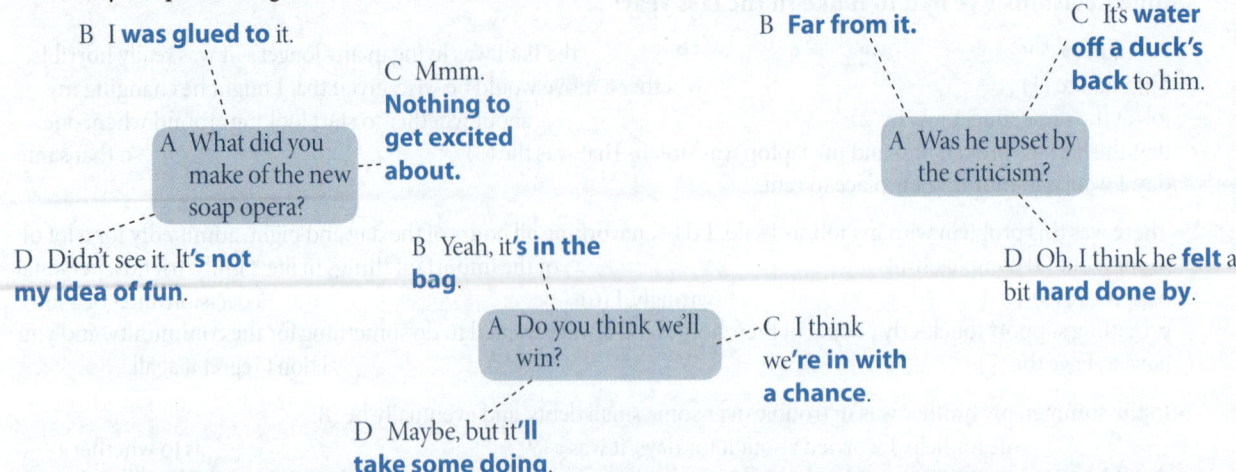

B I **was glued to** it.

C Mmm. **Nothing to get excited about.**

A What did you make of the new soap opera?

D Didn't see it. It**'s not my Idea of fun**.

B Yeah, it**'s in the bag**.

A Do you think we'll win?

C I think we**'re in with a chance**.

D Maybe, but it**'ll take some doing**.

B **Far from it.**

C It's **water off a duck's back** to him.

A Was he upset by the criticism?

D Oh, I think he **felt** a bit **hard done by**.

Glossary

be glued to sth	be paying all your attention to sth.
nothing to get excited about	sth that is not particularly good or interesting. SYN **nothing to write home about**.
not be your idea of fun	not be sth that you enjoy, though others might enjoy it.
be in the bag	If sth **is in the bag**, you are sure to get it or achieve it.
be in with a chance (**of doing sth**)	have the possibility of succeeding or achieving sth.
take some doing	be difficult to do, or involve a lot of effort or time.
far from it	used to say that the opposite of what sb says is true. SYN **quite the opposite/reverse**.
(**like**) **water off a duck's back**	used to say that sth, especially criticism, has no effect on sb.
feel/be hard done by	feel/be unfairly treated.

1 Circle the correct answer(s). Both answers may be correct.

1 Moira felt a bit hard done *by | for* when her boss criticized her.
2 Was Harry unhappy about the exam paper? ~ *Far from it. | Quite the opposite.*
3 I was *glued | stuck* to that programme about elephants last night.
4 Are you sure you'll get that contract? ~ Yeah, it's in the *packet | bag*.
5 What did you think of the book? ~ Nothing to *write home about | get excited about*.
6 You can say what you like to him. ~ Yeah, it's like water off a duck's *beak | back*.

2 Respond to the questions using idioms from above, and using the information in brackets to guide you.

▶ Did you watch the programme? ~ Yes, I was glued to it. (yes, I was fascinated by it)
1 Do you fancy going to the opera? ~ .... (not the sort of thing you like)
2 Were you disappointed with the result? ~ .... (not at all)
3 Do you think he'll win? ~ .... (he has a possibility of winning)
4 What did you think of the film? ~ .... (not very good at all)
5 Were you upset? ~ .... (yes, I was unfairly treated)
6 Do you think you'll succeed? ~ .... (it'll require a lot of effort)
7 Were you upset by the criticism? ~ .... (you're not affected by it)
8 Will she get the job? ~ .... (yes, it's a certainty)

B Say it another way

Idioms often give you an opportunity to say something in a slightly different way.

Do you fancy a coffee?

I wouldn't say no.

What time are you going? … Danny?

I'm sorry, I **was miles away**.

We'd better **make a move** or we**'ll be pushed to** get there on time.

I asked him if he could help with the arrangements but he **didn't want to know**.

I can't see what else to do, so let's **leave it at that**.

You won some money last time, but I wouldn't **push your luck**.

Dad was **none too pleased** about me borrowing the car.

When we go to the gym, Michael just **does his own thing**.

Glossary

I wouldn't say no	= yes, please.
be miles away	be thinking about sth else.
make a move	leave a place.
be (hard) pushed to do sth	have (a lot of) difficulty in doing sth.
not want to know	refuse to listen or get involved.
leave it at that	do or say nothing more.
push your luck	take more risks than are sensible.
none/not too pleased	annoyed.

spotlight *thing(s)*

Thing(s) occurs in many idioms, e.g.:
He likes to do his own thing. = likes to do what he wants or what interests him.
You must be seeing things. = must be imagining you can see things that aren't there (also **be hearing things**).

---

3 Find a mistake in each sentence. Cross out any unnecessary words, or write the correct words at the end.

▶ If they offered me a free flight, I wouldn't say ~~not~~. *no*

1 I think we'll be hardly pushed to get home by seven o'clock. ....
2 I asked her if we could wait in here, but she didn't want to know it. ....
3 We'd better make a move on, or we'll miss our train. ....
4 Let's give him one more try, then leave it at this. ....
5 He was very helpful last time, but you shouldn't push the luck. ....
6 There's no one at the door; you must hear things. ....

4 Replace the part of the response in italics with an idiom that keeps a similar meaning.

▶ Is she going to open another shop? ~ Maybe, but she's *taking a big risk*. *pushing her luck*

1 What did Pat say? ~ Er … I'm sorry, I was *thinking about something else*. ....
2 Is that a deer outside the window? ~ You must be *imagining it*. ....
3 Shall we try talking to her again? ~ No, let's *say nothing more*. ....
4 Would you like a coffee? ~ Hmm, *that would be nice*. ....
5 Do you want another cup of tea? ~ No, I'd better *go*. ....
6 Does he do the same as the rest? ~ No, he just does *what interests him*. ....
7 How did she react when you told her? ~ She was *annoyed*. ....
8 Can you finish it today? ~ I think *that will be difficult*. ....

50 I can use common spoken responses

A Making positive noises

In the responses below, the main stress falls on the underlined syllable.

I've brought my umbrella. **Just as <u>well</u>**.

Do you mind me coming this early? No, **not in the <u>least</u>**.

Shall we go? Yeah, **ready when <u>you</u> are**.

How's the course going? **So far, so <u>good</u>**.

We could take the train. **<u>That</u>'s an idea**.

Is it a difficult game? No, **there's nothing <u>to</u> it**.

Sorry, I didn't give you the money for my sandwich. It's OK. **Forget <u>it</u>**.

It's a public holiday, so everything will be closed. Mmm, **<u>that</u> figures**.

Has the scheme been a success? Yes, **very <u>much</u> so**.

I've got Friday off. **Lucky <u>you</u>**.

Glossary	
(it's/that's) **just as well**	it is lucky that sth has or hasn't happened, otherwise there would be problems.
not in the least	used to emphasize the answer 'no'. SYN **not at all**.
ready when you are	INF used to tell sb that you are ready to do sth with them whenever they are ready.
so far, so good	INF used to say things have been successful up to now.
that's an idea	INF used to reply in a positive way to a suggestion.
there's nothing to it	INF = it's very easy.
forget it	INF used to tell sb not to worry about sth.
that figures	used to say that sth seems logical and reasonable.
very much so	INF used to emphasize your agreement or approval.
lucky you	INF used to say you think sb is lucky to have or do sth.

1 Match 1–8 with a–h.

1 You must be happy in the new place. ....
2 Will I be able to do it? ....
3 I think we should go. ....
4 Was he worried about it? ....
5 We could buy him a watch. ....
6 I took the laptop out of the car. ....
7 Can I pay you for the tickets? ....
8 How's your French class going? ....

a Ready when you are.
b That's just as well.
c That's an idea.
d So far, so good.
e Yes, very much so.
f No, not in the least.
g Yeah, there's nothing to it.
h No, forget it.

2 Complete the dialogues with a suitable idiom.

1 I'm going to spend a week in the south of France. ~ Wow, ...
2 Do you mind if we work in the library? ~ No, ...
3 If she's coming by bus, she won't be here until six. ~ Yeah, ...
4 Are you getting on OK? ~ Yeah, ...
5 How much do I owe you for the meal? ~ It's OK. ....
6 I'm not sure if I'll be able to use this new software. ~ Don't worry. ....
7 I'll be away for a couple of days, so I've locked the windows. ~ Yeah, ...

B Negative or angry responses

‘ Are you coming for an early morning swim? ~ **No <u>fear</u>**. ’

‘ I don't want to go out with you this evening. ~ **Please your<u>self</u>**. ’

‘ Can I have this chocolate? ~ **Don't you <u>dare</u>**! ’

‘ Michael never thanks people for things. ~ **That's a load of <u>rubbish</u>**! ’

‘ I'm going to the dentist this afternoon. ~ Ooh, **rather you than <u>me</u>**. ’

‘ I want to get tickets for that concert. ~ **<u>You'll</u> be lucky**. ’

‘ You've eaten all the biscuits! ~ **So <u>what</u>?** ’

‘ Marianne? ~ Oh, **<u>now</u> what?** ’

‘ Val says she'll be late. ~ **That's not <u>my</u> problem**. ’

Glossary

no fear	INF used to say that you definitely do not want to do sth. SYN **no way**.
please yourself	INF used to tell sb you are annoyed and do not care what they do.
don't you dare	INF used to tell sb strongly not to do sth.
that's/what a load of rubbish/nonsense	INF, IMPOLITE used to say that you think sth is untrue or stupid.
rather you/him, etc. **than me**	INF used to say that you would not like to do sth that sb else is going to do.
you'll be lucky	INF used to tell sb that what they want probably will not happen.
so what?	INF used to say you think sth is not important, especially after sb has criticized you for it. SYN **what of it?**
now what?	INF used when you are annoyed because sb is always asking you questions or interrupting you. SYN **what is it now?**
that's not my problem	INF = I don't care about sth that is sb else's problem (also **that's his/her**, etc. **problem** = they must solve their own problems.)

3 Circle the correct answer(s). Both answers may be correct.

1 You've put on weight. ~ *So what? | Now what?*
2 I don't want to go. I'd rather stay here. ~ *That's not my problem. | Please yourself.*
3 I'm going to tell Dan you went out with Tony. ~ *No fear. | Don't you dare!*
4 I've got too many things to do. ~ *That's your problem. | That's not my problem.*
5 Minus 10 degrees and I'll be sleeping in a tent tonight! ~ *You'll be lucky. | Rather you than me.*
6 Your English pronunciation sounds funny. ~ *What of it? | So what?*

4 Read what people say to Sam. Write Sam's responses. (Sam is lazy and in a bad temper.)

▶ I don't think I'll come to the concert tonight. ~ Sam:' *Please yourself* !'
1 I'm going to pass all my English exams. ~ Sam:' _____.'
2 Are you going on that ten kilometre walk? ~ Sam:' _____.'
3 Can I finish your drink? ~ Sam:' _____!'
4 Your girlfriend's a lot younger than you. ~ Sam:' _____?'
5 I always forget to set my alarm clock and then I oversleep. ~ Sam:' _____.'
6 I'm going to attend extra English classes. ~ Sam:' _____.'
7 Sam! Sam! Come over here! ~ Sam:' _____?'
8 Everyone says you have a very bad temper. ~ Sam:' _____!'

Formal spoken English

Some idioms are commonly heard in more formal spoken contexts such as parliamentary debates, television and radio broadcasts, ceremonies, lectures, and so on.

With all due respect to the Prime Minister, it is the people of this country who have, **in large part**, suffered **at the hands of** his government, and I am sure they will want to **take issue with** his last remark.

Thousands of people gathered to **pay their respects to** the many local servicemen who **laid down their lives for** their country.

Terrorists still **hold sway** in many of the rural areas and **therein lies** the problem. They have already **laid waste to** much valuable farmland, and we could be facing yet another drought. Any hopes that this awful situation might **be at an end** look premature.

James Maplin's groundbreaking research not only **gave rise to** his highly esteemed books and **set the seal on** a glittering academic career, it also put us **on the threshold of** a major breakthrough in the treatment of Parkinson's Disease. I now **have the honour of** introducing Professor Maplin …

I would like to **pay tribute to** the young police officer who, **paying no heed to** his own safety, went to the help of our daughter and saved her from certain death. It was an act of considerable bravery, way **beyond the call of duty**, and we will forever **be in his debt**.

Glossary

with (all due) respect (to sb)	used as a polite formula when you are going to disagree with sb.
in large part	to a great extent. SYN **in large measure**.
at the hands of sb	because of sb's actions (*they suffered/died* **at his hands**).
take issue with sth/sb (over/about sth)	start disagreeing or arguing with sb about sth.
pay your respects (to sb)	show your respect for sb by visiting them, going to their funeral, attending a memorial service, etc.
lay down your life (for sb/sth)	die in order to protect or save sb/sth.
hold sway	have power or influence over a group of people or a region.
therein lies sth	used to indicate the result or consequence of a situation or an action.
lay waste to sth	completely destroy a place or area.
be at an end	If sth **is at an end**, it has finished.
give rise to sth	cause sth to happen or exist.
set the seal on sth	make sth definite or complete.
on the threshold of sth	at the beginning of sth.
have the honour of doing sth	be given the opportunity of doing sth that makes you feel proud.
pay tribute to sb	say or do sth to show your respect and admiration for sb.
pay heed to sb/sth	give careful attention to sb/sth (**pay no heed to sb/sth** give no attention to sb/sth).
beyond the call of duty	(of an action) performed with greater courage or effort than is usual or expected.
be in sb's debt	feel grateful to sb for their help, kindness, etc. (also **be in debt to sb**).

1 Match 1–8 with a–h.

1	have	a	rise to something
2	pay	b	the seal on something
3	take	c	waste to something
4	give	d	the honour of doing something
5	hold	e	tribute to somebody
6	set	f	issue with somebody
7	lay down	g	sway
8	lay	h	your life for something

2 The same word is missing in each pair of sentences. What is it?

1 a Many have suffered .... the hands of the militia.
  b The fighting could be .... an end.
2 a The two young men came and .... their respects to their father.
  b Carl .... no heed to the warnings he had received.
3 a Thousands .... down their lives.
  b The army .... waste to large parts of the territory.
4 a I would like to take issue .... your comments about local residents.
  b .... respect, sir, I don't believe your suggestion will be acceptable.
5 a We were very much .... their debt for their help in winning the election.
  b Humans are .... large part responsible for the global warming crisis.

3 Which word is missing in each definition?

1 If you *lay waste to* something, you .... it.
2 If you are *on the threshold of* something, you are at the .... of something.
3 We use *with all due respect* when we are going to .... with someone.
4 If something *gives rise to* something, it causes it to ....
5 If you *take issue with* somebody, you .... with them.
6 If you *have the honour of* doing something, you have the opportunity to do something which makes you feel ....

4 Replace the words in italics with a more formal idiom that has a similar meaning.

▶ She *showed her admiration for* him in her farewell speech. paid tribute to ....
1 We could be *at the beginning* of a new era. ....
2 Many people have suffered *because of* the rebels. ....
3 The army still *has power* over much of the country. ....
4 Dr Ellis *took no notice of* the calls for his resignation. ....
5 The disease spread *to a great extent* because of poverty. ....
6 So many soldiers *died* in the two world wars. ....
7 I will always *feel grateful to him*. ....
8 They *damaged or destroyed* large areas of the town. ....
9 That is where I *disagree* with the council leader. ....
10 The fireman's bravery was *more than we should expect of anyone*. ....

5 Complete the texts.

‘With all due (1) ...., this is where I take (2) .... with the Prime Minister because this government has not taken any decisive action, and therein (3) .... the problem. It was the government's failure to control lending which gave (4) .... to this crisis in the first place, and now the Prime Minister calmly tells us that our problems could be at an (5) .... What nonsense!’

The brigade gathered to pay their (6) .... to the officer who (7) .... down his life in order to save the lives of others. One soldier who survived as a result of the officer's gallantry paid this special (8) .... to Corporal Ben Williams. 'I had the (9) .... of serving under Corporal Williams, and for those of us who are here today, in large (10) .... because of his bravery, we salute you.'

52 I can use idioms in a legal context

A Reporting a court case

Idioms commonly found in a legal context tend to be more formal.

RADIO REPORT Mr Ryan, **of no fixed abode**, appeared before magistrates having been charged with **breach of the peace**. **Under oath**, Mr Ryan denied that he had been causing a disturbance or that he had attempted to attack …

WITNESS STATEMENT On the day **in question** I encountered Mr Ryan at the entrance to the supermarket. He was clearly **under the influence** and was being abusive, so I **took the liberty of** trying to move him. He did **not take kindly to** this, and started to punch me. However, **by virtue of** my size, and being sober, I was able to restrain him.

POLICE STATEMENT We are now working **in conjunction with** the council to reduce drinking in public places, but are not yet **at liberty to** say precisely what steps will …

Glossary

of no fixed abode	FML = having no permanent home.
breach of the peace	LEGAL the crime of noisy or violent behaviour in a public place.
under/on oath	LEGAL having made a formal promise to tell the truth in a court of law.
in question	FML The **day**, **man**, etc. **in question** is the day, man, etc. being discussed (in this case the day of the alleged crime).
under the influence	having had too much alcohol.
take the liberty of doing sth	FML do sth without permission.
not take kindly to sth/sb	FML find it difficult to accept sth/sb because they annoy you.
by virtue of sth	FML because of sth; as a result of sth.
in conjunction with sb/sth	FML together with sb/sth.
at liberty (to do sth)	FML having permission to do sth.

1 Paraphrase the phrases in italics in more everyday English. Look at the example first.

▶ What does it mean, *he didn't take kindly to it?* It means he was very annoyed by it.
1 What do they mean, *he was of no fixed abode?* ....
2 What did he mean by *under the influence?* ....
3 What's meant by speaking *under oath?* ....
4 What did she mean, *by virtue of her experience?* ....
5 What's *breach of the peace?* ....
6 What does he mean, *he's not at liberty to tell us?* ....

2 Complete the sentences.

1 He's been found guilty of .... of the peace.
2 If you drive while under the ...., you could get into trouble.
3 The authorities did not take .... to my criticism.
4 The newspaper is not at .... to publish the names before the trial.
5 If you give evidence in a court of law, remember that you are under ....
6 The official wasn't there, so I .... the liberty of consulting the prisoner's notes.
7 They are funding the development in .... with the local council.
8 On the day in ...., I didn't see the two men leave the house.

B Read the small print

Fairfax vindicated in court decision

In his **summing-up**, the local magistrate acknowledged that Fairfax Ltd may have violated **the spirit of the law**, but they had acted fully **in accordance with the letter of the law**. He said that although Mrs Wilson refused to pay the money demanded by Fairfax Ltd **in good faith**, she had **entered into** an agreement with the company **of her own free will**, and must **abide by** it. Sadly, it was her failure to read **the small print** in that agreement which **had been her undoing**. He therefore ruled that Fairfax Ltd had not tried to obtain money **under false pretences**, and were entitled to claim what rightfully belonged to them.

Glossary	
summing-up	LEGAL a statement made by a judge, magistrate, or lawyer that gives a summary of the evidence in a court. **sum up** v.
in accordance with sth	FML in a way that follows a rule or sb's wishes.
in good faith	believing that what you are doing is right.
enter into sth	FML take part in a formal arrangement, activity, or discussion.
of your own free will	freely and willingly and not in response to force.
abide by sth	obey a rule, decision, instruction, etc.
the small print	the details of sth, often in a contract, that are written in small letters and may include conditions that limit your rights.
be sb's undoing	be the cause of sb's failure.
under false pretences	If you do or get sth **under false pretences**, you do or get it by tricking or deceiving people.

spotlight The law

The spirit of the law is the real meaning or intention of a law, even if the way it is written does not express this. **The letter of the law** is the exact words that are used in a law rather than its general meaning.

3 Complete the sentences.

1 He followed the letter of the law, but I believe it was against the .... of the law.
2 If you .... into an agreement with someone, you have to .... by it.
3 When you are signing a contract, it is very important to read the .... print.
4 The burglar left fingerprints at the scene of the crime; that was his ....
5 Mary had no idea the document was a forgery; she signed it in good ....
6 He can't complain; he went there of his own free ....
7 The judge will .... up the evidence tomorrow in court.
8 It is claimed the man obtained the money under false ....

4 Paraphrase the sentences on the left using more formal or legal language. Start with the words given.

▶ It was the reason why he failed.   It was *his undoing* ....
1 He wanted to do it; no one made him.   He did it of ....
2 She did exactly what the law says.   She followed the ....
3 He got the money by tricking her.   He got the money under ....
4 He did exactly what Mrs Hart wished.   He acted in ....
5 The judge explained when going over the evidence.   The judge explained in his ....
6 Miles did it because he thought it was right.   Miles did it in ....
7 I wish I hadn't taken part in the discussion.   I wish I hadn't ....
8 They promised to obey the rules.   They promised to ....

53 I can use more formal prepositional verbs

The majority of phrasal verbs are either neutral or informal in style. A small number of prepositional verbs, however, range from neutral to formal, and are used more commonly in written English or more formal spoken English. In most cases, this is because the base verb is more formal, e.g. *allude*, *engage*, etc.

If multinational companies **adhere to** the European Court's decision, they may have to **dispose of** assets which will **deprive** them **of** significant sources of income.

Britain is having to **contend with** an ageing population, the implications of which could **impinge upon** almost all of us in one way or another over the next 20 to 30 years.

In the past the company **prided itself on** being a major employer in the area, but last week it reluctantly agreed to **dispense with the services of** three of its regional managers.

Banks are **resigning themselves to** the fact that they will **be subjected to** much closer scrutiny if the government **embarks upon** its plan of tighter financial regulation.

Jonathan Brannon's solicitor **alluded to** the fact that he and his ex-wife **were** still **engaged in** a dispute over the ownership of their former home.

A spokesperson said he did not **subscribe to** the view that the club's action **had amounted to** unfair dismissal.

Glossary

adhere to sth	obey a law, rule, agreement, etc. SYN **abide by sth**.
dispose of sth/sb	get rid of sth that you no longer want or cannot keep.
deprive sb of sth	prevent sb from having, using, or doing sth.
contend with sth	have to deal with a problem or difficult situation.
impinge on/upon sb/sth	have an effect on sb/sth, usually in a negative way. SYN **impact on sb/sth**.
pride yourself on sth/on doing sth	be proud of sth / doing sth.
dispense with sb's services	stop employing sb or dismiss sb from their job.
resign yourself to sth	accept sth unpleasant that cannot be changed or avoided.
subject sb to sth	(often passive) make sb suffer or experience sth unpleasant.
embark on/upon sth	start to do sth new or difficult.
allude to sth	refer to sth indirectly.
be engaged in sth	take part in sth; be involved in sth (also **engage in sth**).
subscribe to sth	agree with an idea, opinion, or theory.
amount to sth	be the same as or equal to something else.

spotlight verb + *on/upon*

The choice between *on* and *upon*, e.g. *embark* **on/upon**, is often one of style: *upon* is generally more formal than *on*. Other examples include:

She wouldn't *enlarge on/upon* her remarks. = say more about them.

He *called on/upon* the government for more support. = asked the government.

They didn't wish to *dwell on/upon* the consequences. = spend time thinking about something difficult or unpleasant.

1 Choose the most suitable ending (a–h) for each of the sentence beginnings (1–8).

1 They have dispensed with ....
2 You must abide by ....
3 I don't subscribe to ....
4 They were deprived of ....
5 She's about to embark on ....
6 There are risks in disposing of ....
7 We had to contend with ....
8 They have called on ....

a food and water.
b a number of problems.
c nuclear waste.
d her services.
e the terms of the contract.
f other countries for assistance.
g that theory.
h a new career.

2 A preposition is missing in each sentence. Where does it go? Write it at the end.

▶ The suggested changes will not impinge greatly ⟨ people's lives. *on* ....
1 I don't subscribe that point of view at all. ....
2 When are they aiming to embark the new project? ....
3 They were deprived even the most basic essentials. ....
4 We had to contend sub-zero temperatures. ....
5 My mother prides herself her cooking. ....
6 Even without interest, the repayments amount a large sum of money. ....
7 Are they still engaged discussions? ....
8 After the death of her husband, Martha resigned herself a lonely existence. ....

3 Complete the sentences with verbs from the box in the correct form.

subject resign deprive dispose amount impinge adhere engage

1 If you put the plants in that corner, they will be .... of light.
2 Investors have .... themselves to the fact that profits have fallen in value.
3 When the animal dies, the vet will .... of the body.
4 Many of the prisoners were .... to torture.
5 I've been .... in a lengthy dispute with the tax office.
6 Whether he resigned or was sacked, it .... to the same thing.
7 Any cuts in this department will .... upon the rest of the organization.
8 Competitors must .... to the rules, otherwise they will be disqualified.

4 Replace the parts of the sentences in italics with a more formal prepositional verb that keeps a similar meaning.

▶ The people have *had to do without* basic human rights. *been deprived of* ....
1 I asked her to *say a bit more about* her theory. ....
2 I have never *held* the view that punishment is an effective deterrent. ....
3 The court has called upon member states to *stick with* their decision. ....
4 We may have to *deal with* uncompromising attitudes on both sides. ....
5 The managers are going to *get rid of* some clerical staff. ....
6 Let's not *think any more about* past problems. ....
7 His decision to resign *is the same thing as* an admission of failure. ....
8 The group *are proud of* their attention to detail. ....

5 Rewrite the sentences on the left using a more formal prepositional verb.

▶ Let's not think about this any more.   Let's not *dwell on this* .
1 We no longer need these old files.   We can ....
2 It won't have an effect on my decision   It won't ....
3 He had to go through a tough interview.   He was ....
4 She's proud of her loyalty.   She ....
5 Will they do what is stated in the rules?   Will they .... ?
6 She mentioned your comments indirectly.   She ....

FOR SALE £1500 **o.n.o.**

Situations Vacant

|This area is strictly **out of bounds**|

Lyncombe Road, 3-bed house, **UNDER OFFER**

> The policyholder must notify us **in the event of** any change in occupancy. Upon receipt of this notice we **reserve the right to** amend the terms and conditions of this insurance.

Students will only receive a discount **on production of** a valid ID card.

There is no service charge and tipping is **at** your **discretion**.

We look forward to hearing from you **at your earliest convenience**.

To whom it may concern
I have known Margaret Bond for over ten years, and in that time she …

KEEP YOUR DISTANCE

Glossary

for sale	available for sb to buy; **o.n.o./ono** = or nearest offer.
situations vacant	the title of a section in a newspaper where jobs are advertised.
out of bounds	If a place is **out of bounds**, you are not allowed to go there.
under offer	If a house is **under offer**, sb has agreed to buy it.
in the event of sth	= if sth happens.
reserve the right to do sth	= make use of a formal right to do sth if necessary.
on production of sth	when you show sth.
at sb's discretion	according to what sb decides or wishes to do.
at your earliest convenience	FML = at the earliest suitable time for you.
To whom it may concern	FML used at the beginning of a notice or document (e.g. a personal reference) when it is not addressed to a particular person.
keep your distance	make sure you are not too near sb/sth.

1 **Complete the sentences.**

1 Please notify your local authority in the .... of any change in your circumstances.
2 The management reserves the .... to refuse admission.
3 Passengers will only be allowed on the platform on .... of a valid ticket.
4 You can't go in there. The sign clearly says 'out of .... !'
5 .... sale: 2008 Ford Mondeo, in excellent condition. £4,000 ono.
6 We look forward to hearing from you at your earliest ....
7 I believe the apartment for sale is now .... offer.
8 Bail is granted at the .... of the court.

2 **Cover the glossary and answer the questions.**

1 What does 'o.n.o.' mean? ....
2 What might be 'under offer', and what does it mean? ....
3 What kind of thing would you find under 'situations vacant'? ....
4 What would you find written under 'to whom it may concern'? ....
5 What might be 'at your discretion' in a café or restaurant? ....
6 Where would you see a 'keep your distance' sign? ....

Review: Styles of language

Unit 49

1   **Complete the answers to the questions below using idioms from the table. You can move horizontally or vertically, backwards or forwards.**

I	I	WAS	MILES	THING
WOULDN'T	SAY	NO	AWAY	OWN ↑
IT'S	IN	HE'S	DO ⟶	HER ↑
NONE	THE	GLUED	LEAVE	IT
TOO	BAG	TO	IT	AT
PLEASED	FAR	FROM	IT	THAT

▶ Would she like to come on a walk? ~ No, she'd rather *do her own thing* .
1   Is he enjoying the film? ~ Yes, .
2   Would you like a sandwich or something? ~ Hmm, .
3   What happened when she saw the mess? ~ Well, she was .
4   Are you sure you've got the job? ~ Yeah, .
5   I think that's the best we can do. ~ Fine, let's .
6   So, what do you think we should do? ~ Pardon? Oh, sorry, .
7   Did she accept that she was wrong? ~ No, .

2   **Match the opposites.**

▶ He's decided to stay here. OPP *f*
1   He said it was really exciting. OPP
2   He loves doing it. OPP
3   He's unlikely to succeed. OPP
4   He won't take risks. OPP
5   He'll find it easy. OPP
6   He joins in with the crowd. OPP
7   He listened carefully. OPP

a   He pushes his luck all the time.
b   He didn't want to know.
c   He does his own thing.
d   He'll be hard pushed to do it.
e   He's in with a chance.
f   He's going to make a move. ✓
g   He said it's nothing to write home about.
h   It's not his idea of fun.

Unit 50

1   **Tick the correct stimulus from speaker A to match the response from speaker B.**

1   A   *I'm going to clean out the dustbin.* ☐ *I'm going out for dinner.* ☐
    B   Rather you than me.
2   A   *I've won some money on the lottery.* ☐ *I hope I win the lottery.* ☐
    B   You'll be lucky.
3   A   *Are you frightened of the dark?* ☐ *Are you going out in the dark?* ☐
    B   No fear.
4   A   *How's the new job?* ☐ *Is it far to the office?* ☐
    B   So far, so good.
5   A   *Is the new restaurant nice?* ☐ *Is the climb very difficult?* ☐
    B   No, there's nothing to it.
6   A   *Would you like a coffee?* ☐ *Is it OK if I don't come with you tonight?* ☐
    B   Please yourself.
7   A   *Did you enjoy the film?* ☐ *What did you think of the film?* ☐
    B   Very much so.

2 Correct one mistake in each dialogue.

1 Can I take the car tonight? ~ You don't dare! ....
2 Shall we make a move? ~ Ready as you are. ....
3 They say the club's going to close down. ~ What's a load of rubbish! ....
4 I've bought some extra food for tonight. ~ Just so well; Maki and Lita are coming. ....
5 It's after 6.00 – he must have gone home. ~ Yeah, this figures. ....
6 I've got to tell Martin I don't want to see him again. ~ Rather you or me. ....

Unit 51

1 Rewrite the sentences on the left using a more formal phrase.

▶ The fault lies to a great extent with the boss.   The fault lies in *large part with the boss* .
1 We're at the beginning of a new era.   We're on ....
2 He didn't listen to my advice.   He paid ....
3 They died for their country.   They laid ....
4 I'm sorry but I have to disagree with you.   With all ....
5 The soldiers completely destroyed the town.   The soldiers laid ....
6 She showed a huge amount of courage.   She went beyond ....

2 Put the words in order and add one word.

▶ disagree | due | you | with | all | I | with *With all due respect, I disagree with you.*
1 to | our | widow | we | respects | the ....
2 further | to | could | rise | problems | delays ....
3 over | issue | expenses | I | took | her | the | claim ....
4 died | soldiers | to | he | had | tribute | the | who ....
5 meeting | honour | President | we | the | of | the ....
6 government | hands | has | the | of | suffered | country | the | this ....

Unit 52

1 Complete the crossword. The letters in the grey squares spell out a phrase. What is it, and what does it mean?

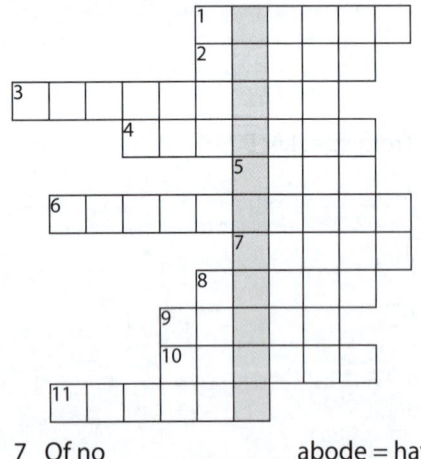

1 Not take .... to something = not want to accept a situation because it annoys you.
2 .... into an agreement = take part in an official agreement.
3 A .... = a statement in court, given by a judge, magistrate, or lawyer, which provides a shortened version of the evidence.
4 Your .... = the thing that causes you to fail at something.
5 Under .... = having made a formal promise to a court of law to tell the truth.
6 In .... with someone's wishes = in a way that fulfils someone's wishes.

7 Of no .... abode = having nowhere permanent to live.
8 Under .... pretences = by tricking or deceiving someone.
9 The small .... = the details in a document which affect your rights.
10 Follow the .... of the law = interpret the law very literally and follow its precise wording.
11 .... of the peace = noisy or violent behaviour in a public place.

The phrase in the grey squares is ....

Unit 53

1 Put the dominoes in the correct order to make a joined sequence of idioms. Write the correct order of dominoes below.

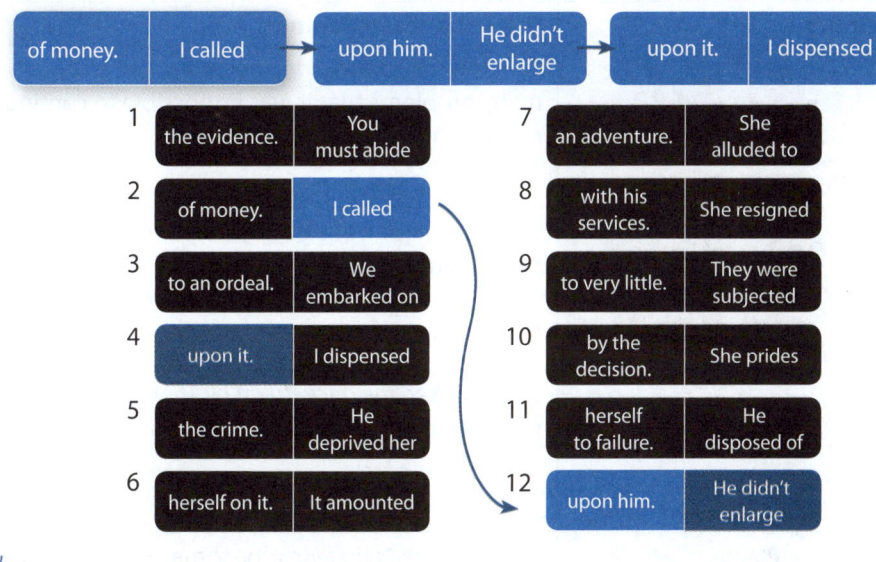

2 , 12 , 4 , ... , ... , ... , ... , ... , ... , ... , ... , ...

2 Circle the correct word. In some sentences both words may be correct.

1 The results were terrible, but they decided not to *dwell* / *impinge* on them for long.
2 Mr Ellis *referred* / *alluded* to the crime in a very roundabout way, but he refused to *enlarge* / *call* upon it.
3 Many local people have *contended* / *resigned* themselves to a second-rate rubbish collection service, and furthermore have to *dispense* / *contend* with litter in the streets for weeks on end.
4 Rankin was *deprived* / *disposed* of his freedom, but he still *took part* / *engaged* in illegal activities.
5 We *call* / *embark* upon the government to *adhere* / *abide* to the agreed regulations.

Unit 54

1 True or false? Write T or F. If the meaning is false, write the true meaning.

Phrase	Meaning?	T/F	True meaning
▶ in the event of fire	= when you are building a fire	F	*if a fire happens / if there is a fire*
1 situations vacant	= empty accommodation		
2 at your discretion	= according to the law		
3 to whom it may concern	heading seen on a personal reference for a job		
4 out of bounds	= out of control		
5 O.N.O.	= or new offer		
6 at your earliest convenience	= as soon as you are able to do something		
7 keep your distance	= stay close to something		

Literal meaning	Metaphorical meanings
*The book's **falling apart**.*	*Things went downhill and her marriage **fell apart**.* = had so many problems that it was impossible to continue existing (a relationship / sb's world **falls apart**).
*This lift **is going down**.*	*Their standards **have gone down** in recent months.* = become worse in quality. *The computer system **has gone down**.* = stopped working temporarily.
*The building **is being knocked down**.*	*She **knocked** the price **down** by 15 per cent.* INF = reduced the price by 15 per cent. **knockdown** ADJ (**knockdown** prices).
*Goats **feed on** grain and grasses.*	*Terrorism **feeds on** fear.* = becomes stronger because of fear. (**feed on sth** is often DISAPPROVING.)
*I **soaked** it **up** with a sponge.*	*We wandered around, **soaking up** the atmosphere.* = absorbing it into our senses, body, and mind (**soak up** the sun).
*The water **spilled over**.*	*The violence could **spill over** into neighbouring areas.* = spread and begin to affect other areas. *His emotions **spilled over** after his big win.* = he was unable to control his emotions.
Mind the... ***Stand back** from the platform edge.*	*You should **stand back** and consider your future.* = think about it as if you are not involved in it.
*You need to **tighten up** the screws.*	*Airlines need to **tighten up** rules on baggage allowance.* = make rules stricter or harder to avoid.
*Turn the clock **around/round**.*	*They **turned** the failing company **round**.* = made it successful again. *They can **turn** repairs **around** in a few days.* = complete them in a few days.
*She **wrapped** it **up** for me.*	*The police have **wrapped up** the enquiry.* = INF completed the enquiry (also **wrap up** a meeting / a deal).

1 Tick the sentences which refer to a physical action.

1 If you go to the market late, they usually knock things down by quite a lot. ☐
2 I hardly touched the bookshelf, but it just fell apart. ☐
3 Turn it round so that we can't see the label on it. ☐
4 I think that just about wraps up the meeting for today. See you tomorrow. ☐
5 Stand back and let these people go by. ☐
6 The oil was everywhere, but they tried to soak it up with a cloth. ☐
7 I'm afraid I can't answer your query right now; the computer's just gone down. ☐
8 I was boiling the milk and forgot about it. It spilled over and made a terrible mess. ☐

2 The same word is missing in each pair of sentences. Write it in.

1 a These rules need to be _____ up.
   b Once the screws are _____ up, it'll be safe.
2 a The computer system suddenly _____ down yesterday.
   b After Mr Austin left, standards at the company really _____ down.
3 a Trouble _____ over into the next region.
   b Her emotions _____ over and she broke down in tears.
4 a I managed to knock them _____ to €150, which was great.
   b The lift was going _____ when it suddenly stopped.
5 a Do you think they'll be able to _____ the firm around?
   b They work very fast; they can _____ around a big repair in 24 hours.
6 a The police decided to wrap _____ the investigation.
   b Wander around and just soak _____ the atmosphere of the town.
7 a What exactly do baby fish _____ on?
   b Current government policies _____ on fear of the recession.

3 Write sentences using words from each column.

Let's tighten	back	the regulations
The standard's gone	down	and think about it
They knocked	apart	the shopping centre
Just stand	on	since she lost her job
Her life has fallen	up	in recent years
The towel soaked	up	insects
They feed	down	the moisture

4 Complete the Words of Wisdom with a suitable phrasal verb.

🍃 Words of Wisdom 🍃

• 'When you are confused about life, (1) _____ and reflect on your past.'

• 'When you are really tense, go outside, (2) _____ the sun and meditate for a while.'

• 'If your relationship is (3) _____ , you both need to seek advice from an expert.'

• 'To (4) _____ a failing business _____ , you often need to change the person in charge.'

• 'Jealousy (5) _____ insecurity. Don't let yourself worry; be open with your partner.'

• 'Poor sleep at night can mean that the previous day's problems (6) _____ to the next.'

• 'When money is short, standards tend to (7) _____ in business. Don't let this happen.'

5 ABOUT YOU Look at the Words of Wisdom in Exercise 4. Do you agree or disagree with them? Write your answers in your notebook giving your reasons, or talk to another student.

56 I can use idiomatic noun phrases

A Bad news stories

Dictionaries may show these noun phrases as idioms or as separate entries, e.g. *lame duck* may be entered as a noun (**lame duck**), or an idiom at the entry for **lame**.

> … The mayor claims that the row over his financial dealings is **a storm in a teacup**, and that he has been a victim of **a hatchet job** in the Daily Globe. He strongly denies any **conflict of interest** between his political role and his business dealings, though many are pointing **the finger of suspicion** in his direction …

> … While the academic books department of the company is not yet **a lost cause**, sharply falling sales are a big concern. The company has recently spent €50,000 to give them **a fighting chance** of survival, but that is **a drop in the ocean** compared to what is needed …

> … Plans to use part of **the green belt** for a new bypass have been **a** political **hot potato** for many years, and with the current council leader virtually **a lame duck**, this may not be the right time to pursue them.

Glossary

a storm in a teacup	a lot of anger or worry about sth that is not important (also **a fuss about nothing**).
a hatchet job (**on sb/sth**)	INF a strong written attack on sb or their work.
a conflict of interest	a situation in which sb has two different jobs or roles, and this may affect their ability to choose or act fairly in either.
the finger of suspicion	If **the finger of suspicion** is pointing at sb, they are suspected of committing a crime or being responsible for sth bad.
a lost cause	sth that has no chance of succeeding.
a fighting chance	a chance to achieve sth if you work very hard at it.
a drop in the ocean	a very small amount that will have little or no effect.
the green belt	an area of protected land around a city where building is not allowed.
a hot potato	an issue that causes angry debate and is difficult to deal with.
a lame duck	a person who is no longer successful or effective in a particular role.

1 Is the meaning similar or different? Write S or D.

1	The project can never succeed now.	The project's a lost cause.	......
2	The row's just a storm in a teacup.	The row's just a lot of fuss about nothing.	......
3	He wants to build on the green belt.	He wants to build on the park near the town centre.	......
4	The offer was a drop in the ocean.	The offer hardly made any difference.	......
5	The article was a hatchet job.	The article was very complimentary.	......
6	There's no conflict of interest there.	There was no fighting there.	......

2 Complete the dialogues. You will need more than one word.

► They're not allowed to build on that open space. ~ No, it's in the green belt .

1 I've a strong feeling that he's guilty. ~ Yeah, ... is pointing at him.

2 I think they just might succeed. ~ I agree, they've got ....

3 Nobody wants to tackle the budget problems. ~ Yes, it's a bit of ....

4 $10,000 won't help the company at all. ~ No, it won't, it's just ....

5 She's a politician but also has shares in the firm. ~ Yeah, I think there's ....

6 The prime minister's hopeless and he'll lose the election. ~Yes, he's ....

7 They're getting upset about nothing. ~ I know. It's just ....

8 There's no hope that the business will recover. ~ No, sadly it's ....

B Better news stories

Inspection gives financial service industry **a clean bill of health**

NEW TENNIS CLUB GETS NADAL'S **SEAL OF APPROVAL**

Car rally hailed **a roaring success**

NEW CHILDREN'S CENTRE WILL PROVIDE '**A HEAD START** IN LIFE'

Cricket win is **a shot in the arm** for New Zealand

Trade in endangered species '**a thing of the past**'

Working mothers can achieve **a happy medium**

Audiences wowed by **thrills and spills** of Winter Olympics

U-TURN ON IMMIGRATION POLICY

Glossary

a clean bill of health	a statement that sb is healthy or that an organization is operating correctly or is in good condition.
a/the seal of approval	a statement that gives a positive opinion of sth that sb has done.
a roaring success	an event or project that is extremely successful.
a head start	an advantage that helps you to be successful.
a shot in the arm	sth that quickly gives you more energy, confidence, etc.
a thing of the past	a thing that no longer exists or happens.
a/the happy medium	a way of doing sth that is between two extreme positions or is satisfactory to everyone.
thrills and spills	INF an exciting mix of dangerous activities.
a U-turn	a sudden or complete change of policy or opinion. SYN **a volte-face**.

spotlight French phrases

Many French phrases, e.g. **a volte-face**, are used in English. **A coup d'état** is the sudden overthrow of a government by force or by revolution. **A faux pas** is an embarrassing mistake.

3 Match 1–8 with a–h.

1 The plan will give the company a shot ....
2 The race had all the thrills and ....
3 You have to find a happy ....
4 Some say that loyalty at work is a thing ....
5 The business has been given a clean ....
6 The children were given a head ....
7 They did a complete volte- ....
8 The boss gave our plan the seal ....

a of the past.
b start by having private lessons.
c of approval, so we start next week.
d face and began to oppose the war.
e in the arm which will improve profits.
f medium between work and play.
g spills we expected.
h bill of health.

4 Put the words in order and add one word.

▶ fair | the | spills | of | the | and | enjoy   *Enjoy the thrills and spills of the fair* .
1 roaring | birthday | the | was | party | a   .
2 on | turn | did | the | policy | government | a | the   .
3 a | find | he's | to | medium | trying   ?
4 bill | get | hope | to | health | we | a | of   .
5 in | a | has | there | been | d'état | Birania   .
6 shot | a | the | company | our | needs | in   .
7 interview | at | terrible | made | the | I | a | faux   .
8 the | of | letter-writing | is | past | a   ?

C Colours

Do you know your colour idioms?

Are you **the black sheep of the family**?

Would you be happy if you had **green fingers**? Why / why not?

If you were given **the red-carpet** treatment, would you be pleased?

Have you ever had **a black eye**? How come?

Do you enjoy dealing with **red tape**?

Is it ever justifiable to tell **white lies**?

If you ended up with **a white elephant**, what could you do with it?

What would be **a golden opportunity** for you?

Have you ever bought anything on **the black market**?

Glossary

the black sheep (**of the family**)	a person who is different from the rest of the family and who is considered bad or embarrassing.
green fingers	A person with **green fingers** is good at making plants grow.
the red carpet	a very special welcome given to an important visitor (*the red-carpet treatment*; *put out* **the red carpet**).
a black eye	a bruise around your eye caused by an accident or sb hitting you.
red tape	official rules or procedures that seem unnecessary and cause delays.
a white lie	a lie told to avoid making sb else upset.
a white elephant	a thing that is completely useless or no longer needed, and may have cost a lot of money.
a golden opportunity	a specially good chance to do sth. (**The chance of a lifetime** is the opportunity to do sth that you will not be able to do again.)
the black market	the illegal buying and selling of goods or currency that are officially controlled and hard to obtain.

5 Are the colours correct? Change any that are wrong.

▶ the ~~white~~ market *black*

1 a gold opportunity ....
2 a black lie ....
3 the red carpet treatment ....
4 a blue eye ....
5 a pink elephant ....
6 the black sheep of the family ....
7 brown fingers ....
8 red tape ....

6 Complete the sentences with a colour idiom.

1 He didn't buy the TV legally. I think he got it on ....
2 I walked into a door, and the next morning I had ....
3 When my long-lost brother came to visit, we put out ....
4 She grows these vegetables herself; she's got ....
5 He's been given a round-the-world ticket – it's ....
6 They built a new shopping centre but no one goes there; it's just ....
7 We never talk about my cousin Donald. He's ....

7 ABOUT YOU Write your answers to the questions at the top of the page in your notebook, or talk to another student.

57 I can use prepositional idioms

A Book titles

On the Scrapheap
The lost generation of miners

IN THE NICK OF TIME
A daring adventure on Everest

Under One Roof
Families in the crowded inner city

Behind Closed Doors
How big business really works

From the Horse's Mouth
Testimonies of wartime courage

Out of the Ordinary
Children with special talents

Within your Rights
A guide to workplace legislation

Computing Essentials **in Plain English**

Good Health Guide
Answers **at your fingertips**

Strictly **by the Book**
A parent's guide to child-rearing

Glossary

on the scrapheap	INF If sb/sth is **on the scrapheap**, they are no longer wanted or useful.
in the nick of time	INF just in time to prevent sth bad from happening.
under one roof	in the same home. SYN **under the same roof**.
behind closed doors	without the public knowing what is happening.
(straight) from the horse's mouth	INF Information coming **from the horse's mouth** comes from sb who is directly involved.
out of the ordinary	unusual or different.
(be) within your rights	(have or) having the moral or legal authority to do sth.
in plain English	simply and clearly expressed.
at your fingertips	near you or available for you to use immediately.
by the book	If you do sth **by the book**, you follow rules and instructions in a strict way.

1 **Is the meaning the same or different? Write S or D.**

1 He told me what happened himself.   I heard about it from the horse's mouth.   ....

2 Something unusual happened.   Nothing out of the ordinary happened.   ....

3 What happened in private?   What happened behind closed doors?   ....

4 She's within her rights to do that.   She's right to do that.   ....

5 It needs to be written in plain English.   It needs to be written in correct English.   ....

6 We got out in the nick of time.   We got out in no time at all.   ....

2 **Rewrite the sentences using the word in capitals. Keep a similar meaning.**

▶ The enquiry was held in private. DOORS _The enquiry was held behind closed doors._

1 I haven't got the facts readily available. FINGERTIPS ....

2 I didn't see anything unusual. ORDINARY ....

3 We do everything in the correct way. BOOK ....

4 We arrived at the very last minute. TIME ....

5 Twelve people are living together in the flat. ROOF ....

6 Hundreds of workers will lose their jobs. SCRAPHEAP ....

7 You have the authority to claim for this. RIGHTS ....

8 She expressed the ideas clearly and simply. PLAIN ....

B A conversation

JO   Has Helmut seen anything of Katrina recently?

JIM   Well, apparently she rang him **out of the blue** the other day, hoping he was free for dinner. And in fact, he was **at a loose end**, but he told her he was **up to his eyes in** work.

JO   Very wise. So did she want to meet up **for old times' sake**, do you think?

JIM   **In all probability**, yeah. But **between you and me**, I think he'd be **off his head** to go back to her.

JO   Too right. That relationship was a disaster **right from the outset**. And **in his heart of hearts**, he knows that.

Glossary

out of the blue	unexpectedly; without warning.
at a loose end	having nothing particular to do.
up to your eyes in sth	INF having a lot of sth to do or deal with.
for old times' sake	so that you can remember a happy time in the past.
in all probability	= it is very likely.
between you and me	used when you are telling sb sth that you do not want anyone else to know. SYN **between ourselves**.
(right) from/at the outset	from/at the very beginning. SYN **(right) from/at the word go** INF.
in your heart (of hearts)	used for talking about true or secret feelings.

spotlight Phrases with *head*

You must be off your head. INF = crazy. SYN **out of your mind** INF.
The talk went over my head. = was too difficult for me to understand.
I was covered from head to toe *in dust.* = all over my body.

3 Complete the phrases with the correct prepositions.

1 .... all probability
2 .... you and me / .... ourselves
3 .... your mind / .... your head
4 .... head .... toe
5 .... a loose end
6 .... the outset / .... the word go

4 Complete the sentences using the phrases from Exercise 3.

1 You paid €100 for that shirt? You must be .... !
2 I got caught in a thunderstorm and I was completely soaked ....
3 Why don't you come over this evening, if you're ....
4 I would say that ...., we should be home before the weekend.
5 He thinks he's got the job, but ...., his chances are slim.
6 It was clear .... that the idea wasn't going to work.

5 ABOUT YOU Complete the questions. Then write your answers to the questions in your notebook, or talk to another student.

1 When did you last get a call from an old friend out of the .... ? Who was it?
2 Are you at a loose .... this weekend? If so, what might you do?
3 Are you up to your .... in work at the moment?
4 Have you watched a TV programme recently that went over your .... ?
5 Do you ever listen to pieces of music for old times' .... ?
6 Did you enjoy studying English right from the word .... ? Why?/Why not?

C States

I want it **off my hands**.

The lights are **on the blink**.

It's **on its last legs**.

The interior's not **in** very **good nick**.

I can't keep it **on the road**.

I'm **in the doghouse** at home.

My temper sometimes **gets** me **into hot water**.

I feel **on edge** the whole time.

I'm **in a rut** at work.

I'm **at a crossroads**. What next?

Glossary

on the blink	INF (of electrical equipment) not working properly.
in good/excellent/bad nick	INF in good/excellent/bad condition.
on the road	(of a car) in good condition so that it can be legally driven. OPP **off the road**.
on its last legs	INF If sth is **on its last legs** it is going to stop functioning very soon.
in the doghouse	INF, often HUMOROUS If you are **in the doghouse**, sb is annoyed with you because you have done sth wrong.
on edge	tense, nervous, or irritable. (If you are **on tenterhooks**, you are anxious because you are waiting to find out about sth.)
in a rut	living or working in a situation that never changes. (👁 See page 162.)
at a/the crossroads	at a point in your life when you must make an important decision.
be in/get (sb) into hot water	INF be in or get (sb) into trouble.

spotlight *hands*

The children are off my hands. = no longer my responsibility.
Inflation is getting out of hand. = difficult or impossible to control.
A nurse will be on hand at the event. = available to help.

6 Tick the phrases which are informal.

1 No one was on hand to help. ....
2 My son's in hot water at work. ....
3 The car's off the road at the moment. ....
4 The flat's in very bad nick. ....
5 The project will be off my hands soon. ....
6 I'm on tenterhooks about the results. ....
7 The TV's on the blink again. ....
8 This old radio is really on its last legs. ....

7 Circle the correct preposition.

1 My life is *at | on* a crossroads at the moment.
2 I once went to a party which got out *of | off* hand.
3 I don't feel I'm *on | in* a rut at the moment.
4 My computer is *on | in* its last legs.
5 My car/bike is *in | on* excellent nick.
6 My TV/MP3 player is *on | in* the blink.
7 I'm *in | on* edge at the moment, waiting for news of something.
8 I wish someone was constantly *on | in* hand to help me with my English.

8 ABOUT YOU Are the sentences in Exercise 7 true for you? If not, change them so that they are true. Write your answers in your notebook or tell a partner.

58 I can use similes

A Similes with (as) ... as ...

My mother struggled a bit after her accident, but she's **fit as a fiddle** now.

I didn't think Leo would know, but he gave me the answer **quick as a flash**.

Come on, you can do this – it's **as easy as pie**.

I'm not sleeping on that bed again – it's **as hard as nails**!

That young niece of yours is **bright as a button**.

I was quite worried when I saw Kate; she was **white as a sheet**.

I love my little brother – he's **daft as a brush** and he makes me laugh.

The captain stayed **cool as a cucumber** in spite of all the pressure.

Lucy's **thin as a rake**. She needs to put on a bit of weight.

Do you want to borrow my suitcase? It's **good as new**.

Glossary

(as) **fit as a fiddle**	fit and in good health (**fiddle** INF a violin).
(as) **quick as a flash**	very quickly.
(as) **easy as pie**	very easy.
(as) **hard as nails**	very hard and uncomfortable.
(as) **bright as a button**	(usually of a child or young person) very bright and intelligent.
(as) **white as a sheet**	looking very ill or very frightened.
(as) **daft as a brush**	very silly.
(as) **cool as a cucumber**	very calm and controlled, especially in a difficult situation.
(as) **thin as a rake**	very thin.
(as) **good as new**	in very good condition, as it was when it was new.

spotlight Similes

A simile is a phrase that compares one thing with another thing, and many are formed with **as** + adjective + **as** + noun. These are used to emphasize the adjective (e.g. if a child is **as good as gold**, they are very good). In spoken English, the first **as** is often omitted.

1 Correct the final word in each sentence.

▶ Jemima's little girl's as bright as a ~~sheet~~. _button_
1 He picked out the correct pictures as quick as a fiddle. ....
2 We had to sit down but the sofa was hard as pie. ....
3 My mother's in her 70s but she's fit as a flash. ....
4 He'd heard the bad news, but he came into work cool as a brush. ....
5 The tests are easy as new. ....
6 She's nice to the customers, but she's daft as a cucumber. ....

2 Answer the questions with a simile with the opposite meaning.

▶ It was incredibly difficult, wasn't it?   No, _it was easy as pie_ .
1 Was it comfortable to sit on?   No, ...
2 Did she get very excited?   No, ...
3 Did he look well?   No, ...
4 Isn't David's little girl a bit slow at school? No, ...
5 I believe he's in very bad health, isn't he?   No, ...
6 Hasn't Lilia put on weight?   No, ...

B Similes with *like*

We can also make comparisons using **like**. These similes can be used for humorous or ironic effect.

I know what my wife's thinking – I can **read** her **like a book**.

We tried these new pills on the dog and they **worked like a dream**.

Don't mention the government to my uncle; it**'s like a red rag to a bull**.

Of course, as soon as I told Martha the news, it **spread like wildfire**.

I tried to explain it all to Dan, but it **was like banging my head against a brick wall**.

My father **'s like a bull in a china shop**, so don't ask him to deal with a sensitive problem.

I can't leave work early; my boss **watches me like a hawk**.

Asking Barry to pay for anything **is like getting blood out of a stone**.

We'll never find that contact lens – it**'s like looking for a needle in a haystack**.

I thought this jacket would be too big, but it **fits like a glove**.

Glossary

read sb like a book	be able to understand easily what sb is thinking or feeling.
work/go like a dream	work very well.
be like a red rag to a bull	be likely to make sb very angry.
spread like wildfire	(of news, etc.) become known by more and more people very quickly.
be (like) banging your head against a brick wall	INF be frustrating because you are making no progress in what you are trying to do.
be like a bull in a china shop	be careless in the way you move or insensitive in your behaviour.
watch sb like a hawk	watch sb very carefully.
be like getting blood out of a stone	be almost impossible to obtain.
be like looking for a needle in a haystack	be almost impossible to find.
fit (sb) like a glove	be the perfect shape or size for sb.

3 Circle the correct answer.

1 If someone watches you like a hawk, they watch you *from a distance | carefully*.
2 If something is like getting blood out of a stone, it is *difficult to obtain | likely to be valuable*.
3 If somebody can read you like a book, they know what you are *doing | thinking*.
4 If someone is like a bull in china shop, they're *strong and careful | clumsy and careless*.
5 If something fits like a glove, it *fits perfectly | is a bit tight*.
6 If something works like a dream, it works *well | well for a short period then fails*.
7 If something is like looking for a needle in a haystack, it is very *difficult to find | interesting*.

4 Complete the sentences using the pictures to help you.

1 My mother watches me like a ....
2 I was amazed – Mary's skirt fitted me like a ....
3 Getting Jerome to say thank you is like getting blood out of a ....
4 Mention the word 'feminism' to her and it's like a red rag to a ....
5 Finding that one earring will be like looking for a .... in a ....
6 Dealing with those children is just like banging your .... against a ....

59 I can use fixed phrases with two key words

A Sound patterns

Dictionaries may enter these phrases as idioms or collocations. The meaning is sometimes clear, e.g. **scrimp and save**, and sometimes idiomatic, e.g. **bread and butter**. However, the combination of words is not obvious, so you will need to learn these expressions.

There are rooms above the café where you can stay. They're fairly **cheap and cheerful**, and I noticed a bit of **wear and tear** on the furniture when we were there recently. But they can't afford to spend much on the rooms as well as the café, which is their real **bread and butter**.

My local team has been beaten **fair and square** in their last four games, so there's rather an atmosphere of **doom and gloom** around the club at the moment.

Ciaran **was born and bred** in the west of Ireland. His family were poor and his parents had to **scrimp and save** to provide for them all. It was hard for his mother, who was very **prim and proper**, but for most families it **was** just **part and parcel of** growing up in that area.

Glossary	
cheap and cheerful	not of great quality, but enjoyable and good value.
wear and tear	small marks and damage that appear over time as a result of normal use.
bread and butter	a person or company's main source of income.
fair and square	in an honest way and without any doubt.
doom and gloom	a feeling that a situation is very bad and without hope.
be born and bred …	used to say where sb was born and grew up.
scrimp and save	spend money only on what is absolutely necessary.
prim and proper	very careful about your appearance and behaviour, and easily shocked by what other people do or say.
be part and parcel (of sth)	be an aspect of sth that has to be accepted.

> **spotlight** Sound patterns
>
> A common feature of fixed phrases joined by *and* is that the first or last sounds in the two words are the same, e.g. *prim and **p**roper*, *doom and gloom*.

1 Complete the phrases.

1 scrimp and ....
2 born and ....
3 doom and ....
4 cheap and ....
5 wear and ....
6 prim and ....
7 fair and ....
8 part and ....

2 Complete the fixed phrase in the sentences.

1 He was .... and .... in Paris, but lives in Cannes nowadays.
2 There's bound to be some .... and .... on these boots after six months.
3 We lost the match .... and .... ; I have no complaints.
4 A lot of families have to .... and .... to buy things in a recession.
5 The economic prospects are not great, but it's not all .... and ....
6 He makes a bit of money from music, but accountancy is his real .... and ....
7 Injuries are .... and .... of being a professional sportsman.
8 It's not luxurious, but our local hotel is .... and .... , and a nice place to stay.

3 ABOUT YOUR LANGUAGE Do you have similar phrases in your language? If so, do some of them also have sound patterns similar to these?

B Paired words and repeated words

Does he clean that car every day? ~ Yes, it's **his pride and joy**.

Have they chosen good colour schemes? ~ Er … actually, I think they're a bit **hit and miss**.

Did you buy anything at the auction? ~ Nothing much – just a few **bits and pieces**.

Is your boss always like that? ~ Yes. Basically, **divide and rule** is the way he operates.

Is Helena making progress? ~ Yes, her English has come on **in leaps and bounds**.

Did he give a speech? ~ Yes, but thankfully it was **short and sweet**.

Did you enjoy the conference? ~ Yes, **all in all** I think it was very successful.

Will Carol move to the city? ~ No, she's a country girl **through and through**.

Glossary

sb's pride and joy	a person or thing that gives sb great pleasure or satisfaction.
hit and miss	unpredictable; sometimes succeeding and sometimes failing.
bits and pieces/bobs	INF small individual things of no great value. SYN **odds and ends**.
divide and rule	a way of controlling people by encouraging them to fight and argue among themselves.
in/by leaps and bounds	quickly or by a large amount (usually used when talking about sb's progress).
short and sweet	not long or complicated.
all in all	having considered everything. SYN **all things considered**.
through and through	used to say that sb has all the qualities of a particular type of person.

spotlight Repetition

There are many phrases, such as **all in all**, which use the same word twice: **little by little** (= gradually), **step by step** (= moving slowly from one stage to the next), **day by day** (= in small slow stages as each day passes), **head to head** (= competing directly), etc.

4 Find six phrases using words from the box.

leaps   short   divide   odds   hit   pride   sweet   joy   ends   rule   bounds   miss

....

....

....

5 Complete the sentences with a suitable fixed phrase. Keep a similar meaning.

▶ My eyes gradually got used to the lights.   My eyes got used to the lights *little by little*   .
1 I'm taking a few small things of no value.   I'm taking a few ....
2 Some of her ideas are good, some are not so good. Her ideas are a bit ....
3 He's made a huge amount of progress.   He's come on ....
4 The letter was simple and concise.   The letter was ....
5 It was a great success, everything considered. It was a great success ....
6 We'll be competing directly with them.   We'll be competing ....
7 That boat's the thing that gives him most pleasure. That boat is his ....
8 Everything about her is Irish.   She's Irish ....
9 We must do this carefully from one stage to the next. We must do this ....
10 His policy is to get them fighting among themselves. His policy is ....

60 I can use sayings and proverbs

A Words of wisdom

A number of common sayings give advice, or say something that is often thought to be true.

TEN Words of Wisdom

Saying	Meaning
Nothing ventured, nothing gained.	You have to take risks if you want to achieve sth.
People (who live) in glass houses shouldn't throw stones.	People who have faults should not criticize other people for having the same faults.
A leopard cannot change its spots.	People can't change their character, especially a bad character.
Too many cooks spoil the broth.	If too many people are involved in sth, it won't be done well. (**Broth** is a soup.)
Strike while the iron is hot.	Make use of an opportunity immediately.
You can't teach an old dog new tricks.	You can't make people change their ideas, ways of working, etc. when they've had them a long time.
You can't make an omelette without breaking eggs.	You can't achieve sth important without a few problems or unpleasant effects.
(There's) no time like the present.	Now is the best time to do sth, not in the future.
Many hands make light work.	A job is made easier if a lot of people help.
One good turn deserves another.	You should help sb who has helped you.

1 Answer the questions.

1 Which two idioms are saying something very similar about people's character?
.... / ....

2 Which two idioms appear to be saying completely opposite things?
.... / ....

3 Which two idioms express the importance of taking action now?
.... / ....

4 Which two idioms talk about the way we behave towards others?
.... / ....

2 Which idiom best summarizes each of these situations?

1 It will be difficult setting up a new business, but why not give it a try? ....
2 If we want to move forward, we must cut costs and get rid of some staff. ....
3 Maria did my shopping for me, so I said I'd help her with her homework. ....
4 If everyone lends a hand, we can clean up the flat in an hour or so. ....
5 My mum's overcooked vegetables all her life; she won't change now. ....
6 It took us a long time to clean the flat because we all got in each other's way. ....
7 He complains about me smoking, but I've seen him with a packet of cigarettes! ....
8 Let's buy that flat now, before prices start to go up. ....

3 ABOUT YOU Which idioms express the best advice or the most truth, in your opinion? Write your answers in your notebook, or talk to another student.

B First part only

There are some sayings where you only need to say the first part. The second part (shown in brackets below) is usually omitted. When you just say the first part, your voice often rises on the final word.

Saying	Example	Meaning
when in Rome (do as the Romans do)	*They use chopsticks here. ~ Well, **when in Rome** …*	In a foreign country or unfamiliar situation, you should behave in the same way as the people around you.
a bird in the hand (is worth two in the bush)	*I had an offer of £200 for my bike, but I think I'll wait for a better offer. ~ Well, **a bird in the hand** …*	It is better to have sth that you can be certain of than to risk losing it by trying to get sth much better.
two's company (three's a crowd)	*Can I come with you and Mel? ~ No, **two's company** …*	People in a romantic relationship don't want a third person with them.
better the devil you know (than the devil you don't)	*Would you like a new boss? ~ Not really. **Better the devil you know** …*	Someone you don't like but know may be better than somebody you don't know who might be worse.
an eye for an eye (and a tooth for a tooth)	*If a gang member is beaten up, the rest take revenge. It's **an eye for an eye**.*	Used to say that you should punish sb by doing to them what they have done to you.
don't count your chickens (before they're hatched)	*I'm sure I'll get that job. ~ **Don't count your chickens** …*	Don't be too confident about a future event before it has happened.
the grass is always greener (on the other side of the fence)	*My life seems so boring compared with my sister's. ~ Well, as they say: **the grass is always greener** …*	Used to say that people always think others are in a better situation than they are.
the spirit is willing (but the flesh is weak)	*Do you fancy a game of squash? ~ Well, **the spirit's willing** …*	Used for telling sb that you would like to do sth but do not have the energy or strength to do it.
birds of a feather (flock together)	*Everyone here is rich. ~ Well, **birds of a feather** …*	People of the same sort are usually found together.

4 Match 1–6 with a–f.

1 The grass is always greener ....
2 The spirit's willing ....
3 Two's company ....
4 Don't count your chickens ....
5 Birds of a feather ....
6 A bird in the hand ....

a before they're hatched.
b is worth two in the bush.
c on the other side of the fence.
d flock together.
e three's a crowd.
f but the flesh is weak.

5 Which saying best summarizes each of these situations?

1 If they attack us, we attack them. It's as simple as that. ....
2 You say the exam was easy, but you haven't got the results yet. ....
3 I don't like the present leader, but the next might be even worse. ....
4 Now we're in Poland, we're meant to kiss friends three times. ....
5 Jane and her boyfriend don't want a younger sister following them around. ....
6 I've got a well-paid job, but Ingrid's job sounds much more interesting. ....

6 ABOUT YOU Is there much truth in any of the sayings in the table? Do you particularly agree or disagree with any of them? Write your answers in your notebook, or talk to another student.

Review: Types of idiom

Unit 55

1 Match the verbs in the box with their literal and metaphorical meanings below.

> stand back   fall apart   spill over   wrap sth up

1 break into pieces. _____
2 cover something, e.g. by putting paper or cloth round it. _____
3 move away from something, especially something dangerous. _____
4 think about a situation as if you are not involved in it. _____
5 spread and begin to affect other areas. _____
6 have so many problems that it is impossible to continue. _____
7 finish something. _____
8 accidentally flow out of a container. _____

2 Complete the phrasal verb in each sentence.

1 You just need to _____ up the two screws on either end.
2 This company is in such a mess, it will take a genius to _____ it around.
3 He's too close to the situation. He needs to _____ back and be more objective.
4 These birds mostly _____ on worms and small insects.
5 Trouble started in the main square, then _____ over into the neighbouring streets.
6 They _____ down the old factory to make way for a new supermarket.
7 They can't answer our query right now: their computers have _____ down.
8 I _____ up my girlfriend's present last night, and gave it to her this morning.

Unit 56

1 Match 1–8 with a–h.

1 a lame _____   a elephant
2 a happy _____   b start
3 a black _____   c bill of health
4 a white _____   d in the ocean
5 a drop _____   e medium
6 a clean _____   f duck
7 a fighting _____   g eye
8 a head _____   h chance

2 Complete the texts.

> John Denham's new film has been a roaring (1) _____ with the public, and has even earned the (2) _____ of approval from most of the critics. This is just the (3) _____ in the arm the British film industry was looking for, and Denham is sure to get the red-(4) _____ treatment when he arrives at the Vienna Film Festival later today.

> The (5) _____ of suspicion is again pointing at MPs who continue to hold influential posts in business while working as MPs. The issue has been a hot (6) _____ for years, and critics believe that it must create a (7) _____ of interest. However, in an interview yesterday, a senior minister dismissed the allegations as a (8) _____ in a teacup.

3 Complete the idioms in the questions.

1 Is there anything you would buy on the _____ market?
2 In what circumstances would you tell a _____ lie?
3 Is letter-writing a _____ of the past?
4 Have you ever missed a _____ opportunity?
5 Do you often get annoyed by _____ tape?
6 How important is it to protect the _____ belt?
7 Is promotion of organic food just a _____ about nothing?
8 Is the attempt to halt global warming a _____ cause?

4 ABOUT YOU Write your own answers to Exercise 3 in your notebook, or talk to another student.

Unit 57

1 Cross out the noun or noun phrase which does <u>not</u> follow the words in italics.

1 Someone or something is *at*:
   a) your fingertips b) the outset c) all probability d) a crossroads
2 Someone or something is *in*:
   a) a rut b) closed doors c) plain English d) the doghouse
3 Someone or something is *on*:
   a) its last legs b) edge c) tenterhooks d) the blue
4 Someone or something can be *out of*:
   a) their heart b) their mind c) the ordinary d) hand
5 Someone or something can be *on the*:
   a) scrapheap b) road c) nick of time d) blink

2 Complete the idioms with adjectives from the box.

| last   deep   closed   good   plain   old   loose   same |

1 behind _____ doors
2 under the _____ roof
3 in _____ English
4 on its _____ legs
5 for _____ times' sake
6 at a _____ end
7 in _____ water
8 in very _____ nick

3 Complete the definitions.

▶ If something is *on its last legs*, it is old and will probably stop working soon .
1 If something goes *over your head*, it is _____ .
2 If something is *on the blink*, it isn't _____ .
3 If something is *out of the ordinary*, it is _____ .
4 If someone is *in hot water*, they are _____ .
5 If you are *at a loose end*, you have _____ .
6 If someone is *off their head*, they are _____ .
7 If something is *in good nick*, it is _____ .
8 If something is true *from the word go*, it is _____ .

Unit 58

1 Change one letter in each sentence to create correct similes.

▶ She's as bright as a mutton, and doing brilliantly at school. _button_
1 He got back from the expedition looking thin as a cake. ....
2 We must get a new bed; this one's as hard as rails to sleep on. ....
3 Look at this wetsuit – it hits like a glove. ....
4 I'd ask him to pay, but it's like getting flood out of a stone. ....
5 She won't do as I say. It's like banging your head against a brick hall. ....
6 He thinks I don't understand him, but I can lead him like a book. ....
7 Raising the subject of politics is like a red bag to a bull with him. ....
8 The boy was as white as a sheep, and I was worried he might faint. ....

2 Complete the sentences using a simile.

1 If a rumour gets around fast, it spreads ....
2 If something is hard to find, it's like looking for .... needle ....
3 If something is in very good condition, it's as good ....
4 If someone is very calm under pressure, they're as cool ....
5 If someone is very clever, they're bright ....
6 If something is very simple, it's easy ....
7 If someone is suspicious of you, they might watch you ....
8 If someone responds very fast, they answer you as quick ....

Unit 59

1 Put the dominoes in the correct order to make a joined sequence of idioms. Write the correct order of dominoes below.

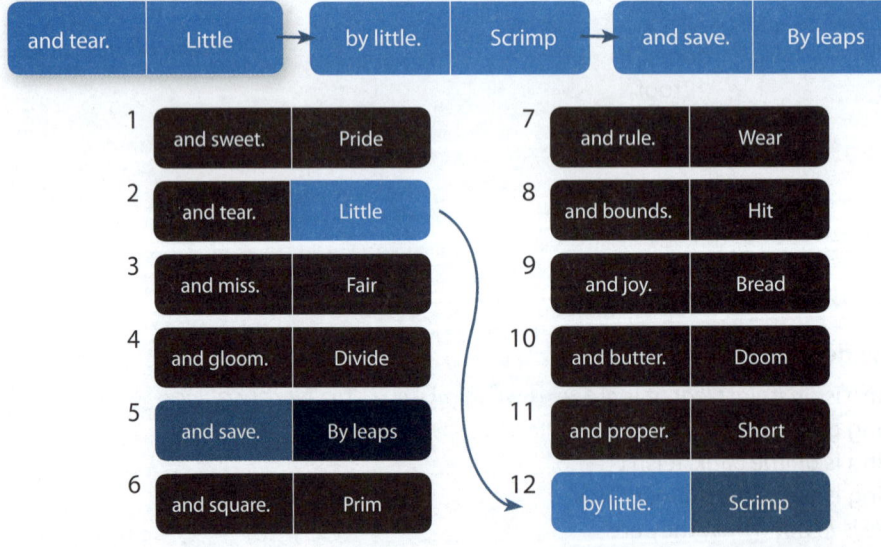

2 , 12 , 5 , ... , ... , ... , ... , ... , ... , ... , ... , ... , ...

2 Are the sentences true or false? Write T or F.

1 If someone's prim and proper, they are careful about what they say or do. ....
2 If you're going to buy a few bits and bobs, you're being very specific. ....
3 If you have to scrimp and save, you need to be careful with money. ....
4 If someone was born and bred in Thailand, they spent their childhood there. ....
5 If you're worried about your bread and butter, you're hungry. ....
6 If you explain something step by step, you explain the whole thing quickly. ....
7 If someone's a city person through and through, they are most at home in the city. ....
8 If life is all doom and gloom for someone, they're very happy at the moment. ....
9 If your phone service is quite hit and miss, it needs to be improved. ....
10 If two teams go head to head, they compete with each other. ....

Unit 60

1 Write your answers.

▶ What can't you count before they're hatched? *Your chickens.*
1 What can't a leopard change? ....
2 What should you strike while it's hot? ....
3 What can't you teach an old dog? ....
4 What happens with too many cooks? ....
5 What's the advantage of many hands? ....
6 What shouldn't people in glass houses do? ....

2 Here are the second parts of some idioms that are often omitted when we speak. Write the first part.

▶ *Birds of a feather* .... flock together.
1 .... before they're hatched.
2 .... , three's a crowd.
3 .... , do as the Romans do.
4 .... , but the flesh is weak.
5 .... than the devil you don't.
6 .... on the other side of the fence.
7 .... is worth two in the bush.
8 .... and a tooth for a tooth.

Idioms – some interesting histories

How did English idioms come into use? Here we show the meanings behind some idioms, and how some of them developed.

beat about the bush (Unit 35)

This phrase refers to a technique used for hunting. Some hunters in the forest beat the trees or bushes to scare the birds or animals, which were then shot by other hunters as they tried to escape. **Beating about the bush** was therefore a preparation for catching the birds or animals, but without actually achieving it. If people **beat about the bush**, they keep talking, but without getting to the main point.

be in the doldrums (Unit 18)

The **doldrums** is a 19th-century expression meaning a state of inactivity or laziness. Sailors used it to refer to certain areas of the ocean near the Equator where lack of wind made it difficult to sail. A business that is **in the doldrums** is not doing well.

drive a wedge between people (Unit 7)

A **wedge** is a piece of wood or metal with one thin end and one thick end; you use it to keep two things apart or to split wood. If you **drive a wedge between** two people, you make them start disliking or feeling suspicious of each other.

in a rut (Unit 57)

A **rut** is a deep track made by a wheel in muddy ground which it is then difficult to get the vehicle out of. If you are **in a rut**, you are living or working in a situation that never changes.

quick/slow off the mark (Unit 30)

In athletics, the **mark** is the starting point in a race, or the line that indicates it, so someone who is **quick off the mark** makes a quick start. You can also describe someone as being **quick** or **slow off the mark** when they are quick or slow in responding to a situation.

rest on your laurels (Unit 19)

Laurel leaves were used in Roman times to make a crown for the winner of a race or competition. If you **rest on your laurels**, you enjoy your success, but stop trying to improve your performance.

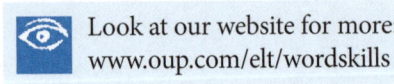

Look at our website for more:
www.oup.com/elt/wordskills

Answer key

Unit 1

1
1 get out of bed on the wrong side
2 not out of the woods
3 take a back seat
4 my heart sank

2
1 sore (a sore point)
2 stroke (hasn't done a stroke of work)
3 thing (the next thing I knew)
4 foot (put my foot in it)
5 Having (Having said that)
6 more (more than happy)
7 pushed (we'll be hard pushed to …)
8 much (I thought as much)
9 serves (it serves her right for …)
10 personally (take it personally)

3
1 The style is INFORMAL, and *on* is optional.
   (= continue doing sth in a determined way,
   even though it is difficult)
2 **if my memory serves me correctly** could also
   be **if my memory serves me well/right**. (used
   for saying that you think you have remembered
   sth correctly)
3 **keeping up with the Joneses**: the style
   is INFORMAL and usually DISAPPROVING. (=
   trying to have all the possessions and social
   achievements that your friends and neighbours
   have)
4 **the last straw** could also be **the final straw**, or
   even **the straw that breaks the camel's back**.
   (= the last in a series of bad events, that makes
   it impossible for you to accept a situation any
   longer)
5 **rest assured (that)** is FORMAL. (= be completely
   certain or confident (that))

4
1 hit the ground running, sort out the sheep from
   the goats; put a brave face on it; throw in the
   towel; were all in the same boat; Kevin's bark
   was worse than his bite.
2 a throw in the towel
   b sort out the sheep from the goats ('separate
      the sheep from the goats' is also possible)
   c Kevin's bark was worse than his bite
   d hit the ground running
   e were all in the same boat
   f put a brave face on it

Unit 2

1
1 track   3 chip   5 corner/spot
2 sleeve   4 dust   6 chest

2
1 She's in the driving seat.
2 I'm sure we're on the right track.
3 Strike while the iron is hot.
4 Wait for the dust to settle.
5 The company is on the ropes.
6 She's in a tight corner/spot (right now).
7 He has / He's got a chip on his shoulder.
8 She plays her cards close to her chest.

3
The common idea with the **head** idioms is of
using your brain or intelligence. The common idea
linking the **heart** idioms is emotions or feelings.
have your head screwed on INF be able to make
sensible decisions.
lose your head become unable to act in a calm,
sensible way.
use your head think carefully so that you
understand sth or avoid making a mistake.
break sb's heart make sb feel extremely unhappy.
(When used without further explanation, the
reference is to sb ending a romantic relationship.)
take sth to heart be very affected or upset by sth
that sb has said or done.
not have the heart to do sth not be able to do
sth because you know that it will upset sb else.
I let my heart rule my head = I act according to
what I feel, rather than doing what I think is sensible.

4
Ships and sailing: take the wind out of sb's sails,
learn the ropes
Radio and telecommunications: be on the same
wavelength, get your wires crossed
Horseriding: be in the saddle, keep a tight rein on
sth/sb
Weapons and war: bite the bullet, beat a hasty
retreat

5
1 be in the saddle
2 learn the ropes
3 be on the same wavelength
4 beat a hasty retreat
5 take the wind out of sb's sails
6 keep a tight rein on sth/sb
7 get your wires crossed

Unit 3

1

1	around	4	in	7	into
2	to	5	on	8	down
3	up	6	for		

2

1	dislike	4	persuaded
2	wrong/stupid/bad	5	killed
3	landed	6	wrote

3

1	out	5	down
2	up	6	up
3	around/round	7	down
4	on	8	out of

4

1 watch out for snakes
2 stand out against discrimination
3 let both of them off
4 burst in on us
5 hold it against him

5

1	watch out for sth or sb	4	hold sth against sb
2	burst in on sb	5	let sb off
3	stand out against sth		

Unit 4

1

1 Will there be a union climbdown / a climbdown by the union?
2 Was there a police cover-up?
3 We asked a passer-by.
4 There was a breakout from prison last night. OR There was a prison breakout last night.
5 The judge gave a brief summing-up. OR The judge's summing-up was brief.
6 Will the team give us / provide backup? OR Will backup be provided by the team? OR Will we get backup from the team?

2

1	bystanders/onlookers	5	getaway
2	intake	6	backup
3	climbdown	7	outbreak
4	breakout	8	passer-by

3

1 F 2 F 3 T 4 T 5 F 6 T 7 T 8 F

4

1	were knocked out	5	off-putting
2	worn out	6	breakaway
3	watered down	7	spoken out against it
4	leftovers	8	ongoing

Unit 5

1

1	quick	4	gladly
2	Deep, surface	5	thumb
3	barking	6	tough

2

1	hopping	5	own voice
2	two short planks	6	as a hatter
3	it cool	7	his thumb
4	mad keen on	8	as old boots

3

1 P 2 N 3 P 4 P 5 P 6 N 7 N 8 N

4

1 word (a man of his word)
2 soft (a soft touch)
3 earth (the salt of the earth)
4 creature (a creature of habit)
5 unknown (an unknown quantity)
6 spark (a bright spark)
7 nobody's/no (nobody's/no fool)
8 piece of work (a nasty piece of work)

Unit 6

1

1 Dad went to **great** lengths to help them.
2 We were given a helping **hand** with our writing.
3 They managed to hold their marriage **together**.
4 She doesn't have your best **interests** at heart.
5 I thank my **lucky** stars that I'm healthy.
6 She needs a shoulder to **cry** on.

2

1 turn to
2 sets her apart
3 shoulder to cry on
4 there for me
5 goes to great lengths / goes out of his way
6 went out of her way / went to great lengths
7 thank my lucky stars
8 hold the family together

4

1 T 2 F 3 F 4 T 5 F 6 F

5

1	sure of herself	5	get round
2	his foot down	6	her round your little finger
3	picking on	7	walk all over
4	pushes you	8	have/get his own

Unit 7

1

1 G 2 B 3 B 4 G 5 G 6 G 7 B 8 B

2

1 Janet and Dom (Dom and Janet) are **made** for each other.
2 Do you think they will **get** hitched?
3 You could be storing **up** trouble for later.
4 It isn't easy to walk **away** from an argument.
5 Their marriage went through a bad **patch**.
6 They're living in each other's **pockets**.

4

1 messed her around/about
2 answer to my boss
3 is piling up
4 finished / broken up with Pilar
5 held me back
6 let me down

5

1 finished (finished with him)
2 as (do as I pleased)
3 break-up (break-up)
4 anything / my right arm (I'd give anything / my right arm to)
5 let (let her down)
6 messing (messing her about)
7 sooner (I'd far sooner)
8 myself (please myself)
9 bear (doesn't bear thinking about)
10 arm (I'd give my right arm to)

Unit 8

1

1 (as) miserable as sin
2 On top of
3 your own flesh and blood
4 turned on
5 account for
6 on top of
7 fight like cat and dog
8 There's little/no love lost between them.

2

1	flesh	3	ranks	5	on
2	dog	4	top	6	take

4

1 They lavish far too much money **on** their children.
2 There's a danger they will **put** their son on a pedestal.
3 She's very naughty; they let her get **away** with murder.
4 Since the divorce, he's distanced **himself** from his family.

5 No wonder the child was unhappy; she was **starved** of attention.
6 Try to **make** a point of praising your middle child's creativity.

5

1 pedestal
2 murder
3 result
4 point
5 out
6 starved ('deprived' is also possible)
7 out
8 back
9 lavish

Unit 9

1

1 The news is so bad that I can't take it in.
2 The boy was screaming/laughing/shouting his head off.
3 She was crying her eyes out.
4 I'm at the end of my tether.
5 He went off the deep end.
6 The news stirred up a lot of anger.
7 Please don't wind her up.
8 I'm (feeling) on top of the world.

2

1	up	4	off	7	stir
2	dumps	5	deep	8	top
3	end	6	apparent		

3

1 He poured his heart out to me.
2 Don't take sides on this issue.
3 He must keep his anger in check.
4 Whose side are you on?
5 That's easier said then done.
6 Don't bottle up your feelings.
7 I'm dying for a coffee.

4

1 even keel (on an even keel)
2 sides (sides with)
3 cool (cool down) / calm (calm down)
4 go at (had a go at)
5 dying (I'd been dying to)
6 check (kept his temper in check)
7 flares (flares up)
8 said than done (that's easier said than done)
9 up the wrong way (rubs me up the wrong way)
10 bottle up (bottle up your feelings)

Unit 10

1
1 he's growing fast
2 we don't need it any more
3 put them in the bin
4 it keeps falling over
5 it can go in the lorry
6 someone might steal your wallet
7 fell asleep
8 he was in pain

2
1 T 2 F 3 F 4 F 5 T 6 T 7 T 8 F
9 T 10 F

3
1 take
2 mop
3 curled
4 stuck
5 deal ('hand' is correct in (a), but would be unnatural in (b))
6 roll
7 prop/shore
8 screw

4
1 stick it out
2 spread them out
3 let it down
4 chuck it away / chuck it out / screw it up
5 roll our sleeves up
6 mop it up
7 prop him up
8 curled up (with embarrassment) OR doubled up/over (with laughter)

Unit 11

1
1 lay my ~~hand~~ **hands**
2 fork ~~over~~ £30 **out**
3 pay ~~out~~ **off**
4 on the ~~breadqueue~~ **breadline**
5 to ~~fill~~ back on **fall**
6 be better ~~on~~ **off**

2
1 off   5 worse
2 pretty   6 fall
3 way   7 bail
4 forked/paid

3
1 pay off   3 lay your, bail you
2 pay your own   4 the breadline

4
1 You should err on the side of caution.
2 I went into it with my eyes open.
3 He opened an account off his own bat.
4 He could land himself in trouble.
5 She held on to her oil shares.
6 We don't have much money to play with.

5
1 add   4 went   7 err
2 comes/came   5 play   8 bat
3 fruit   6 put

Unit 12

1
1 F 2 T 3 F 4 F 5 T 6 F

2
1 sense   3 matter   5 come
2 leg   4 splash   6 set

4
1 got **behind** with
2 living from hand **to** mouth
3 the same **old** story
4 **to** say the least
5 going **cheap**
6 The last **I** heard
7 living **beyond** his means
8 put a deposit **down** / put **down** a deposit

5
1 He got caught up in something illegal.
2 He's in arrears with his rent.
3 I'm putting aside €100 a month.
4 She put down a £25 deposit.
5 It's the same old story.
6 She's living beyond her means.

Unit 13

1
1 off-colour   3 don't know 5 become ill
2 the bathroom   4 unwell   6 fall over

2
1 starting to **wear** off now
2 death warmed **up**
3 coming **down** with a cold
4 blacked **out**
5 **take** it easy
6 his **usual/normal** self

3
1 weather   3 going
2 come   4 off, easy

4
1 G 2 B 3 B 4 B 5 B 6 G 7 B 8 G

5

1	sorry	5	swell	9	go
2	went	6	checked	10	mend
3	side	7	away		
4	wood	8	gone		

Unit 14

1

1	crow	4	cutting	7	flagged
2	murder	5	drop	8	pulled
3	snail's	6	cut		

2

1	get from A to B	4	blocked me in
2	murder	5	cutting it fine
3	As the crow flies	6	miles from anywhere

4

1 G 2 B 3 B 4 G 5 G 6 B

5

1	a gear	4	the end of the road
2	a green light	5	the rails
3	ticking over	6	steam

6

1	the green light	4	the end of the road
2	down that road	5	up a gear
3	us on the map	6	down the road

Unit 15

1

1 Sam ~~cleaned~~ it all off **polished**
2 we can ~~set~~ up with him **settle**
3 I could eat a ~~house~~ **horse**
4 grab a ~~mouth~~ to eat **bite**
5 burnt to a ~~chip~~ **crisp/cinder**
6 making my ~~taste~~ water **mouth**
7 eats like a ~~mouse~~ **horse**
8 by word ~~or~~ mouth **of**

2

1	picks at	5	like a bird
2	full / full up	6	settle up
3	leftovers	7	a bite / a bite to eat
4	by word of mouth		

3

1	looking foolish	5	being overambitious
2	seeming innocent	6	energy
3	TV	7	events getting worse
4	having influence		

4

1 the best thing since sliced bread
2 bitten off more than she can chew
3 eating out of his hand

4 crying over spilt milk
5 egg on their face(s)
6 a couch potato
7 of the frying pan, (and) into the fire
8 full of beans

Unit 16

1

1 U 2 U 3 P 4 P 5 U 6 P 7 U 8 P

2

1 colours (with flying colours)
2 of trying (it's not for want of trying)
3 me off (told me off)
4 my head (it went over my head)
5 apply (apply himself)
6 him back (it's … holding him back)
7 signs of (showing signs of)
8 new leaf (turned over a new leaf)
9 marked me (marked me down)
10 or tail of it (can't make head or tail of it)
11 of course / of routine (as a matter of course / of routine)
12 socks up (pull his socks up)

3

1 coming on
2 make head or tail of this
3 night after night
4 next to nothing
5 scraped through
6 holding him back
7 cut out
8 running
9 apply myself
10 in/by leaps and bounds

4

1	told	4	a) on, bounds; b) signs
2	socks	5	matter
3	flying	6	show

Unit 17

1

1 take sth in your stride
2 get your foot in the door
3 keep your ear to the ground
4 put all your eggs in one basket
5 keep your feet on the ground
6 make a name for yourself

2

1	foot	4	options	7	grapevine
2	stride	5	ground	8	alone
3	name	6	pinning	9	keep

4

1 tricks of the ~~business~~ **trade**
2 ~~some~~ of the furniture **part**
3 it'll ~~make~~ some doing **take**
4 pass it ~~through~~ to the others **on**
5 under her ~~arm~~ **wing**
6 close ~~by~~ ten years **on**
7 he got the ~~pull~~ **push/boot/elbow**
8 throw his ~~size~~ about **weight**

5

1 some doing
2 fit
3 weight around/about
4 -end job
5 push/elbow/boot
6 the tricks
7 his wing
8 furniture

Unit 18

1

1 The deal has fallen / is going to fall through.
2 We survived thanks to the government.
3 Michael White is on the verge of resigning.
4 There are fears that the company could go to the wall.
5 A management buyout emerged at the eleventh hour.
6 Their future hangs in the balance.
7 The government will bail them out.
8 The company had pulled out of the deal.

2

1 buyout
2 hanging
3 pull out
4 stand
5 go
6 verge
7 through
8 bailout
9 shore / prop

3

1 G 2 G 3 B 4 G 5 B 6 B 7 G 8 B

4

1 we brought someone/somebody in
2 it caught us on the hop
3 it has fallen off
4 it's in the doldrums
5 it's slimmed down
6 they've bucked / they're bucking the trend
7 we did it up ourselves
8 it's making a comeback / it's coming back into fashion

Unit 19

1

1 a short space of ~~the~~ time
2 cut out ~~of~~ the middleman
3 *Correct.*
4 rest ~~up~~ on your laurels
5 *Correct.*
6 going ~~on~~ strong

7 *Correct.*
8 the going ~~pay~~ rate

2

1 middleman
2 at the right time
3 space of time
4 on our laurels
5 success
6 rate
7 off
8 strong

3

1 boat
2 In
3 *Both are correct.*
4 top-heavy
5 false
6 water
7 corners
8 sell up

4

1 An opportunity to do something.
2 Because they don't want a situation that is becoming unsuccessful to get worse.
3 The past. / A past event.
4 Annoyed or upset.
5 Yes, because I'd be in trouble.
6 *Most likely answers are:* cut back on staff, sell poorer quality food/drinks.

Unit 20

1

1 S 2 S 3 D 4 D 5 S 6 D

2

1 ~~do~~ a big thing **make**
2 take ~~out~~ any more **up**
3 stresses me ~~up~~ **out**
4 something ~~down~~ those lines **along/on**
5 like a bomb has ~~exploded~~ it **hit**
6 raised an ~~eyelash~~ **eyebrow**

3

1 It's no big deal if you can't do it.
2 The office looked like a bomb had hit it.
3 We need something on these lines.
4 They made a big deal/thing of / out of it.
5 John's taken over the cooking from me.
6 This table takes up too much room/space.

4

1 my first thought was to **buy** in a lot
2 Look – it's no **big** deal!
3 some of her **tried** and tested recipes
4 start **trying** out new things
5 pitch **in** and give me a hand
6 shopping **like** mad
7 I was so **stressed** out I had to go
8 organized and **clear** up the cooking stuff
9 as I **went** along
10 she took **over** from me in the kitchen
11 dished everything **up**, it looked fabulous

5

1	out, tried	3 as you	5 top
2	save their life	4 pitch	6 make a

Unit 21

1

We set up camp near a lake.
They rolled up late as usual.
Try not to tire yourself out.
The cash came in handy.
You should go easy on the cakes.
Don't take the easy way out.

2

1 wore herself out/was worn out/tired herself out
2 came in handy/useful
3 rolled up
4 put it up
5 keep an eye
6 easy on
7 make do
8 it behind

3

1 G   2 G   3 B   4 G   5 B   6 B

4

1 the rain held **off**
2 it just **tipped** down
3 being **soaked** to the skin
4 stumbled **on/across** an incredible band
5 going **down** a storm
6 kicked **off** with an amazing version
7 the high **point** came when they
8 went down pretty **well** too
9 putting **on** a real show

Unit 22

1

1 G   2 B   3 G   4 G   5 B   6 G   7 B   8 B
9 G   10 B

2

1	bland **blind**	4	mine **mind**
2	sell **tell**	5	fall **call**
3	blew **flew**	6	slapped **snapped**

3

1	in the eye	4	pick you up / call for you
2	bag/bundle	5	his eyes off
3	round to	6	chatted away

4

1	had in the mind	7	the same like
2	picked me all up	8	flew well by
3	could tell him	9	chatted himself away
4	got him round to	10	look at him

5 had big bags   11 on the playing cards
6 to get wind me up

5

1	dates	4	come
2	wound, bundle	5	call
3	make		

Unit 23

1

1 g   2 d   3 e   4 b   5 a   6 h   7 c   8 f

2

1	big	4	but	7	off
2	shelf	5	limit	8	wouldn't
3	better	6	popped		

3

1 She really spoke **from** the heart.
2 The good weather really **made** my day.
3 You can get this medicine **off** the shelf.
4 Mum **goes/went** on and on about tidying my room.
5 Winning was the icing on the **cake**.
6 It's **not** every day you win the lottery.
7 Please raise **your** glasses to the happy couple.
8 The ceremony **went** off without a hitch.

4

1	broke, tears	5	hear of
2	glowing terms	6	big day
3	shut, up	7	bottom, heart
4	break, bank	8	sky, limit

Unit 24

1

1	get	3	dead	5	time
2	safety	4	took	6	worse

2

1 and **catch** up on
2 always **brought** out the worst
3 under **no** obligation
4 I had **nothing** to lose
5 Go **for** it!
6 **there** is safety
7 a **whale** of a time

3

1	look great	4	aren't	7	older
2	older	5	under	8	terrible
3	don't enjoy	6	in good shape		

4

1	look, keeps	4	pushing, up
2	now, bones	5	million, takes years off
3	years, shape	6	friends

Unit 25

1

1 off	3 ground	5 aside
2 in	4 below	6 a par

2

1 hit	3 way	5 off
2 bench	4 par	6 on

3

1 We're on a par with Everton.
2 The coach brushed the comments aside.
3 We are in contention for the title.
4 He's confident the strategy will pay off.
5 We're gaining ground on the league leaders.
6 Is he going to gamble on Palmer tonight?

4

1 P   2 U   3 U   4 P   5 P   6 P   7 U   8 P

5

1 came	4 held	7 striking
2 dug	5 out	8 running
3 eased	6 hook	

Unit 26

1

1 cuff	5 without
2 the best	6 miss out on it
3 from the beginning	7 think about
4 later	8 eyes

2

1 off the wall	4 feedback
2 off the cuff	5 flash by / fly by
3 it in mind	6 all along

3

1 eye to eye	3 lined, cater	5 pat
2 miss, knows	4 bounce	6 back, bear

4

1 We must bridge the gap between rich and poor.
2 I didn't see eye to eye with the teacher.
3 She opened my eyes to more important things.
4 We came away with a lot of new ideas.
5 I gave an answer off the top of my head.
6 The organizers deserve a pat on the back.

5

1 by	3 wall	5 thought
2 know	4 for	6 away

Unit 27

1

1 less	3 is	5 get rid of it
2 stop	4 known	6 disappears

2

1 He put pressure on her to change her mind. OR He put her under pressure …
2 His comments were off the record. OR His comments weren't intended to be on the record.
3 We need to do this, and the sooner the better.
4 He's a household name.
5 The secrets have recently leaked out.
6 The incident will soon blow over.
7 She blew it (up) out of (all) proportion.
8 His comments have stirred up a lot of anger.

3

1 D   2 S   3 D   4 D   5 S   6 S

4

1 open	5 under the carpet
2 mixed	6 true
3 speak	7 brunt
4 without fire	8 lengths

Unit 28

1

1 the robbers	4 secret information
2 under-age drinking	5 gambling
3 *Both are logical.*	6 production

2

1 in, for	4 at	7 in, of
2 on, for	5 in, of	8 in
3 in	6 with	

3

1 lying (lying in wait for)
2 make/run (make/run off with)
3 possession (in possession of)
4 wake (in the wake of)
5 lookout (had been on the lookout for)
6 crack (crack down on)

4

1 d   2 f   3 e   4 a   5 b   6 c

5

1 gradually	4 make it stricter
2 are found innocent	5 a warning
3 increasing	6 more responsibly

6

1 They're going to phase the scheme out. OR … phase out the scheme.
2 The policeman went under cover (as a criminal).
3 He led the boy astray.
4 She wants to clear her name.
5 The police are pressing / have pressed charges (against him).
6 They are going on the offensive (against him).

Unit 29

1
1 turnout
2 join/combine
3 made
4 boarded up
5 go ahead
6 event
7 broke
8 walks of life

2
1 calling
2 passed/went off
3 go-ahead
4 bring/put, end
5 In the
6 forces
7 our way
8 turned out

3
1 a sit-in
2 spread
3 to
4 *Both are possible.*
5 *Both are possible.*
6 down

4
1 They will never back down.
2 Keep it to yourself.
3 We will certainly press ahead with our plans.
4 He always stood up for his beliefs.
5 Why did they cordon off the café?
6 How will we spread the word?
7 The talks paved the way for the reforms.
8 It's very hard to get our message across.

Unit 30

1
1 level ('equal' is also possible)
2 advantage
3 reasonable/logical
4 bad
5 reacting/responding
6 criticized/attacked
7 thinking
8 better

2
1 fire
2 slow
3 up
4 final
5 boils
6 plucked

3
1 put
2 *Both are correct.*
3 having
4 give
5 *Both are correct.*
6 words
7 call
8 run and run

4
1 house, order
2 benefit, doubt
3 jump, bandwagon
4 have, field
5 wake-up call
6 give/budge/move, inch
7 war, words
8 bode well

Unit 31

1
1 different
2 dispute
3 urgent
4 possible
5 continue/proceed
6 part of what they want

2
1 free up
2 can ill
3 standing firm
4 press on / press ahead
5 (being) poles apart / (being) at loggerheads / (being) locked in battle
6 meet each other halfway
7 hang in the balance

3
1 battle
2 bullet
3 guns
4 in both camps
5 battle
6 line

4
1 broken ranks
2 foot in both camps
3 running battle over this (for ages)
4 bite the bullet and raise taxes
5 siding with the Opposition
6 sticking / going to stick to her guns (on this)
7 a losing battle
8 the firing line

Unit 32

1
1 N   2 N   3 P   4 P   5 N   6 N

2
1 break
2 wildest
3 rise
4 head
5 pieces
6 knocked

3
1 A lot of actors fall by the wayside.
2 We must tread carefully.
3 He was successful, but it came at a price. OR His success came at a price.
4 It was beyond my wildest dreams.
5 Holly went to pieces.
6 I'm sure Jason will rise to the occasion (on the night).

4
1 tries, does
2 shadow
3 past, through
4 its toll, a heavy toll
5 set
6 line, road

5

1 news **got/leaked** out
2 fight her **way** through
3 in the public **eye**
4 coupled **with** the birth
5 had **set** her back
6 taken a heavy **toll** on her
7 determined to **bounce** back
8 not **cast** a shadow

Unit 33

1

1 hard to ~~get~~ to terms **come**
2 wiped ~~off~~ by earthquakes **out**
3 wreaking ~~damage~~ on **havoc**
4 roof caved ~~down~~ **in**
5 caught up ~~on~~ the forest fires **in**
6 started to ~~make~~ hold **take**

2

1 in the grip   5 caught up
2 ripped through   6 caved in
3 wreaked havoc   7 loss of life
4 swept away

3

1 away   4 for   7 away
2 in   5 at   8 for
3 off   6 to

4

1 The train came/ground to a standstill.
2 We were cut off.
3 They towed the car away to the police station.
4 I headed for the hospital.
5 They turned us away from the building.
6 The food is running low. OR We're running low on food.
7 We'll be cut off for the foreseeable future.
8 I was caught unawares by the snow. OR The snow caught me unawares.

Unit 34

1

1 They give you information you need.
2 Yes, you are (it means they keep you up-to-date with information).
3 Angry or annoyed.
4 Persuading them that you are / something is right.
5 That you understand the situation.
6 Noticed something, a detail perhaps (and you may have acted on it).
7 You tell them what you are thinking or feeling.
8 No.

2

1 in   3 up   5 basis
2 posted   4 picture   6 over/round
  ('informed' is
  also possible)

4

1 no   4 yes   7 no
2 yes   5 no   8 no
3 perhaps   6 yes

5

1 I keep my cards close to my chest.
2 I got the wrong end of the stick.
3 I gave it away.
4 I wanted to mull it over.
5 I kept it to myself. OR I kept her in the dark.
6 I read between the lines.
7 It doesn't occur to me that I'm being secretive.
8 It makes no odds to me what people think.

Unit 35

1

1 D 2 S 3 D 4 S 5 S 6 D

2

1 butting   3 beating, point   5 back
2 missed   4 word   6 devil's, sake

4

1 gone   4 deserve   7 evil
2 grips   5 politically
3 justifies   6 part

5

1 can't teach an old dog new tricks
2 get what we deserve
3 a necessary evil
4 life after death
5 gone too far
6 politically correct / PC
7 get to grips with it
8 gone/going off the rails

Unit 36

1

1 time/money   4 PC
2 ideas/thoughts   5 savings/experience
3 *All are correct.* 6 ease/rest

2

1 wing   3 run   5 for
2 sit, notice 4 loosen   6 mind

4

1 N 2 P 3 P 4 N 5 N 6 P

5

1 life (the shock of my life), through (sit through), nod (nod off)
2 truth (nothing could be further from the truth), jumped/butted (jumped/butted in)
3 wreck (a nervous wreck), pare (pare it down), sight (lose sight of)

Unit 37

1

1 F 2 T 3 T 4 T 5 F 6 T

2

1 at home
2 with open arms
3 start/begin with
4 of her
5 was in his mouth
6 it by ear
7 a start
8 the word go

4

They arrived in dribs and drabs.
Don't rush into a decision.
We're forging ahead with the plans.
The situation was left hanging for days.
She rambled on for hours.
The meeting ran over by half an hour.
Don't hold the floor so others can't speak.

5

1 The measures will be to the detriment of patient care.
2 The chair laid down the rules of the meeting.
3 Dad rambled on about the wedding.
4 Don't rush into it / anything / a decision.
5 The money was released in dribs and drabs.
6 They threw together a video. OR They threw a video together.
7 We're forging ahead with the project.
8 I don't want to leave the situation hanging.

Unit 38

1

1 terms
2 purposes
3 equal
4 belief
5 speaking

2

1 name
2 equal
3 push/pinch
4 contrary
5 knowledge
6 intents

3

1 He told me what he thought of me in no uncertain terms. OR He told me in no uncertain terms what he thought of me.
2 It's common knowledge that they're married.

3 We can get six people round the table at a push/pinch. ('only just' fulfils the same function as 'at a push/pinch')
4 I'll sell the car as a last resort / if all else fails.
5 Strictly speaking, a tomato is a fruit.
6 Contrary to popular belief, he's not Welsh.

4

1 ~~little~~ (it's the least I can do)
2 ~~and~~ (last but not least)
3 ~~worst~~ (worse luck)
4 ~~I~~ (I'll give you that)
5 ~~later~~ ((a bit) late in the day)
6 ~~have~~ (you'll be lucky)
7 ~~quite~~ (it's all very well)
8 ~~everything~~ (for all she cares)

5

1 stay in, worse luck
2 safely, thank goodness
3 it's the (very) least I can do
4 abroad for all I care
5 is better in Spain, I'll give you that
6 be lucky to find a taxi

Unit 39

1

1 into the bargain
2 well and truly
3 ever so
4 by far / far and away / without (a) doubt
5 no wonder
6 on end

2

1 It's by far / far and away / without (a) doubt the best part of town.
2 He gave me a discount, and wrapped it up nicely into the bargain.
3 Karoly's ever such a generous guy.
4 Unfortunately the party was well and truly over when we arrived.
5 I think it's without (a) doubt / by far / far and away her most interesting novel.
6 I've been back there three times today as it is; I don't want to go again.
7 She ate some seafood that was off, so no wonder she's feeling ill.
8 It's not just any silk. It's the finest silk you can buy.

3

1 c 2 g 3 e 4 b 5 f 6 h 7 d 8 a

4

1 She'd give her right arm to go waterskiing.
2 They'll have to pull out all the stops.
3 They're up in arms over/about it.
4 I couldn't believe my ears when I heard the news.
5 They're streets ahead of me.
6 That boy doesn't do a stroke of work.
7 She came down on him like a ton of bricks.
8 I avoided her like the plague.
9 These guys don't half work hard.
10 All hell broke loose.

Unit 40

1

1 spare	4 death	7 facing
2 light	5 hush/cover	
3 on	6 kept/hid	

2

1 She wanted to spare her feelings.
2 She didn't want to let on to people.
3 He was scared to death. OR His father scared him to death.
4 He didn't want to lose face. / He wanted to save face.
5 She couldn't face up to it.

4

1 ~~in~~ his conscience **on**
2 when it comes **to** helping
3 I wasn't **born** yesterday
4 gave the game ~~up~~ **away**
5 ~~packs~~ of lies **a pack**
6 pull the wool over my ~~ears~~ **eyes**
7 difficult to live **with**
8 my aunt ~~looked~~ through it **saw**

5

1 live with
2 a pack of lies
3 have it on my conscience
4 went (as) red as a beetroot
5 gloss over
6 When it comes to

Unit 41

1

1 D 2 S 3 S 4 D 5 D

2

1 They're neck and neck.
2 They're gaining ground.
3 It could tip the balance in your favour.
4 The race is hotting up.

5 She'll be hard to beat.
6 He's a dark horse.
7 She slipped up. / She made a slip-up.
8 I think he's got something up his sleeve. OR … has something up his sleeve. OR … has kept something up his sleeve.

3

1 shot	3 true	5 off
2 safe	4 shave/call	6 balance

4

1 gave	3 pulled	5 price
2 down	4 looking	6 dream

Unit 42

1

1 no	3 yes	5 no
2 no	4 no	6 yes

2

1 laugh	3 flat	5 beyond a joke
2 my leg	4 in cheek	6 stitches

4

1 famous ~~lost~~ words **last**
2 fell off the back of a ~~train~~ **lorry**
3 but no one's ~~here~~ **home**
4 my ~~beautiful~~ sleep **beauty**
5 What ~~plane~~ is he on? **planet**
6 as ~~clean~~ as mud **clear**
7 for reasons ~~better~~ known to himself **best**
8 a ~~cry~~ of nature **call**

5

1 I dread to think.
2 No, it was (as) clear as mud.
3 I need my beauty sleep.
4 That's the kiss of death, then.
5 They fell off the back of a lorry.
6 What planet is he on?
7 Famous last words.
8 A call of nature, I think/expect.

Unit 43

1

1 daylight	4 *Both are correct.*
2 squeeze	5 past
3 feet	6 for

2

1 put it past her
2 rip-off
3 robbery
4 beyond me
5 fell for / was taken in by

6 to death of it / to the back teeth of it
7 squeezed another €20 out of OR squeezed it out of
8 out on

4
1 let us alone
2 be fair enough
3 take it out personally
4 all in for
5 all dead set
6 jumped in down

5
but he's **dead** set against that
argue the **toss** with him
The thing is, **no** disrespect to Dad
and **to/let's** be fair
pulled my arguments to **pieces/shreds**
and that's **putting** it mildly
I think he takes that **personally**
won't get a job in the City, **let** alone become

Unit 44

1
1 your wit about you **wits**
2 an event of fire **the**
3 miss out of **on**
4 stay a good chance **stand**
5 no hurt in asking **harm**
6 makes sensible to **sense**
7 note for what **of**
8 wouldn't harm to **hurt**

2
1 swept
2 keep
3 times
4 no harm
5 note
6 essence
7 event
8 missing out

3
1 we're in the **same** boat
2 get so **worked** up
3 **For** what it's worth
4 pills **keeps** me from
5 stands to **reason** that
6 by any **stretch** of the imagination
7 if all **else** fails
8 you **could** do worse

4
1 I feel for her at this time.
2 We're both in the same boat.
3 Your best bet is to say nothing.
4 Try not to get worked up about the plan.
5 You could do worse than stay in a B and B.
6 If all else fails, you can refuse to work.

Unit 45

1
dig your heels in OR dig in your heels
a storm in a teacup
take the bull by the horns
fall into the trap of doing sth
have a chip on your shoulder
sit tight

2
1 He fell into the trap of doing everything himself.
2 She's made her choice; she must act on it.
3 He's got a chip on his shoulder.
4 I would sit tight (and do nothing).
5 He's digging his heels in. OR He's digging in his heels.
6 She has to think through what might happen. OR … to think it through.
7 You'll have your work cut out.
8 I was asked to sort out the problem. OR … sort the problem out.
9 It's a storm in a teacup.
10 He's going to take the bull by the horns.

3
1 off his
2 sail through
3 in a (terrible) state
4 get over
5 recipe for
6 finished with
7 came
8 pull himself

4
1 frame
2 coming
3 hanging
4 state
5 sail
6 world
7 day

Unit 46

1
1 this is life **that's**
2 write the experience out **off**
3 she's no stopping her **there's**
4 throws him into it **himself**
5 she looked to it **took**
6 luck's by his side **on**

2
1 carried away
2 's too short
3 like a duck to water
4 wasn't on your side
5 and breathes
6 goes on
7 came, way
8 element

3
1 S   2 S   3 D   4 S   5 D   6 D   7 S   8 S

4

1 light
2 running through
3 slipped
4 dwelling
5 live
6 jumping/leaping
7 face
8 putting
9 out

Unit 47

1

1 yes
2 no
3 no
4 no
5 no
6 yes

2

1 weigh, rushing
2 go
3 gut
4 turn
5 go
6 of your convictions

4

1 d 2 e 3 f 4 a 5 c 6 b

5

1 give
2 blind eye
3 step
4 put
5 toss
6 minds
7 two evils
8 draw

Unit 48

1

1 e 2 d 3 a 4 f 5 b 6 c

2

1 stick, out
2 get, into, no excuse
3 life, limb
4 bluff
5 hedged, put
6 play, split

4

1 thrives on
2 made up
3 down to
4 seek out
5 err on the side of caution
6 shed light on
7 a long shot
8 Not necessarily

5

1 seek
2 thrive
3 make-up
4 take, long
5 risk
6 run ('take' is also possible)

Unit 49

1

1 by
2 Both are correct.
3 glued
4 bag
5 Both are correct.
6 back

2

1 No, it's not my idea of fun.
2 Far from it. / Quite the opposite. / Quite the reverse.
3 Yes, he's in with a chance.

4 It was nothing to write home about / nothing to get excited about.
5 Yes, I felt hard done by.
6 Yes, but it'll take some doing.
7 No, it's (like) water off a duck's back (to me).
8 Yes, it's in the bag.

3

1 be hardly pushed **hard**
2 didn't want to know it
3 make a move on
4 leave it at this **that**
5 push the luck **your**
6 must hear things **be hearing**

4

1 miles away
2 seeing things
3 leave it at that
4 I wouldn't say no
5 make a move
6 his own thing
7 none too pleased / not too pleased
8 I'll be (hard) pushed to do that

Unit 50

1

1 e 2 g 3 a 4 f 5 c 6 b 7 h 8 d

2

1 lucky you
2 not at all / not in the least
3 that figures
4 so far, so good
5 Forget it
6 There's nothing to it
7 just as well

3

1 So what?
2 *Both are correct.*
3 Don't you dare!
4 *Both are correct.*
5 Rather you than me.
6 *Both are correct.*

4

1 You'll be lucky.
2 No fear. / No way.
3 Don't you dare!
4 So what? / What of it?
5 That's your problem. / That's not my problem.
6 Please yourself. / Rather you than me.
7 Now what? / What is it now?
8 That's/What a load of rubbish/nonsense!

Unit 51

1

1 d 2 e 3 f 4 a 5 g 6 b 7 h 8 c

2

1	at	3 laid	5 in
2	paid	4 with	

3

1	destroy	4	happen/exist
2	beginning	5	disagree
3	disagree	6	proud/happy

4

1 on the threshold
2 at the hands of
3 holds sway
4 paid no heed to
5 in large part/measure
6 laid down their lives
7 be in his debt / be in debt to him
8 laid waste to
9 take issue
10 beyond the call of duty

5

1	respect	5	end	9	honour
2	issue	6	respects	10	part/measure
3	lies	7	laid		
4	rise	8	tribute		

Unit 52

1

1 It means he had no permanent home.
2 It means drunk, or having had too much alcohol.
3 It means having made a formal promise to tell the truth in a court of law.
4 It means because of her experience.
5 It means noisy or violent behaviour in a public place.
6 It means he's not free or allowed to tell us.

2

1	breach	4	liberty	7	conjunction
2	influence	5	oath	8	question
3	kindly	6	took		

3

1	spirit	4	undoing	7	sum
2	enter, abide	5	faith	8	pretences
3	small	6	will		

4

1 his own free will
2 letter of the law
3 false pretences
4 accordance with Mrs Hart's wishes
5 summing up
6 good faith
7 entered into the discussion
8 abide by the rules

Unit 53

1

1 d 2 e 3 g 4 a 5 h 6 c 7 b 8 f

2

1 subscribe **to** that point of view
2 embark **on/upon** the new project
3 deprived **of** even the most
4 contend **with** sub-zero temperatures
5 prides herself **on** her cooking
6 amount **to** a large sum
7 engaged **in** discussions
8 resigned herself **to** a lonely existence

3

1	deprived	5	engaged
2	resigned	6	amounts/amounted
3	dispose	7	impinge
4	subjected	8	adhere

4

1 enlarge on/upon
2 subscribed to
3 abide by / adhere to
4 contend with
5 dispense with the services of
6 dwell on/upon
7 amounts to
8 pride themselves on

5

1 We can dispose of these old files.
2 It won't impinge on/upon my decision. OR It won't impact on my decision.
3 He was subjected to a tough interview.
4 She prides herself on her loyalty.
5 Will they adhere to the rules? OR Will they abide by the rules?
6 She alluded to your comments.

Unit 54

1

1	event	4	bounds	7	under
2	right	5	For	8	discretion
3	production	6	convenience		

2

1 or nearest offer
2 Usually a flat or house, and it means someone has agreed to buy it.
3 Job advertisements.
4 A personal reference or a public notice.
5 Giving a tip.
6 On the back of a lorry, van, car, etc.

Unit 55

1

Sentences referring to a physical action are: 2, 3, 5, 6, 8.

2

1 tightened	4 down	7 feed
2 went	5 turn	
3 spilled	6 up	

3

Let's tighten up the regulations.
The standard's gone down in recent years.
They knocked down the shopping centre.
Just stand back and think about it.
Her life has fallen apart since she lost her job.
The towel soaked up the moisture.
They feed on insects.

4

1 stand back
2 soak up
3 falling apart
4 turn, around/round
5 feeds on
6 spill over
7 go down

Unit 56

1

1 S 2 S 3 D 4 S 5 D 6 D

2

1 the finger of suspicion
2 a fighting chance
3 a hot potato
4 a drop in the ocean
5 a conflict of interest
6 a lame duck
7 a storm in a teacup / a fuss about nothing
8 a lost cause

3

1 e 2 g 3 f 4 a 5 h 6 b 7 d 8 c

4

1 The birthday party was a roaring **success**.
2 The government did a **U**-turn on the policy.
3 He's trying to find a **happy** medium.
4 We hope to get a **clean** bill of health.
5 There has been a **coup** d'état in Birania.
6 Our company needs a shot in the **arm**.
7 I made a terrible faux **pas** at the interview.
8 Letter-writing is a **thing** of the past.

5

1 a ~~gold~~ opportunity **golden**
2 a ~~black~~ lie **white**
3 *Correct.*
4 a ~~blue~~ eye **black**
5 a ~~pink~~ elephant **white**
6 *Correct.*
7 ~~brown~~ fingers **green**
8 *Correct.*

6

1 the black market
2 a black eye
3 the red carpet
4 green fingers
5 a golden opportunity / the chance of a lifetime
6 a white elephant
7 the black sheep (of the family)

Unit 57

1

1 S 2 D 3 S 4 D 5 D 6 D

2

1 I haven't got the facts at my fingertips.
2 I didn't see anything out of the ordinary.
3 We do everything by the book.
4 We arrived in the nick of time.
5 Twelve people are living under one roof. / … under the same roof.
6 Hundreds of workers will be on the scrapheap.
7 You are within your rights to claim for this.
8 She expressed the ideas in plain English.

3

1 in	3 out of, off	5 at
2 between	4 from, to	6 at/from, from

4

1 out of your mind / off your head
2 from head to toe
3 at a loose end
4 in all probability
5 between you and me / ourselves
6 at/from the outset / from the word go

5

1 blue	3 eyes	5 sake
2 end	4 head	6 go

6

The following phrases are informal: 2, 4, 7, 8.

7

1 at	4 on	7 on
2 of	5 in	8 on
3 in	6 on	

Unit 58

1

1 ~~fiddle~~ **flash**
2 ~~pie~~ **nails**
3 ~~flash~~ **fiddle**
4 ~~brush~~ **cucumber**
5 ~~new~~ **pie**
6 ~~cucumber~~ **brush**

2

1 it was (as) hard as nails
2 she was (as) cool as a cucumber
3 he looked/was (as) white as a sheet
4 she's (as) bright as a button
5 he's (as) fit as a fiddle
6 she's (as) thin as a rake

3

1 carefully
2 difficult to obtain
3 thinking
4 clumsy and careless
5 fits perfectly
6 well
7 difficult to find

4

1 hawk
2 glove
3 stone
4 bull
5 needle, haystack
6 head, brick wall

Unit 59

1

1 save
2 bred
3 gloom
4 cheerful
5 tear
6 proper
7 square
8 parcel

2

1 born and bred
2 wear and tear
3 fair and square
4 scrimp and save
5 doom and gloom
6 bread and butter
7 part and parcel
8 cheap and cheerful

4

1 leaps and bounds
2 short and sweet
3 divide and rule
4 odds and ends
5 hit and miss
6 pride and joy

5

1 bits and pieces / bits and bobs / odds and ends
2 hit and miss
3 by/in leaps and bounds
4 short and sweet
5 all in all / all things considered
6 head to head
7 pride and joy
8 through and through
9 step by step
10 divide and rule

Unit 60

1

1 A leopard cannot change its spots. / You can't teach an old dog new tricks.
2 Too many cooks spoil the broth. / Many hands make light work.
3 Strike while the iron is hot. / (There's) No time like the present.
4 People who live in glasshouses shouldn't throw stones. / One good turn deserves another.

2

1 Nothing ventured, nothing gained.
2 You can't make an omelette without breaking eggs.
3 One good turn deserves another.
4 Many hands make light work.
5 You can't teach an old dog new tricks. ('A leopard cannot change its spots' would not be as suitable here, as the sentence is about a way of doing sth, not character.)
6 Too many cooks spoil the broth.
7 People who live in glass houses shouldn't throw stones.
8 Let's strike while the iron is hot.

4

1 c   2 f   3 e   4 a   5 d   6 b

5

1 (It's) An eye for an eye (and a tooth for a tooth).
2 Don't count your chickens (before they're hatched).
3 Better the devil you know (than the devil you don't).
4 When in Rome … (do as the Romans do).
5 Two's company (three's a crowd).
6 The grass is always greener (on the other side of the fence).

Answer key to review units

Introduction to idioms and phrasal verbs

Unit 1

1

1 foot	5 side	9 bark
2 right	6 keep	10 sinks
3 next	7 hit	11 towel
4 sore	8 stroke	12 seat

The expression in the grey squares is 'fixed phrases'.

Unit 2

1

1 e 2 h 3 d 4 g 5 b 6 c 7 f 8 a

2

1 cards, chest   4 screwed
2 strike   5 heart, head
3 corner/spot   6 heart

Unit 3

1

1 to it
2 for pickpockets/thieves/cheats, etc.
3 on me
4 out on her
5 a warning
6 it means

2

1 put down   5 put down
2 came up   6 took against
3 ate up   7 eat in
4 puts himself down   8 talked me into going

Unit 4

1

Phrasal verb	Phrasal noun
look on	onlooker
break out	outbreak
sum up	summing-up
stand by	bystander

Phrasal verb	Phrasal adjective
speak out	outspoken
water sth down	watered down
wear sth out	worn out
go on	ongoing
put sb off	off-putting

2

1 knocked out   3 cover-up   5 get away
2 leftover   4 backup   6 worn out

People

Unit 5

1

I would choose Amy (a bright spark), Syd (tough as old boots), Don (nobody's fool), and Brenda (salt of the earth).
I wouldn't choose the others because on a difficult demanding journey you probably wouldn't want Ollie (an unknown quantity), or Bill (thick as two short planks, so not very bright). Alec (a creature of habit) would find it difficult not knowing what to expect every day, and Mandy (a cold fish) would not be good company. Clive (likes the sound of his own voice) might become irritating, and Isabel (doesn't suffer fools gladly) might cause friction in the group.

2

1 mad   4 wire   7 thumb
2 temper   5 touch   8 cool
3 piece   6 hatter

Unit 6

1

1 He never lifts a finger (to help).
2 She'll stop at nothing (to get what she wants).
3 They went to great lengths to help us.
4 Her generosity is what sets her apart.
5 Call me if you need a shoulder to cry on.
6 My sister takes me for granted.

2

1 on   4 turn, shoulder   7 way
2 up   5 hand   8 take
3 finger   6 foot

Unit 7

1

1 finished	4 made	7 messed
2 break-up	5 himself	8 away
3 patch	6 meet	

2

1 of the moment
2 a wedge between them
3 sooner you came alone
4 other's pockets
5 the knot
6 anything / my right arm to meet George Clooney

Unit 8

1

1 b 2 b 3 a 4 b 5 a 6 a 7 b 8 a

2

1 Shan distanced herself from the group.
2 I lavished praise on my son.
3 Dara is starved of affection (by her parents).
4 He's my own flesh and blood.
5 She got away with murder.
6 Those kids fight like cat and dog (all day long).

Unit 9

1

1 U 2 H 3 U 4 U 5 H 6 U 7 U 8 U

2

1 head	4 sides	7 eyes/heart
2 easier	5 rub	8 dying
3 pour	6 apparent	

Unit 10

1

1 She's rolling up a picture.
2 She's dealing out cards.
3 She's sticking her tongue out. OR She's sticking out her tongue.
4 He's zipping up his jacket.
5 Somebody has propped the tree up.
6 She's curled up on the sofa.
7 I'm mopping up some water.
8 I'm throwing something away.

2

1 help a company in difficulty
2 start a difficult task
3 make a mess of it
4 embarrassed
5 continue to do sth difficult or boring
6 complete

Everyday life

Unit 11

1

1 play	4 bail	7 bear
2 goes	5 landed	8 put
3 fork	6 fall	

3

1 his own way	5 worse off
2 err, caution	6 paid, off
3 own bat	7 his eyes
4 comes	8 the breadline

Unit 12

1

1 in the lap of luxury
2 (him) an arm and a leg
3 more money than sense
4 was going cheap
5 puts (some) money aside
6 set foot in/inside that nightclub

2

1 object	4 arrears	7 mouth
2 least	5 lane	8 means
3 heard	6 story	

Unit 13

1

Groups with possible titles
Feeling unwell: out of sorts, under the weather, off-colour
Getting better: on the mend, pull through, take a turn for the better ('come round' would also be possible here)
Lose/gain consciousness: pass out, black out, come round

2

1 It's touch-and-go whether he'll survive.
2 He started to throw up.
3 She (suddenly) took a turn for the worse.
4 I think he's going downhill.
5 It won't go away.
6 Check it out – to be on the safe side.

Unit 14

1

1 She dropped me off at 3.00.
2 I was cutting / had cut it fine.
3 He's running/run out of steam.
4 It's five miles as the crow flies.
5 She drives at a snail's pace.

2

1 ticking   3 gear   5 blocked
2 murder   4 road

Unit 15

1

1 beans   3 milk   5 butter, mouth
2 egg   4 eating   6 bitten, chew

2

1 I'm full up
2 I could eat a horse
3 settle up
4 (By) word of mouth
5 leftovers
6 grab/have a bite
7 's a couch potato
8 is making my mouth water OR looks mouth-watering

Unit 16

1

9, 6, 1, 11, 5, 7, 3, 8, 10, 2

2

1 through   4 on
2 for   5 out
3 off   6 back

Unit 17

1

1 Don't throw your weight around/about.
2 I heard about it on the grapevine.
3 Don't put all your eggs in one basket.
4 When I started the job, Bill took me under his wing.
5 He got his foot in the door of the firm.
6 They gave me the boot/elbow.
7 Keep your ear to the ground.
8 He keeps his feet on the ground.

Unit 18

1

1 verge   5 eat   9 comeback
2 buyout   6 hop   10 bailout
3 stand   7 trend   11 slim
4 shore   8 win

The idiom in the grey squares is 'go to the wall'. (If a company **goes to the wall**, it fails because of lack of money.)

Unit 19

1

1 space   5 retrospect   9 sell
2 success   6 laurels   10 step/jump
3 corners   7 boat
4 deep   8 flooded

Events

Unit 20

1

1 had hit it
2 over
3 it out
4 (out) of it
5 a cat
6 eyebrow
7 those / these / the same lines
8 off my shoulders / off my mind

2

1 mad/crazy   4 stressed   7 deal, deal
2 save   5 in   8 tested
3 off   6 dish

Unit 21

1

1 c   2 g   3 e   4 a   5 b   6 h   7 f   8 d

2

1 It tipped down.
2 I stumbled on/across the book.
3 We got soaked to the skin.
4 That tin opener came in handy/useful.
5 I wore myself out. OR I was worn out.
6 The band went down a bomb.
7 We can make do with two assistants instead of three.
8 I have my doubts about Jeremy.

Unit 22

1

1 b   2 a   3 a   4 b   5 a   6 b   7 b   8 a

2

1 blind   6 chatted
2 bag/bundle   7 flew/flashed
3 picked   8 made
4 bags   9 cards
5 shell

Unit 23

1

1 pop the question	5 break the bank
2 the sky's the limit	6 in glowing terms
3 propose a toast	7 the icing on the cake
4 speak from the heart	8 get the better of

2

1 peg	4 up	7 praises
2 hitch	5 day	8 day
3 hear	6 tears	

Unit 24

1

1 pushing	4 years on
2 and bones	5 for it
3 million dollars	6 of shape

2

1 We had a whale of a time.
2 I must get in touch with Stephanie.
3 You're under no obligation to do it.
4 I'll be happy to see the back of him.
5 We're just good friends.
6 I wouldn't be seen dead in that place.
7 There's nothing better than a day on the beach.
8 I just want to catch up on/with the latest news.

Unit 25

1

1 effort	6 standard/level
2 equally	7 risk ('chance' is also
3 no	possible)
4 unimportant	8 substitute ('reserve' is
5 strong	also possible)

2

1 off	4 par	7 off
2 contention	5 off	8 plot
3 ground	6 hook	

Unit 26

1

1 second	4 missed	7 cater
2 lined	5 bounce	8 came
3 flash/fly	6 bridge	

2

1 bear something in mind
2 a pat on the back
3 off the top of your head
4 food for thought
5 know your stuff
6 off the wall
7 eye to eye
8 off the cuff

What's in the news?

Unit 27

1

2, 12, 3, 7, 5, 8, 4, 11, 1, 9, 6, 10, 2

2

1 stirring	4 open, overstepped
2 over, go	5 pressure, sooner
3 out, weren't/wasn't	6 feelings, stamp

Unit 28

1

1 in **possession** of	5 going **on** the offensive
2 clean up **their** act	6 **on** the lookout
3 go **under** cover	7 held up **at** gunpoint
4 **lying** in wait	8 in the **wake** of

2

1 tipped off	5 on the up
2 leading him astray	6 nip it in the bud
3 broad daylight	7 crack down
4 in the clear	

Unit 29

1

1 stand up	7 bring
2 spread	8 turned out
3 pave	9 break up
4 made	10 pass/go off
5 cordoned off	11 board up
6 calling on	

Unit 30

1

1 boils **down** to
2 the **benefit** of the doubt
3 they wouldn't **give/budge/move** an inch.
4 In the **final** analysis
5 put its own **house** in order
6 just **plucked** the figures
7 just didn't **add** up
8 to capitalize **on** this success

2

1 have a field day
2 a wake-up call
3 neck and neck
4 come under fire
5 a war of words
6 stop the rot
7 climb on the bandwagon
8 quick off the mark

Unit 31

1

1 D 2 S 3 D 4 D 5 S 6 D 7 S 8 D

2

1 open	4 crying	7 ahead
2 apart	5 up	8 camps
3 step	6 side	

Unit 32

1

1 price	4 tread	7 public
2 break	5 bounce	8 cast
3 build	6 rise	9 beyond

The word in the grey squares is 'celebrity'.

2

1 taken its ~~heavy~~ toll
2 Smoking ~~is~~ coupled with
3 gone ~~up~~ to her head
4 fight ~~for~~ our way
5 try ~~to~~ my upmost
6 went to ~~the~~ pieces

Unit 33

1

1 halt/standstill	4 havoc
2 risk	5 hold
3 future	6 terms

2

1 caught unawares
2 thick and fast
3 ground/came to a halt/standstill
4 towed away
5 snowed in
6 cut off (by the snow)
7 in the grip of

Communication

Unit 34

1

1 keep	4 hold	7 on
2 let	5 odds	8 picture
3 over	6 up	

2

1 I can't take it all **in**.
2 Reading **between** the lines, he doesn't like our idea.
3 It occurred **to** me that she could be wrong.
4 It makes **no** odds to him if we lose.
5 She plays her **cards** close to her chest.
6 It's a secret, so **keep** it to yourself.

Unit 35

1

1 you'll ~~take~~ what you deserve **get**
2 get ~~round~~ the point **to**
3 he ~~got~~ off the rails **went** / **has gone**
4 *Correct.*
5 stop beating about the ~~bushes~~ **bush**
6 the ~~ending~~ justifies **end**
7 a necessary ~~devil~~ **evil**
8 *Correct.*
9 believe in ~~live~~ after death **life**
10 *Correct.*
11 teach an old ~~cat~~ new tricks **dog**
12 try to ~~save~~ the last word **have**

2

1 disagree with her just for the sake of it
2 his behaviour is excessive
3 meant to avoid offending anyone
4 interrupting
5 to win the argument
6 accept that she has lost the argument

Unit 36

1

1 e 2 a 3 f 4 g 5 d 6 b 7 h 8 c

2

1 from the truth	5 winged
2 cross	6 spare
3 at rest/ease	7 of his life
4 wreck	8 rooting

Unit 37

1

1 We're on the same wavelength.
2 They welcomed me with open arms.
3 I'll play it by ear.
4 My heart was in my mouth.
5 It was a meeting of minds.
6 He just threw the dish together. OR He just threw something together.

2

1 forge ahead	5 hold the floor
2 lay down	6 detriment
3 from the word go	7 to start/begin with
4 in dribs and drabs	8 run over

The phrasal verb in the grey squares is 'ramble on'.

Unit 38

1
1 failed / not worked / not succeeded
2 annoyed/irritated
3 relieved and pleased
4 not really / not truly
5 clearly/directly
6 irritation/annoyance
7 not interested
8 annoyed/unhappy

2
1 in no uncertain terms
2 worse luck
3 at a push
4 I'll give you that
5 it's the least I can do
6 contrary to popular belief
7 thank goodness
8 to all intents and purposes

Unit 39

1
1 lost **for** words
2 It's **by** far the best
3 came **down** on me
4 so **no** wonder
5 to get **without** a doubt
6 for weeks **on** end
7 cartridge **into** the bargain
8 This is **not** just any / isn't just any

2
1 does a stroke
2 arms about/over
3 ever
4 a house on
5 head and shoulders
6 my right arm
7 couldn't believe my
8 pulled out all the

Human behaviour

Unit 40

1
1 up   3 on   5 face
2 to   4 over   6 comes

2
1 spare   4 game
2 kept   5 daylights
3 gloss   6 live

Unit 41

1
1 avoid   7 decided
2 mistake   8 past event
3 progress   9 level
4 risks   10 catching up
5 succeed, difficult 11 try
6 advantage   12 exciting

Unit 42

1
1 clear as mud   5 laugh your head off
2 a call of nature   6 falls flat
3 pull someone's leg 7 the kiss of death
4 tongue in cheek   8 I dread to think

Unit 43

1
1 put   6 squeeze ('get' would
2 rip   also be correct)
3 fair   7 robbery
4 all   8 toss
5 take

Unit 44

1
1 miss   4 wits   7 bet
2 makes   5 stand   8 event
3 harm   6 worth   9 fails

Unit 45

1
1 a real ~~fish~~ on his shoulder **chip**
2 take the ~~cow~~ by the horns **bull**
3 digging his ~~toes~~ in **heels**
4 she'll ~~fly~~ through **sail**
5 a storm in a ~~saucer~~ **teacup**
6 have your ~~job~~ cut out **work**
7 ~~stepped~~ into the trap **fallen**
8 just sit ~~loose~~ **tight**

2
1 act on
2 got over
3 pull yourself together
4 It's not the end of the world.
5 sail through the exam
6 has been off his food
7 came up
8 sort out

Unit 46

1

1 C 2 C 3 P 4 C 5 P 6 P 7 C 8 P
9 C 10 P

2

1 short, on
2 conclusions, away
3 stopping him, himself into it
4 her head in the sand, up to it

Unit 47

1

1 weigh up
2 two minds
3 final/last straw
4 lost sight
5 Rightly or
6 rushed into
7 courage of your convictions
8 turned to
9 toss-up
10 step in
11 draw a line

Unit 48

1

1 light
2 chance
3 safe
4 bluff
5 into
6 neck
7 put
8 down

2

1 on
2 on, of
3 at
4 out
5 at
6 out
7 on
8 up

Styles of language

Unit 49

1

1 he's glued to it
2 I wouldn't say no
3 none too pleased
4 it's in the bag
5 leave it at that
6 I was miles away
7 far from it

2

1 g 2 h 3 e 4 a 5 d 6 c 7 b

Unit 50

1

1 I'm going to clean out the dustbin.
2 I hope I win the lottery.
3 Are you going out in the dark?
4 How's the new job?
5 Is the climb very difficult?
6 Is it OK if I don't come with you tonight?
7 Did you enjoy the film?

2

1 ~~You don't~~ dare **Don't you**
2 Ready ~~as~~ you are **when**
3 ~~What's~~ a load of rubbish **That's/what**
4 Just ~~so~~ well **as**
5 ~~this~~ figures **that**
6 you ~~or~~ me **than**

Unit 51

1

1 the threshold of a new era
2 no heed to my advice ('no attention' would also be correct but less formal)
3 down their lives for their country
4 due respect, I have to disagree with you
5 waste to the town
6 the call of duty

2

1 We **paid** our respects to the widow.
2 Delays could **give** rise to further problems. OR Problems could **give** rise to further delays.
3 I took issue **with** her over the expenses claim.
4 He **paid** tribute to the soldiers who had died.
5 We **had** the honour of meeting the President.
6 The country has suffered **at** the hands of this government. or This country has suffered **at** the hands of the government.

Unit 52

1

1 kindly
2 enter
3 summing-up
4 undoing
5 oath
6 accordance
7 fixed
8 false
9 print
10 letter
11 Breach

The phrase in the grey squares is 'in good faith'. (If you have done something **in good faith**, you have done it believing that it is right.)

Unit 53

1

4, 8, 11, 1, 10, 6, 9, 3, 7, 5, 2

2

1 dwell
2 *Both are correct*, enlarge
3 resigned, contend
4 deprived, *both are correct*
5 call, adhere (NOT 'abide to')

Unit 54

1

1 F. It is the title of a newspaper section where jobs are advertised.
2 F. It means according to what you decide or want to do.
3 T
4 F. It means you are not allowed to go in a particular place.
5 F. It means 'or nearest offer'.
6 T

Types of idiom

Unit 55

1

1 fall apart	5 spill over
2 wrap sth up	6 fall apart
3 stand back	7 wrap sth up
4 stand back	8 spill over

2

1 tighten	6 knocked ('pulled' is also possible)
2 turn	
3 stand	7 gone
4 feed	8 wrapped
5 spilled	

Unit 56

1

1 f 2 e 3 g 4 a 5 d 6 c 7 h 8 b

2

1 success	4 carpet	7 conflict
2 seal	5 finger	8 storm
3 shot	6 potato	

3

1 black	4 golden	7 fuss
2 white	5 red	8 lost
3 thing	6 green	

Unit 57

1

These noun phrases do not follow the words in bold:

1 c all probability	4 a their heart
2 b closed doors	5 c nick of time
3 d the blue	

2

1 closed	4 last	7 deep
2 same	5 old	8 good
3 plain	6 loose	

3

1 too difficult for you to understand
2 working well
3 unusual
4 in trouble
5 nothing particular to do
6 crazy
7 in good condition
8 true from the beginning

Unit 58

1

1 cake **rake**	5 hall **wall**
2 rails **nails**	6 lead **read**
3 hits **fits**	7 bag **rag**
4 flood **blood**	8 sheep **sheet**

2

1 like wildfire
2 a, in a haystack
3 as new
4 as a cucumber
5 as a button
6 as pie
7 like a hawk
8 as a flash

Unit 59

1

5, 8, 3, 6, 11, 1, 9, 10, 4, 7, 2

2

1 T 2 F 3 T 4 T 5 F 6 F 7 T 8 F
9 T 10 T

Unit 60

1

1 Its spots.	4 They spoil the broth.
2 The iron.	5 They make light work.
3 New tricks.	6 Throw stones.

2

1 Don't count your chickens
2 Two's company
3 When in Rome
4 The spirit's willing
5 Better the devil you know
6 The grass is always greener
7 A bird in the hand
8 An eye for an eye

List of spotlight boxes

Word list / Index

Here is an index of all the idioms and phrasal verbs, in alphabetical order according to the first word. The numbers are unit numbers. (If you cannot remember the first word, see the list of key words on page 202.)

Key words

If you cannot remember the first word of an idiom, look here for other key words that are used in the idiom. The numbers are unit numbers

abode 52
accordance 52
act 28
advocate 35
afford 31
ahead 19
air 7, 30
alight 21
all 38, 41, 43
all out 25
alone 17, 43
analysis 30
any 39
anything 7
anywhere 14
apart 31
approval 56
arm 7, 12, 39, 56
arms 37, 39
arrears 12
assured 1
astray 28
away 49

back ADJ 1
back N 24, 26, 34, 42
back seat 1
back teeth 43
bad light 46
bad patch 7
bag 22, 49
balance 18, 31, 41
bandwagon 30
bank 23
bargain 39
bark 1
basket 17
bat 11
battle 31
beans 15
bear 7, 41
beating 41
bed 1
bee 43
beetroot 40
begin 37
behind 21
belief 38
believe 39
belt 56

bench 25
benefit 30
best 24
best bet 44
best shot 41
best thing 15
bet 44
bets 48
better 13, 23, 24, 27
better off 11
beyond 12, 42, 43
big deal 20
bill 56
bird 15, 60
bit much 49
bite 1, 15
blind 47
blink 57
blood 8, 58
blue 57
bluff 48
boat 1, 19, 44
bobs 59
bomb 20, 21
bones 24
bonnet 43
book 57, 58
boot 17
boots 5
born 40
bothered 22
bounds 16, 54, 59
brave face 1
bread 15
breadline 11
break 32
breaking 60
breathe 46
bred 59
brick wall 58
bricks 39
bright 58
broad daylight 28
broke 1
broth 60
brunt 27
brush 58
bud 28
budge 30
bull 45, 58

bullet 2, 31
bush 35
but 23
butter 59
button 58
cake 23
call 30, 41, 51
camel's back 1
camps 31
cards 2, 22, 34
care 38
carefully 32
carpet 27, 40, 56
cat 8, 20
caught up 12, 33
cause 56
caution 11, 48
chance 44, 48, 49, 56
change 60
charges 28
cheap 12
check 9
cheek 42
cheerful 59
chest 2, 34
chew 15
chickens 60
china shop 58
chip 2, 45
cinder 15
clear 28, 42
closed doors 57
colour 13
colours 16
combine 29
comes 40
common 38
company 60
concern 54
conclusions 46
conjunction 52
conscience 40
considered 59
contention 25
convenience 54
convictions 47
cooks 60
cool 5, 58
corner 2

luck 38, 49
lucky 38, 50
lucky stars 6
luxury 12

mad 5, 20
made 7
map 14
mark 27, 30
market 19, 56
matter 16, 42
means 12, 35
measure 51
medium 56
meet 22
melt 15
memory 1
mend 13
message 29
middleman 19
mildly 43
miles 49
milk 15
million dollars 24
mind 20, 22, 26, 36, 45, 46, 47, 57
minds 37
minutes 12
miserable 8
miss 47, 59
mixed feelings 27
moment 7
money 11, 12, 48
more exciting 24
mouth 12, 15, 37
move V 30
move N 49
much 50
mud 42
murder N 8, 14

nails 58
name 17, 27, 28, 38
nature 42
necessarily 48
neck 48
need 31
needle 58
need-to-know 34
nerves 22
new 58
new leaf 16
new tricks 35, 60
next thing 1
nick 57
no 49
no one 42

nobody 42
none 26
nonsense 50
normal self 13
note 44
nothing 6, 12, 16, 24, 50, 56
now 50
numbers 24

oath 52
object 12
obligation 24
occasion 32
ocean 56
odds 34
off 45
offensive 25
offer 54
old dog 35, 60
old times 57
omelette 60
on 42, 46
o.n.o. 54
open ADJ 11
open N 27
open arms 37
opportunity 56
opposite 49
options 17
ordinary 57
other one 40
OTT 20
outset 57
own 8, 25, 47

pace 41
par 25
parcel 59
part 35, 51, 59
past 43, 56
patch 7
PC 35
peace 52
pedestal 8
peg 23
personally 1, 43
picture 34
pie 15, 58
piece 5
pieces 32, 43, 59
pinch 38
place 19
plague 39
plain 57
planet 42
planks 5

play 11
please 7
pleased 49
plot 25
plunge 24
pockets 7
point 1, 8, 21, 35
popular belief 38
possession 28
posted 34
potato 15, 56
practical joke 42
praises 23
present 60
pressure 27
pretences 52
price 32, 35, 41
pride 59
print 52
probability 57
problem 50
production 54
proper 59
proportion 27
public eye 32
purposes 36, 38
push 17, 38
pushed 1, 49
pushing 24
put 43

quantity 5
question 23, 52
quick 58
quick temper 5

rag 58
rails 14, 35
rake 58
ranks 8, 31
rate 19
reaction 47
reason 9, 44
reasons 42
record 27
red 40, 58
rein 2
resort 38, 44
respect 51
respects 51
rest 36
retreat 2
retrospect 19
reverse 49
right ADJ 1, 19
right N 54

right arm 7, 39
right track 2
rights 57
ring 27
rise 51
risk 33, 48
road 14, 32, 57
robbery 43
Romans 60
Rome 60
roof 57
room 20
ropes 2
rot 30
routine 16
rubbish 50
rule 59
run 30
running 1, 16, 25
rut 57
saddle 2
safe 13, 41, 48
safe side 13
safety 24
said 1
sails 2
sake 35, 57
sale 54
salt 5
same 44
same boat 1
same lines 20
sand 46
sank 1
save 20, 59
say no 49
scrapheap 57
screwed on 2
scum 5
seal 51
seat 1, 2
see 1
seeing 49
self 13
sense 12, 44
separate cover 53
serves 1
services 53
set 43
settle 2
shadow 32
shape 24
shapes 1
shave 41

sheep 1, 56
sheet 58
shelf 23
shell 22
shop 58
short 46
short space 19
shot 41, 48
shoulder 2, 45
shoulders 20, 39
show 16
shreds 43
side 1, 9, 13, 46
sides 9
sight 36, 47
signs 16
sin 8
sit up 36
sizes 1
skin 21, 24
sky 23
sleep 42
sleeve 2
sleeves 10
sliced bread 15
small print 52
smoke 27
snail 14
snowed in 33
socks 16
sooner 7, 27
sorry 13
sorts 13
sound 5
space 19
spare 36
spark 5
speaking 38
spills 56
spilt milk 15
spirit 52
spoil 60
spot 2
spots 60
square 59
stands 44
standstill 33
stars 6
start 37, 56
state 45
steam 14
step 19, 31
stick N 34
sticks V 27

sticky patch 7
stone 58
stones 60
stopping 46
storm 21
story 12
straw 1, 47
stretch 44
stride 17
striking distance 25
stroke 1, 39
strong 19
struck 37
stuff 26
success 19, 56
suffer 5
surface 5
suspicion 56
sway 51
sweet 59
swing 20
tail 16
take 52
taken in 43
tape 56
teach 35, 60
teacup 45, 56
tear V 59
tears N 23
teeth 43
tell 22
temper 5
tenterhooks 57
terms 23, 33, 38
terrible 45
tested 20
tether 9
that 39, 49
there 6
thick 5
thin 58
thin air 30
thing 1, 15, 20, 41, 49
things 38, 49, 59
think 42
thinking 7
thought N 26
thought V 1
three 60
threshold 51
throat 43
thumb 5
tight 45
tight corner 2

tight rein 2
tight spot 2
time 11, 19, 24, 57, 60
times 44, 57
toast 23
toe 57
toll 32
ton 39
tooth 60
top 8, 9, 20, 26, 41
top gear 14
toss 43
toss-up 47
touch 5, 13, 24
tough 5
towel 1
track 2
trade 17
trap 45
treatment 56
trend 18
tribute 51
tricks 17, 35, 60
trim 24
true 27, 41
truly 39
truth 36
trying 16
turn 13, 60
two evils 47

unawares 33
uncertain terms 38
undoing 52
unknown 5
up 28
use 53
useful 21
usual self 13
utmost 32

vacant 54
ventured 60
verge 18
virtue 52
voice 5

wait 28
wake 28
walks 29
wall 18, 26
want 16, 49
warmed up 13
waste 51
water 15, 19, 46, 49, 57
wavelength 2, 37

way 6, 9, 11, 21, 25, 29, 32, 46, 50
wayside 32
weak 60
weather 13
wedge 7
weeks 39
weight 17, 20
well 21, 38, 50
whale 24
white 58
wildest 32
wildfire 58
will 52
willing 60
wind 2
wing 17
wire 5
wires 2
wits 9, 44
woman 5
wonder 39
wood 13
woods 1
wool 40
word 5, 15, 29, 35
word go 37, 57
words 30, 39, 42
work 1, 5, 39, 45
worked up 44
world 9, 45
worse 1, 13, 24, 25, 44
worse off 11
worst 24
worth 44
wreck 36
write 49
wrong 1, 34
wrong track 2
wrong way 9
wrongly 47

years 24
yesterday 40